THE
MAKING OF AMERICA
SERIES

STRATFORD
AND THE SEA

This lithograph from 1900 shows many aspects of the Housatonic estuary: the lighthouse at Stratford Point, a sloop-rigged yacht, oyster steamers C.S. Conklin *and* Florence, *oyster bed marker buoys, working dredges, and a coasting schooner. The inset shows H.J. Lewis's shops.*

FRONT COVER: *This scene at the lower wharf shows the border between Stratford and the sea. The bank highway, known in 1900 as Shore Road, winds behind a row of oyster shacks toward Captain Bond's prizefighter training camp at the former steamboat wharf. On pilings at the shore is the old bait shop cottage, last used as Katherine Hepburn's quarters when she played at the Stratford Shakespeare Theatre. In the foreground rests the fast cutter* Sheldrake, *and rowboats lie along the shoreline. Across the river are piles of oyster shells lying on the marsh now named for the dean of American decoy carvers, Charles Edward "Shang" Wheeler.*

THE
MAKING OF AMERICA
SERIES

STRATFORD
AND THE SEA

LEWIS G. KNAPP
THE STRATFORD HISTORICAL SOCIETY

ARCADIA
PUBLISHING

First published 2002
Reprinted 2006

Published by Arcadia Publishing
Charleston SC, Chicago IL, Portsmouth NH, San Francisco CA

For all general information contact Arcadia Publishing at:
Telephone 843-853-2070
Fax 843-853-0044
E-Mail sales@arcadiapublishing.com
For customer service and orders:
Toll-Free 1-888-313-2665

Visit us on the Internet at www.arcadiapublishing.com

In 1919 local Stratford water was clean enough for residents Ed Brownell, Ray Knapp, Jim Sullivan, and Jack Horsey to dig a basketful of clams apiece.

CONTENTS

ACKNOWLEDGMENTS

My thanks to everyone who helped me create this book: to those who offered information and provided illustrations, to those who worked with me editing, indexing, and gathering illustrations, and especially to those who lived before us, who over past centuries recorded and saved the elements of history so important in assembling this story of Stratford and the sea.

To Marie Blake who searched for illustrations from several sources, to Charlie Lautier, who scanned the files of distant museums, libraries, and historical societies to locate illustrations, then edited the text. But most of all to my wife Vivienne, who not only served as retriever of information and critical editor and advisor, but who put up for several years with my constant disappearance into the shell of authorship, reading and writing for hours at a time, including working at my computer in a shipboard cabin on a trip around the world. To those who gave material to me or to the Stratford Historical Society—such as slides of an overturned dredge from Al and Florence Farnworth, or Captain Hotchkiss's journal from Bruce and Lewis Jersey—that helped build the story. Lewis Barnum's journal sent from San Francisco by his great-grandson Glenn Light provided a whole sub-chapter. Twenty-five years of Captain Sterling's journals, donated by his great-grandson Richard Day Bunnell, were crucial to our story of the China trade. Caroline Davenport Mendillo's photography typified the duck hunters. The late Ray Cable's postcards and Carol Lovell's ability to find anything at the historical society filled out the story.

But I thank especially our antecessors who lived these experiences and documented them in journals, logs, and diaries; in news articles, ledgers, and account books; records of their daily lives through the years. Nathan McEwen's record of his grandfather's travels in the Revolution, Nathan Wells and Lewis Russell's diaries, and Judge Robert Fairchild's notes provided data; as did John Selby's and Curtis Chatfield's account books. Captain Sterling's and Captain Hotchkiss's ships' journals are quoted directly. William Pendleton's 50-year weather record included notes on storms and icing. The memories of the little slave girl Hagar filled in the local scene.

And thanks to the members of the Stratford Historical Society, who for more than 77 years have gathered and protected all these valuable records so we could tell this story of Stratford and the sea.

—Lewis G. Knapp

INTRODUCTION

This is the story of a Connecticut seacoast town that for more than 360 years harvested the bounty of its waters, engaged in seaborne commerce, sent its sons to sea to defend the land or to bring home the riches of the world, and then relaxed in the enjoyment of its shores and water.

New England coastal towns were fashioned by their dependence on the sea. Their fisheries helped feed them and sustain a shipping trade; their farmlands on alluvial soil, fertilized by fish and seaweed, yielded grain and crops; live animals were shipped on deck and casks of salt meat filled holds; manufactured goods—shoes, leather goods, and textiles—all were shipped by sea. Coastal sailing packets and steamboats carried passengers and freight. Shipyards thrived along the shores, generating local wealth. Water resources and seaborne commerce shaped and grew the seaside towns. Stratford was one of these.

Modern Stratford, 19 square miles in area, has 13 miles of shoreline. But residents are cautioned not to eat the fish they catch, or gather shellfish near the shore. Although a few still bathe at the beaches and some still handle sailboats, many have turned to backyard pools or public indoor pools, and large power yachts come air conditioned.

The town's 20-year-old plan for a shoreside greenway/bikeway is unrealized: instead citizens view the water from air conditioned cars. Stratford has grown away from the water and lost touch with its maritime past. Its people have forgotten the nautical history that built their town.

This book *is* that history brought to light. Records from the Stratford Historical Society, town archives, U.S., British, and Norwegian national archives, maritime museums, old newspapers, ships' logs and journals, diaries from family attics, memories of those who were there, and the author's trip around the world, when put together, tell a powerful story of Stratford's evolution as influenced by the sea.

Millions of years of geological processes formed the waters and the land at river's mouth first seen by the settlers of Connecticut in 1637, which led to their resolution in 1638 to form "plantations by the sea." In 1639 Stratford was the first of these. Within a generation the supply of fish—salmon, sturgeon, and shad—of oysters, waterfowl, and Indian corn ground fine at tide mills and grist mills on tumbling streams, provided goods for trade. Master carpenters built sloops and schooners on the riverbank, manned by Stratford sailors to Boston and New York, then to the West Indies and Europe.

Stratford mariners helped shape the outcome of the Revolution, the War of 1812, and the Civil War. Then sailing packets and steamboats expanded coastal trade, and Stratford skippers commanded New York ships that opened up the Orient, to Canton and Manila. Meanwhile at home the annual harvest of anadromous fish was exceeded by the oyster crop, and Stratford oysters travelled across the country and to Europe. The market for waterfowl brought forth the decoy carvers, and Stratford carvers became the best. Finally the Housatonic Boat Club and other clubs brought pleasure boating to the public, the major use of the waters today.

The maritime history of the town *is* the history of the town, and reflects the history of the nation. Stratford is re-learning that its water resources today are beyond value, and it is now working to restore, protect, and preserve them for future generations. The key to understanding is to know the history of Stratford and the sea.

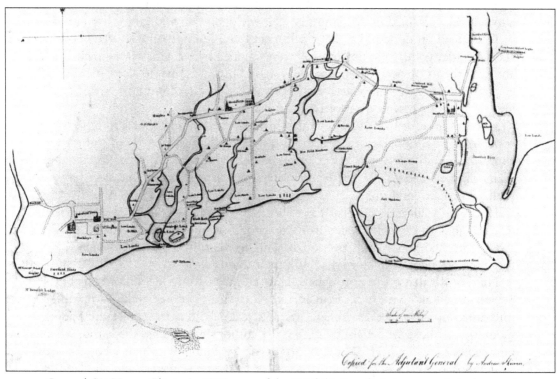

General Sir Henry Clinton's 1779 map of the Fairfield-Stratford shore reveals both towns' natural harbors and accessibility from the sea. (Clements Library, University of Michigan.)

1. The Edge of the Sea

The English settlers of Connecticut trekked through the woods of Massachusetts Bay Colony to found the towns of Hartford, Windsor, and Wethersfield, on a body of water called by the Indians Connecticut, or "Long River." When their men joined Colonel Mason in 1637 to drive marauding Pequot Indians away, and chased them westward down the coast of Long Island Sound, they discovered other, more luxuriant plantation sites along the shore. In 1638 the General Court decreed that the Connecticut Colony settle "these lands at the sea," before the New Amsterdam Dutch or the New Haven colonists moved in. In 1639 three new plantations, Stratford, (Pequannock or Cupheag), Guilford, and Fairfield (Uncoway) were formed, and the first of these was Stratford. For more than 360 years this town has grown and prospered at the edge of the sea.

The Waters and the Land

In the spring of 1639 a group of families who had left their English homes across the ocean reached this wilderness at the edge of the sea, to begin recorded history at the place that would be called Stratford.

Some 18,000 years earlier the last great glacier—the Laurentide Ice Cap, part of the Late Wisconsin Glacier—ground its way south to cover all New England and eventually reached halfway to the equator. As the earth began to warm, the ice sheet retreated northward, and sand and gravel sediment, gathered on the journey south, fell from the melting ice and formed a ridge that we would someday call Long Island. Behind that terminal moraine, receding ice left a basin to form a freshwater lake. As the glacier retreated, its melting waters poured south along some early incarnation of the Housatonic valley into that lake, and then about 8,000 years ago burst through to unite the lake with the ocean and form Long Island Sound.

Rains from the Housatonic watershed rushing to the sound carried soil and nutrients to cover the glacial gravel, creating islands and barrier beaches along the Stratford coast. Behind the barrier beach in Stratford salt and fresh waters merged, providing ideal conditions for the growth of salt-tolerant plants in the mud and silt. Salt cordgrass, salt meadow grass, and blackgrass took root.

Before the coming of the English settlers, the enormous marsh now called Great Meadows had formed. Because primeval forests covered the Housatonic and Naugatuck valleys, spring floods were limited and the summer flow of water was greater than today. This evened out the salinity of the estuary through the year, which aided the oyster crop. Great numbers of anadromous fish—salmon, shad, and sturgeon—swam upriver to spawn at the base of the great falls at New Milford that gave the inland stretch of river the name Pootatuck, or "falls river."

A mile up the river from its mouth, a little inlet on the Stratford side formed a sheltered cove between the gravelly banks, about 2 acres in area and a fathom deep. This the Indian residents called Cupheag, or "the sheltered place." It was fed by three small creeks, from north, west, and south, and being free of marsh was an ideal spot for colonists to keep their boats.

Another 1,000 feet upriver a tiny creek led from a salt pond. Selby's Pond, a glacial kettle of 2 acres of open water surrounded by a 2-acre band of spartina-dominated wetlands, is typical of the upriver tidal marshes. When the colonists arrived in 1639 they found the pond much as it is today, connected by the creek to the river, and highly saline. They used it as a retting (rotting) pool to prepare their flax for scutching (pounding by hand).

Early grants of fishing rights describe the river mouth as an open estuary with two channels, the Milford channel and the Stratford channel. Knell's Island, a 7-acre marsh, stood between. An 1837 coast survey shows Knell's expanded along with two little marshes, Duck Island and Little Duck Island, added to the south. In a redefinition of the Stratford-Milford boundary in 1885, because there was then only one main river channel, Knell's Island and the marsh went to Milford. The general shape of Knell's within the overall Charles E. Wheeler Preserve is visible today, outlined by the reed phragmites growing there.

The enlarged marsh was ideal for waterfowl hunters, as it was an excellent fueling stop for huge migrating flocks of birds. Market hunters carried large-bore guns capable of slaughtering two dozen birds per shot.

After 1824 when the lower wharf was extended into the channel for steamboat landings, eddies formed below it at ebbtide, and the current dropped silt along the west shore and in Mack's Harbor to form new marsh. Those eddies can be observed today.

A trip up the river from its mouth would have revealed a host of bars, flats, and, in the intertidal zone, salt hay islands. In 1964 old Stratfordite Ed Washburn labeled a flat out near the breakwater as Moneymaking Bar, and named Poverty Bar opposite the Birdseye Street launching ramp, Old Centennial Bar opposite Broad Creek where the beacon sat, and Culver's Bar above the railroad bridge. Todd Lovell says the Wheeler Wildlife Preserve held the "shell hole," Duck Island, Broad Creek, Todd's Pond hole, Boathouse Creek, and Knell's Island (later corrupted to Nell's). On the Stratford side below the bridges, Goose Island has nearly disappeared and Brinsmade's Island is gone. Between the railroad bridge and the parkway bridge Peacock Island, Carting Island, Long Island, and Pope's Flat still exist, and on the Milford side is Fowler's Island.

Centuries of mud and silt brought down the river covered the glacial gravel and formed Great Meadows marsh. Fresh Pond is an opening in the marsh, home to crabs, eels, and bird life, all nourished by the marsh's plants.

By the first quarter of the twentieth century, Great Meadows saltmarsh was at the peak of its natural growth. A few manmade scars already marked its surface: William Hopson's dike, cut in 1890, stretched from Lordship northward to the end of Honeyspot Road, and an arrow-straight berm pointing toward the Bridgeport line at Eagle's Nest on Johnson Creek, where West Stratford had become a part of Bridgeport in 1889, was raised to become Lordship Road, and later the trolley right-of-way. The saltmarsh was at its maximum size then, and relatively undisturbed.

It covered 1,400 acres—more than 2 square miles—on the 1911 chart. It reached from Great Neck and Long Beach northward to another lowland stretch then termed Great Swamp, now called Avon Park. It was fed by salt water from the sound through Lewis Gut from Bridgeport Harbor in the west, by brackish water through Neck Creek from the Housatonic in the east, and by fresh water from Stoney Brook, now Bruce's Brook, and several minor brooks and creeks. Its salinity varied, but was generally fewer than 20 parts per thousand, versus 30 at the Race.

Centuries of rotting vegetable matter called detritus had formed a bed of peat atop the baseline sand and gravel, and in most places this was several feet thick. It was detritus that fed a multitude of plants and animals and made the marsh a spot where life began. Each acre produced 3 to 7 tons a year, four times the nutrients of a wheat field.

Throughout the intertidal zone and in the creeks the dominant plant was salt marsh grass or saltwater cordgrass, *spartina alterniflora*. In the earliest days of the Stratford colony this had been the material used for thatching roofs, but it was soon succeeded by wooden shingles. It grows 3 to 6 feet tall, and during the winter months freezes, dies, decays, or is pulverized by wave action into detritus. Digested by bacteria, the shredded parts settle to the bottom or drift away to become food for sea creatures.

To landward of the cord grass, in the upper marsh where the flats are flooded only at high tide grows another spartina: salt meadow grass or salt hay, *spartina patens*. It is a small, fine grass, which grows no higher than 2 feet, and forms an even carpet on the flats. Until the early twentieth century, farmers were still coming down to the marsh to harvest this salt hay for winter fodder and bedding. Nathan Wells's diary from 1866 describes late nineteenth century harvesting. "16 August, commenced mowing on the salt meadows." "23 August, carted the first load of hay from the salt meadows," "6 September, went to Knees and Paws and mowed salt hay yesterday and today, which if I succeed in getting it home in good order will finish all I want for hay this year." "20 October, finished going in the salt meadows."

On the landward side of the salt marsh, wherever freshwater creeks emptied into it, grew meadows of black grass—actually black rush, *juncus gerardi*. Other common marsh plants at Great Meadows were sedge, seaside goldenrod, and glasswort. The seaside goldenrod was attractive to honeybees late in the autumn season, and imparted an almost molasses flavor to the honey. Local beekeepers were wise to harvest their honey earlier in the year to separate this honey from

Salt hay was harvested on bars in the river, then left on elevated ricks until farmers could float hay scows across the marsh at high tide. This hay scow waits at Peck's Mill.

their lighter clover honey. Glasswort, or samphire, was a shrubby little plant with water-filled stems, slightly translucent, that grew on sandy banks at the water's edge. It gave salads a salty taste, and was great for pickling. Nathan Wells wrote on June 10, 1869, "went to Knees and Paws and cut a bag of samphire." "1878, 25 May, went to Long Beach with Ben Wells for samphire." "1880, 3 June, To Knees and Paws for samphire with Lucius Boothe." Each year through 1890 Wells gathered glasswort.

Great Meadows supported all kinds of little creatures. Plankton and small crustaceans—amphipods and isopods, tiny prawns—fed on algae and detritus, and in turn were eaten by crabs and fish and birds. Rock barnacles clung to stones, seaweed, logs, and boat bottoms, passing floating particles through their bodies. Periwinkles, mud snails, and salt marsh snails abounded.

Mussels, clams, and oysters grew in Great Meadows and Lewis Gut. Ribbed mussel, able at low tide to open its shell to air and retain water in its mantle, could survive in the high intertidal zone of the marsh. It had no commercial use, but its filtering action cleansed the high marsh and it was food to migratory birds and wandering rodents.

Both hard shell and soft shell clams lived in Lewis Gut and the creeks that ran through Great Meadows marsh. The hard shell, *mercenaria*, called quahog or littleneck, inhabited the Gut floor, where it dug itself into the mud or sand with its foot or sometimes lay exposed, where barefoot clammers walking through the water could feel for it with their feet. The soft shell clam, *mya*, called long neck or steamer, dug a deeper home in the mud or sand, and reached its siphon through the mud to ingest detritus. When the tide was out and passersby disturbed the steamer, it squirted a jet into the air, earning the name "pissclam." The steamer is delicious steamed and quahogs made wonderful chowders: Nathan Wells's diary tells of nineteenth-century clamming expeditions to the marsh.

The unpolluted marsh was home to many kinds of crabs. Little fiddler crabs dug holes in the inter-tidal mud and peat, where fishermen dug them out (and still do) for blackfish bait. Marsh crabs shared this habitat, but have since become rare in the area. Blue crabs were visible swimming across the tide pools and tidal creeks. They were abundant, and grew to 6 or 7 inches. They are both scavengers and pugnacious predators, feeding on fish, crabs, snails, and mussels, either dead or alive. Blue crabs were a delicacy, and in spite of the painful bite of their pincers, were trapped or netted by the bushel. Boiled in cauldrons on the beach, they could be picked apart for the tasty white meat, and their red shells scattered, recycled to the marsh.

Great Meadows marsh was a nursery for finfish. Killifish and mummichogs—little minnows— darted across tidal pools, gobbling up algae and mosquito larvae, and being swallowed in turn by bluefish, crabs, or egrets. These made great bait for fishermen after tautog, fluke, or summer flounder. Summer flounder itself, a left eye flounder, was found in sandy or sandy-mud bottoms in the estuary, and after winter spawning, young fish drifting in in the spring would grow up in the shallow nursery grounds of the marsh. Winter flounder, a right-eye flounder, spawned in deeper water, but young fish might be found in Lewis Gut. From March to July, when striped bass invaded estuaries to spawn, some found their way into the Great Meadows.

At the onset of the twentieth century, according to old citizens now gone, one prominent inhabitant of the marsh was the diamondback terrapin. It had once been so common that laws were passed limiting the number of times per week that it, or lobster, could be fed to servants. There were enough diamondbacks to make it worthwhile to gather them commercially and ship them to New York, until the price for a dozen females rose to $120 and they were hunted nearly to extinction.

All of these plants and animals made Great Meadows an ideal hunting ground for migratory birds. Although the marshlands on the Milford side of the channel were strong competition, hunters from Bridgeport and West Stratford set up blinds in the Meadows. Competing with the fishermen and hunters, raptors such as ospreys, marsh hawks, and even eagles, hunted fish and birds. At low tide, sandpipers and piping plover raced along the muddy creekbeds, and egret and heron stalked their prey. Small mammals such as muskrat searched for food, largely cordgrass rhizomes and other roots, and in turn were trapped by man for their fur. The marsh was rich with life.

Included in that life was the saltwater mosquito, *aedes solicitans*, the scourge of the marsh. Early colonists were plagued by swarms of greenhead flies and biting midges, but in the spring and again in the fall mosquitoes were the nemesis of all. Congregational revivalist George Whitefield in 1740 blamed the sins of Episcopalians for the outbreaks, but they in turn blamed the heathen Indians.

Harold Lovell told of the time the Cupheag Club was preparing for its annual clambake in Lordship and three clubmembers were sent ahead to dig clams. "They took a huge iron kettle with them. When they began to dig there was a strong breeze. However the wind died, and the mosquitoes arrived in battalions. Finally, in desperation, the men pulled the kettle over themselves. They claimed to hear the mosquitoes drilling through the kettle. As the bills came through, they clinched the bills on the inside. Finally they attached so many mosquitoes that they flew away with the kettle."

Nathan McEwen told the story of the lighthouse keeper's cow. Lighthouse keeper Samuel Buddington had a large family, and he kept a cow for milk. In 1822 the mosquitoes were so numerous that the cow, tormented by their stings, burst out of her barn and dashed across the fields. They followed her in clouds, "and stung her so she swelled as large as a hogshead and died from the effect." Lovell's story is apocryphal but McEwen's is probably true.

In the high marsh, the salt marsh mosquito lays its eggs in small depressions on drying mud, where they remain dry for at least a day. When abnormal tides or spring rains fill these pools with water, the eggs hatch within minutes and grow into adults within a week. The ability of the eggs to survive for weeks—or months—in the mud assures that when a pool forms it is instantly full of "wrigglers." Again in the autumn when high tides combine with autumn rains, the high areas of the marsh that were dry all summer come alive, and the salt marsh mosquito becomes more abundant than at any other time of year.

Nature countered the salt marsh mosquito through predators. The larvae were a favorite food of dragonflies. Where killifish could reach the little high marsh pools they devoured the wrigglers. Ducklings and migratory birds included them in their fare. On summer evenings, flocks of martins, swifts, and swallows swooped and dipped over the marsh, after adult mosquitoes. Nature kept a balance, but swarms of mosquitoes were part of it.

Great Meadows marsh reached its ultimate growth in the first quarter of the twentieth century, but many of its products were no longer important to the people of Stratford who were growing away from their closeness to the shore, and questioning its value. The Great Meadows wetland was increasingly viewed as the Great Meadows wasteland.

THE FIRST AMERICANS AT STRATFORD

Ten thousand years before the Englishmen arrived, the first Americans were already camped along the shore where the river meets the sea. Soon after the glacial ice receded, nomad paleo-Americans followed the herds of animals that

*When the Paugusset tribe of the Mohegan people came east across the hills to the Housatonic, their clans and villages spread along the shore where food was abundant. (*History of the Indians of Connecticut.*)*

Tools of stone, bone, wood, and leather served for hunting, fishing, preparing food and clothing, and, when necessary, waging war. Stone tools were most durable, as evidenced at diggings.

were their food across the continent, as the west dried up and temperatures moderated in the northeast. Clovis points, or folsom points, on exhibit at the Stratford Historical Society museum, testify to the presence of these spear-throwing hunters in this area.

Some time between 7,000 and 3,000 years ago—the date is uncertain—the bow and arrow appeared, and the spear was relegated to spearing or harpooning fish. The bow, usually carved from hickory, was about 4 feet long, strung so tightly that only a strong man could bend it. The arrow was of reed or elder stick, with a carefully shaped hard point attached. Arrowheads of antler, bone, and stone, found embedded in the skeletons of these early men, demonstrate the improved power, range, and accuracy available to the warrior or hunter, and volumes of arrows turned up by the plow identify their villages, campsites, and hunting fields. Farmer "Ike" Lobdell kept a jar of quartz arrowheads in his barn, found when spring rains revealed them lying on top of newly plowed ground. The bow enabled the hunter to bring down such food as deer and moose and bear and beaver, and birds in flight—turkey, goose, duck, passenger pigeon, and heath hen. Wildcats, wolves, and foxes were hunted for their fur. Seasonal trapping expeditions with hand-made spring traps served even better to supply meat for drying into pemmican.

16

Alluvium, swept down the river and deposited along the shore, formed a fertile plain stretching from the Housatonic across Bridgeport harbor and beyond to Ash Creek—called by the natives Poquonnock (pauqu'un-auke), "cleared land," which was kept clear by set fires. On this plain they gathered nuts and berries, and harvested corn, beans, and pumpkin as they needed. Other floodplains along the river itself, as at Oronoque (Woronoke), where the coastal Indian trail crossed the Housatonic, were also planted to corn and beans.

The sparkling clear river was host to migratory fish of many kinds—shad, salmon, sturgeon, bass; alewives, menhaden, smelt, and blues; lamprey eels, flounder, flats, and sole. Weirs of woven stems and branches set in shallows in the channels brought in quantities of anadromous fish coming home to spawn. The creeks and channels of the marshes were filled with crabs and lobster, and diamondback terrapin were common. Clams and scallops were plentiful, but the most abundant food source was the oyster. After a storm it wasn't even necessary to get wet feet to gather them, as they washed up onto the shore.

Before recorded history, this abundance and variety of food brought men to settle along the shore. As they prospered they banded together into families, clans, tribes, and nations.

Who were these precursors of the English settlers who came in 1639? The English planters/settlers/colonists referred to them as aborigines, heathen, or natives, but particularly as Indians. They were not, of course, the people whom Columbus had thought they were, i.e. people of the East Indies, but they had almost certainly come to America from Asia, and were of mongoloid stock, thus related to the East Indian Malaysians. So Indians they were named, and Indians they became.

All the Indians in southern New England spoke variants of a common language, the language of the Algonquian family of nations that covered northeastern North America. In Connecticut these tribes seemed to be a part of the Mohegan Indian people, who spilled through the Taconic range from the Hudson and settled the three river valleys and the Long Island Sound shores near their mouths. With the Sasco tribe, a minor adjunct of the Manhattos, to the west, and the Quinnipiacs to the east, the Housatonic watershed was peopled by a tribe of clans closely related to each other. When first encountered by the English in 1639, the hereditary sachem of this tribe, Ansantaway, resided in Milford, either on Charles Island, or at Milford Point, or at the Wepawaug (place at the narrows) River, thus giving his tribe an early name. His 19-year-old son Okenuk headed a clan in Stratford, at Cupheag, and his other son Towtanimoe headed a village at a place called Paugussett (confluence) in present day Derby. Each of these places gave the clan of Indians that lived there its name, but soon Ansantaway's people at all of these locations were recognized as Paugussetts. At Pequannock (open place) between Stratford (Cupheag) and Fairfield (Unquawa), Queriheag was chief Sagamore. Whether the Pequannocks were under Paugussett rule is not clear, but in later years when they all retreated up the river to Paugussett and beyond, their sagamores Chicken and Siacus were part of the group.

In any case, because their major threats, the fierce Pequots, had been occupied against the Narragansetts to the east, and because food was plentiful, the Native Americans of the lower Housatonic, known to the colonists as the Paugussett family of tribes, were only loosely organized and their camps and villages were spread out near the shores wherever there were springs, planting fields, creeks, and forests.

One of the largest Indian village sites in all New England was spread along the sands of Milford Point and back around the eastern, or Milford, channel of the river. Called "Poconic," it stretched for a mile to the mouth of Beaver Brook, and back for half a mile up a low rise called Eagle Hill.

Early in the twentieth century Stratford resident Franz Goldbach spent his youth following Indian expert Anson Dart from site to site, and was of the last generation able to conduct archeological digs in pastoral Stratford before the sites were destroyed by modern development. Goldbach cites some 15 locations where evidence of Native American presence existed. Hildreth Winton found evidence of settlements beneath the ledge at the top of the hill behind his pie factory in Oronoque and town surveyor William Morehouse remembered as a boy being taken by his father to see Native American wigwams on the hill at Wigwam Lane in the 1860s.

At these encampments along the river or its tributary streams, the clans erected their wigwams and hogans, using bent saplings as frames, and covering them with skins or bark, smooth side inward. When moving camp, they stripped the lodges of bark to transport to the next site, but left the frames in place.

To harvest shad and salmon in their seasons, the clans constructed wiers all up and down the river. These traps of woven stems and branches were placed in shallow spots along the stream, configured to allow fish to enter but not find their way out. In the spring, migrating herring were so abundant that they were simply scooped out of the water at the creek that drained Fresh Pond. Eels were a delicacy speared in creeks and streams, often at the foot of waterfalls. Larger fish were caught with hook and line, from shore or from canoes. Canoes used on the Sound were sometimes made of heavy elm bark, but more often hollowed out of logs. Pine, oak, or chestnut would do, and the time to burn out and shape a 14-foot log into a canoe with tools of shell and stone was some two man-weeks.

The easiest food to harvest was shellfish. Clams and oysters were waiting to be gathered into woven baskets, and were eaten in abundance as evidenced by kitchen middens—shellfish piles—all along the shore. But as colonial Stratford expanded inland, the natives gradually retreated north up the Housatonic valley, and by the late 1700s only small groups returned to Stratford each summer to set up wigwams or live in some abandoned house, to harvest fish or shellfish, or to weave baskets to sell to the white man. A memorial sent by the Mohegans to the state General Assembly in 1789 says it all:

> The times are exceedingly altered, yea, the times are turned upside down; or rather we have changed the good times, chiefly by the help

European settlers did not drive the natives off the land, but their ever-increasing competition nudged them out. Shellfish gatherers built year-round shelters at the shore. The Indians gradually retreated inland and disappeared.

of the white people. For in times past our forefathers lived in peace, love and great harmony, and had every thing in great plenty. When they wanted meat, they would just run into the bush a little way, with their weapons, and would soon return, bringing home good venison, racoon, bear and fowl. If they chose to have fish, they would only go to the river, or along the seashore; and they would presently fill their canoes with variety of fish, both scaled and shell-fish. And they had abundance of nuts, wild fruits, ground nuts and ground beans; and they planted but little corn and beans. They had no contention about their lands, for they lay in common; and they had but one large dish, and could all eat together in peace and love. But alas! it is not so now; all our hunting and fowling and fishing is entirely gone.

PLANTATION BY THE SEA

It was in June 1637 that Englishmen first saw the broad and bountiful waters where the river meets the sea. Captain John Mason, with ninety colonist-soldiers from Hartford, Windsor, and Wethersfield, had driven the defeated Pequots west along the shore past Quinnipiac (soon to be New Haven) and across the mouth of the yet unnamed Housatonic to Sasco swamp in future Fairfield. Stories of

19

abundant fish and shellfish in the dual channels of the mile-wide estuary, of sheltered harbors for their boats, of wild birds in the marshes, of open fields for planting crops, must have spread through the towns on the Connecticut River and prompted plans to settle on "the lands beside the sea."

In the spring of 1639 Reverend Adam Blakeman and a small group of families left the Connecticut River towns and followed Indian trails through the forest, to settle by the river that would be known successively as the Great River, Stratford River, and finally the Housatonic, at an inlet called by the Paugussett Indians Cupheag. At least two of Stratford's early settlers, Robert Rose and Samuel Sherman, had been part of Mason's little army. That year and next, English towns were settled on the shore at Guilford, Branford, Milford, Stratford, Fairfield, Norwalk, and Stamford, by planters from Connecticut and New Haven colonies.

Few of the colonists were shipwrights—they were weavers, masons, and yeomen—but they soon took up the tools of the joiner's trade to build their homes and implements, and some became ships' carpenters, to build the craft they had to have to gather food and transport goods. Others learned to steer their ships along the coast, to trade with other colonies. Although few of the first planters were trained in seamanship, both necessity and their passage across the

In the spring of 1639 Reverend Adam Blakeman and a small group of Englishmen came through the forests from Wethersfield to found a new plantation "at the sea." They called it Pequannock, then Cupheag, then Stratford. (Bill McCracken painting.)

Atlantic were training enough. Most of them had gathered in East Anglia and taken ship for New England from London, Ipswich, and ports between. Others left from Isle of Wight, Plymouth, and Bristol. Passages of two or three months acquainted the emigrants with the perils and hardships of life at sea. A list of ships they came on includes *Arabella* (1630), *Christian*, *Elizabeth & Ann*, and *Lyon* (1632), *Francis* (1634), *Griffen*, *Hector*, *Hopewell*, *Plaine Joan*, *Planter*, *Recovery*, *Safety*, and *Truelove* (1635).

From this experience, and under the tutelage of a few good shipwrights, new shallops, pinks, and pinnaces were launched at yards all along the riverbank, and the Sound became a water highway connecting the New England ports.

How Adam Blakeman and his group of settlers came from Wethersfield and the river settlements to the little harbor of Cupheag is unrecorded, but when Roger Ludlowe came this way that August he "adventured to drive his cattle thither" overland, so some believe that in early spring the Stratford settlers had done the same. There were few boats in the Connecticut Colony at that time—during the Pequot War in 1637 a shallop, a pinnace, and a pink are mentioned—but one may have been used to transport household goods, or perhaps even a framework for the meetinghouse, to the harbor at Cupheag where the group first settled.

One of the first tasks after erecting shelter was to build boats for transport and for fishing. The names of the earliest boatbuilders are lost in time, but in May 1648 Moses Wheeler, born in Kent in 1598 and recently expelled from New Haven for kissing his wife Miriam on Sunday, was granted the right to operate the ferry—called "a skiffer and a horse boat" in the lease.

The will of William Beardsley, dated September 28, 1660 reads, "If Joseph, my sone, please to be an assistant to my wife . . . and leaves the sea, I give to him ye halfe of my acomodations in Stratford; if not, I give him twenty pounds of my share of ye bark, to add to his part."

Thomas Fairchild called himself a merchant in 1662 when he married for the second time in London. After his death in 1670, the inventory of his estate included an uncollected sum of £22 13s, "debts desperate 2,100 [pounds?] of sugar," indicating that he was active in the West Indies trade, as an owner and shipper.

Shipyards became common near the head of navigation as the supply of timber near the river's mouth gave out. From about 1650 Joseph Hawley was building vessels, first in Stratford, then upriver in Derby. Across the river from Derby in Ripton, Dr. Thomas Leavenworth bought a mile of land along the bank at Indian Well. The Leavenworths built a shipyard on the north side of Indian Well brook, and the doctor's son James cut timber up in the White Hills to clear the land and to supply the shipyards.

Thomas Wheeler was a Stratford man in 1654 when he bought 40 acres of land from the Paugussetts in Derby. In 1657 he opened a shipyard there and ran it for three years before selling out to the Bryans of Milford. Alexander Bryan and his son Richard created their own fleet to bring manufactured goods from Europe. When the second meetinghouse was being built in 1679, there was a bill "due to

Mr. Richard Bryan for glace & box, £19 14s 8p," indicating that one of Bryan's ships had returned from England with a cargo of window glass.

In 1696 James Bennett built a vessel in Stratford on the riverbank in Oronoque. In 1737 Matthew Bennett mortgaged "19A near the shipyard, bdd. E on the great river and S on the shipyard brook," where Ryder's Lane shopping center exists today.

Daniel Curtiss's shipyard on the peninsula, called Shipyard Point and formed by Ferry Creek, has remained in operation through the centuries and is now Brewer's Stratford Marina.

Joseph Hawley was an early importer. He was the town innkeeper in the 1660s and at the ordinary he displayed and sold imported cloth, tea, sugar, molasses, indigo, logwood, nails, wines, and rum. Isaac Nichols and Samuel Blagge marketed imported goods as well, and all three seem to have operated their own vessels from time to time. On October 27, 1678 Hawley and his partners had shipwright John Rogers in New London build them a ship called *John and Esther*, to operate out of Fairfield. Hawley's one-eighth share in *John and Esther* cost him £58 1s 2p. In 1680 he sold out to John Prentice.

Benjamin Beach, son of Richard the innkeeper, is said to have been an early shipbuilder and merchant in Stratford. He was granted his first home lot in 1669, and as he prospered he expanded his holdings. When he built the Perry house on South Parade before 1700, he was well off. William Beach, son of Benjamin's cousin Isaac, born in 1694, was in the shipping trade and must have been the richest man in town by 1742; he subscribed more than £1,000 to build the new Episcopal church that year, and had the best pew in the building, next to the minister. After his death in 1751 his sons Abel and Abijah carried on the business, but in 1758 lost their property to the Nicolls.

Richard Blackleach began his career when he bought an eighth interest in "the Katch *Tryall* of Milford" in 1679 for £60. In May 1686 Blackleach and Daniel Shelton were authorized by the proprietors "to build each of them a warehouse and wharf" on the river, providing they allowed townspeople to use it when they themselves were not. Blackleach's wharf seems to have been at the inner end of Mack's Harbor, where the water was then deep enough for commercial vessels. Shelton built his wharf and warehouse at present day Bond's Dock. In December of that year Samuel Wheeler was granted permission to build a wharf between Shelton's and the home of customs officer Richard Butler (now 50 Shore Road.) When Wheeler's widow Elizabeth married Blackleach in 1717 he may have acquired this wharf (where 19 Shore Road is today) but in 1735 it was granted to Daniel Curtiss, then in 1757 to John Brooks and several others, "in case they erect said warff within the space of two years & keep up ye same from time to time & at all times in good repair for laying vessels thereto & unloading them thereupon."

Blackleach and Shelton both became prominent merchants. (Traveler Sarah Knight, who passed through on horseback in 1704 said, "They give the title of 'merchant' to every trader.") By 1699 Shelton was in the top 15 percent in town wealth, and nobody had a larger estate than Blackleach. People were as litigious then as now, and Shelton often found himself in court. On one occasion, the marshal of Fairfield County accepted his land upriver for bail bond. On another Shelton sued the town and won when his horse broke a leg on a town bridge and had to be shot. On a third occasion, he had to petition the assembly to be paid for rum and other "supplies" he had sold seven years earlier to the colony for its troops. In 1696 the court brought a judgement against "Daniel Shilton" for money owed for goods he had ordered.

Blackleach, too, left a trail of lawsuits. In 1690, a man named Jeffries sued him for not honoring a contract to ship some sugar from the West Indies to England. John Butler's widow had to sell part of his estate to pay a debt to Blackleach. In 1698 Will Hoadly of Branford appealed a judgement in favor of Blackleach, who had sold him some slaves.

In 1683 Blackleach petitioned to purchase oil in New York for several soapmakers in the towns of Stratford, Milford, and Fairfield. In 1683, together with his father-in-law and brother-in-law, he had the sloop *Endeaver* built in Middletown. In October 1686 he was in Barbados with Nathan Whelpley, master of the bark *Laurel* of Stratford. In 1689 Blackleach persuaded the colony to appoint him commissary for the army at Albany during a foray against the Indians, but in 1691 the court appointed a committee "to audit the accounts of Comisary

THE VALLEY OF THE HOUSATONIC.

WITH ILLUSTRATIONS BY J. DOUGLAS WOODWARD.

Mouth of the Housatonic.

THERE are few New-England rivers of any considerable length which do not present, in the range of their flow, not only a great variety, but also a striking contrast, of aspects. Rising ordinarily in the hills as sparkling rivulets, they dance and chatter, or foam and fret,

This sketch shows the river as the colonists found it. As it was larger than most rivers at home, they called it Great River, then Stratford River, probably for a town with a fording spot along the River Stour in Suffolk. (Laurie Lofgren.)

23

A view downriver from Oldfield Point shows the merging of sea and shore. At right the common field is farmed; at left a sharpie and a dory rest between trips.

Bleakleach with the country." The town church members bore down on both Shelton and Blackleach in their meeting on August 8, 1701, when they voted "to make Mr. Blackleach and Mr. Shilton remove their pew so a gallery stair can be erected, or a selectman will remove it for them." Blackleach was on better terms with the Congregational Church in 1710 when he was allowed to build a new pew in the meetinghouse, but in his old age he donated land to build the first Anglican Church.

As early as 1659 the General Court named Richard Butler—who lived on what had been Moses Wheeler's home lot, near what would be the lower dock—customs officer in Stratford "for entry and recording such goods as are subject to customs." In 1680, 26 vessels are listed in Connecticut Colony: 3 pinks, 12 sloops, 6 ketches, 2 barks, and 3 ships, the largest being a 90-ton sloop in Hartford, in the transatlantic trade with Bristol. In 1702, there were eight "lawful ports" in Connecticut:

> New London, Saybrook, Guilford, Newhaven, Milford, Stratford, Fairfield and Stamford, at every of which aforesaid ports an officer shall be held and kept for the entring and clearing of all ships and other vessels trading to and from this Colony, to be called and known by the name of the Navall Office; and at one of the ports aforesaid and not elsewhere, all ships or other vessels trading to or from this Colony shall lade and unlade all goods, commodities, wares and merchandise."

In 1714 Benjamin Curtice was the "navall officer" of the Port of Stratford. Vessels reported (or underreported) to the crown were 42 in 1730, and 72 in 1756, including the 90-ton ship *Lion* and the snow *Leopard*.

Goods and wares exported from colonial Stratford's harbors of the Housatonic and Newfield included corn and grain, onions, apples, beef and pork, oysters and shad, bolts of cloth, leather products, and horses. Export of timber and wood products for clapboards, staves, hoops, rails, or building lumber was forbidden by the town in 1690, as nearby forests became depleted. Imports from Europe included wine, nails, iron, glass, delicate fabrics; and from the West Indies came molasses, rum, sugar, salt, hemp, indigo, spices, gunpowder, and fruit. From Boston and New York came trans-shipped imports.

As more bottoms were demanded, the sound of the whipsaw, the thud of adzes, mauls, and axes, and the ring of hammer or beetle on trunnels and caulking irons echoed from the yards at Lower Wharf, Daniel's Point, Near Mill, Oronoque, Indian Well, Derby, and in Pequonnock Harbor.

With hardly any tidal currents, Pequonnock Harbor was popular with sailing skippers. More merchants moved their operations to this harbor and built new warehouses at the Newfield. Just before the Revolution, four or five coasters were delivering produce from Pequonnock Harbor to Boston, and several schooners were delivering grain from Newfield's tidemills to places like St. Kitts, Barbados, and Martinique.

Nathan Lewis of Fairfield, master of the sloop *Daniel*, recorded these typical receipts of cargo from his Stratford relatives on March 25, 1718, "Received of Mr. Joseph Lewis on board the sloop *Daniel* myself master 18 bushels of Indian Corn 16 bushells oates, 160 pounds of flax, goods consigned to myself & to be sold in Boston & returns to be made in money to him in Std. he paying fraight according to custome, the danger of the sea onely excepted," and "Received of Mr. Benjn. Lewis on board of sloop *Daniel*, myself master 40 bushells of Indian Corn, 10 bushells of oates, 120 pounds of flax, goods consigned to myself & to be sold in Boston & the return to be made in money to him in Std, he paying fraight, according custome, dangers onely excepted."

Town records record:

> Theophilus Nickols of Std. for £36 to Lieut. John Wilcockson & ensign Jon Lewis both of Std.- one twenty fourth part of ye good sloop *Rainbow Plantation* as per register, now bound on a Voyage to ye West Indies - together with her Mast Boome & Bowl Split [bowsprit], Ropes, Ankers, Cable, Sales, standing & Running Rigging & all priviliges and appurtanances thereunto belonging 14 March A.D. 1745/6.

In 1722 a Captain Wakeman received £13 for goods transported for John Ebenezer Coe, and Coe's journal for July 1725 states "David Bostick carried to Barbados in the year 1721, 21 pounds of shoe thread to sell and bring the effects to Stratford."

In 1736 Peter Hepburn asked permission to build a warehouse and wharf north of Prince's Wharf, and in 1757 a group built another to the south. Prince's Wharf became Thompson's Wharf, and in 1773 Ebenezer Thompson sold it to Legrand Cannon. Today it is Bond's Dock.

In 1766 John Fairchild of Stratford sent his sloop *Delight* to Barbados and Tortuga from the Connecticut River with a cargo of goods and horses. Arriving at Barbados on February 28, *Delight* had to pay harbor costs of nearly £20, including £5 15s at the collector's office, £5 5s 6p for gunpowder, £3 for stamps at the customhouse, £5 to the fort, and money for the searchers office, naval office, and liquor office—and "toss in cash for an officer." Return cargo included salt (sal Tortuga), sugar, and 1,825 gallons of rum.

In 1768 Abel Beach sold his remaining property at Sandy Hollow and his brig in service to the West Indies to merchant LeGrand Cannon.

Transatlantic commerce also expanded in the late eighteenth century. In 1756 there were 74 ships and vessels listed in the Connecticut Colony, averaging 43 tons displacement. Forty-nine of them were sloops. By the time of the Revolution, nearly this many were registered in the three ports of Stratford alone. Seaborne commerce was a significant contributor to the economy of the coastal towns of the colony of Connecticut.

MANAGING THE RIVER

In 1781 Reverend Peters wrote: "The western river is navigable and called Stratford only for ten miles, where Derby stands: then takes the name Osootonoc. It is 50 miles west from Connecticut River, and half a mile wide."

One bitter winter day in 1757, the Earl of Loudon, on learning that the passage across the Stratford River was clogged with ice, sent word ahead from New Haven that the ferry route was to be cleared overnight that his lordship might safely pass. Like King Canute, he discovered that the waters were not subject to his will. The Stratford River crossing was one of the roughest on the shoreline route from Boston to New York, with winter ice floes, spring floods, and tidal currents up to 7 knots. It took a rough ferryman to tend it. From 1648 to 1690 Moses Wheeler was the man.

He was a large and powerful man. One story tells of the time he was in his cellar when three Indians with tomahawks appeared at the hatchway. Undaunted, he exclaimed "Let's all have a drink," lifted a nearly empty cider cask to his lips, and drank from the bunghole. Noting his muscular build, and thinking the cask was full, the natives slunk away. Moses Wheeler thrived on hard cider and rowing ferries. He lived to be 100 years old.

Wheeler must have satisfied the town, because in 1670 they renewed the lease to "Moses Wheeler, ship carpenter, the ferry, with thirty or forty acres of upland and six of meadows joining to the ferry for twenty-one years." He was obliged to take Stratfordites for "a ha'penny" and their animals for "tuppence," while others paid twopence and fourpence. He was to "Seasonably and readily attend ye ferry and

In 1648 Moses Wheeler became the ferryman. We don't know what the ferry looked like, but it was described as similar to a "gundalow." It lasted for 155 years.

upon call to carry over all passengers, horses, cattel, and things passible there, to keep in repair two boats, ye one to be called ye horse boat; ye other to be called ye skiffer to be always ready for ye ferry in seasonable weather." The franchise was exclusive, and the town agreed to pay for any improvements at the end of 21 years.

To face the winds and currents in the channel, the skiffer must have been a one-man narrow-beam rowing boat, to carry pedestrians across, and the horseboat a large wide-beamed scow, for travellers with horses. Carts and carriages were not ferried until later.

The horseboat might have been propelled in any of several ways. A system described in the Public Records of Connecticut, October 1802, was certainly employed at some period: with a long line secured to one shore, the boat was steered at an angle to the current, forcing it across the stream, then on return it swung back to the bank. Some ferries were actually powered by horses, either hauling on long lines from the shore, or circling a windlass aboard, or on a treadmill powering paddlewheels.

When his second lease expired in 1690, old Moses Wheeler, now 92, sent the town's committee a note saying "For the natural love and affection yt I have to my dearly beloved son Samuel Wheeler, I doe by these presents transmit all my right, title and interest of ye ferry in the bounds aforesaid with all benefits and profitable improvements accrewing thereunto by virtue of any gift, grant or lease whatsoever." The town showed the same love and affection when they agreed to lease the ferry to Samuel, but the General Assembly decided differently. In 1691 they authorized the selectmen of Milford to set up their own ferry on the other bank "in case Mr. Wheeler the present ferryman does not intend to fulfill the articles formerly made." Again in January 1698 the Assembly ruled "judging it very conducible to his Majesties interest and the common benefit of his Majesties subjects in there speedy and comfortable passage over the river" that a ferryman be stationed on the Milford shore, to counter "great complaints of travellers against the said ferry as it is now managed."

Apparently no separate Milford ferry was actually established. Complaints continued that Milford citizens had to pay twice as much for transport as Stratfordites, and westbound travelers had to blow the horn interminably to arouse the ferryman on the Stratford side. This was the situation when Sarah Kemble Knight rode the Post Road with the post rider in 1704. The Stratford ferry did not help her disposition. She wrote:

> Dec. 6th we set out from New Haven, and about 11 same morning came to Stratford ferry; wch crossing, about two miles on the other side Baited our horses and would have eat a morsell ourselves, but the Pumpkin and Indian mixed bread had such an aspect, and the Bare-legg'd punch so awkerd or rather Awful a sound, that we left both, and proceeded forward, and about seven at night come to Fairfield.

When Samuel Wheeler's lease expired in 1712—he himself had died before 1703—Richard Blackleach, Stratford merchant and shipping magnate in the West Indies trade, signed up to operate the ferry for seven years. Immediately, a Milford committee was chosen to "sign an agreement with Mr. Blackleach of Stratford, on ye Towns behalf, whereby ye said Blackleach shall bind himself in a bond of £20 to carry over Stratford Ferry ye Inhabitants and people of Milford for half ye price stated by law, so long as he shall keep ye said ferry.

Still not satisfied with their ferryman, in 1719 Stratford ordered the selectmen to "treat with Mr. Blackleach respecting the ferry lease." He ended up getting them to extend his lease for another 21 years. In February 1736 the property and "ferry boat with oars" went to Josiah Curtis Jr. whom the Assembly allowed to charge 6d pay (produce or goods) or 4d money (metal coin) for man, horse, and load, and 3d pay or 2d money for single man or single horse. This was only half what Saybrook and New London ferries were charging. Magistrates, military men, and postriders went free. The most unpopular customer was postrider Ebenezer Hurd, who would come charging up to the ferry landing gate yelling "Open the gate for the King's Post!" The legislature required "good tight boats sufficient both for largeness, strength and steadiness for the safe transportation of travellers and their horses, supplied with oars and other implements and men who are discreet, strong, and skilled in rowing." The larger boat was described as similar to a "gundalow," a flat-bottomed, shoal-draft double-ender about 50 feet long used to transport farm produce on rivers. Gundalows were propelled by oars and also usually had a pair of square sails on a single mast.

The campaign to add a ferry on the Milford side continued. Finally in 1758 the legislature issued a command: "Whereas it is thought necessary for the public good and benefit, that there be a boat kept on the east side of Stratford Ferry river, for the transportation of travellers across said river on the country or post-road" that the towns of Milford and Stratford "and also Mr. Josiah Curtiss of Stratford that tends the ferry on the west side of the river" appear before the Assembly to discuss the matter. Stratford's representatives and Mr. Curtis opposed the Milford ferry, but it was approved, pending erection of an inn at the ferry, and "keeping a good boat with all proper utensils."

It wasn't as great as Milford had expected. The colonists were in the middle of the French and Indian War, and Josiah Curtis had been compelled to ferry troops across the river for free. In 1757 and 1758 he counted 192 colonials and 320 regulars in Colonel Frasier's regiment, all non-paying. Curtis asked the legislature for £5 6s 9d, but was finally given £1 1s 4d, not much for all his rowing.

Captain Peter Hepburn of Milford remained eager to start the ferry on the Milford side, "in expectation of keeping a public house of entertainment at said ferry," and was finally appointed innkeeper in 1761. The Milford ferry operated until 1798, when the town voted to sell the ferry house and lands for £750 to Joshua Hopkins, who had just picked up the lease for the Stratford side operation, which he ran until the bridge was built.

Crossings farther up the river also had their ferries. In 1716 Sergeant Joseph Hawkins of Derby was authorized to keep a boat for hire at Derby Narrows to the Stratford (Ripton) side. In 1737 his son Moses was the ferryman, and after his death in 1745, his son Joseph. Derby Neck became known as Hawkins Point, and the ferry, taken over by John Stephens in 1762, ran to well after 1800 as the Huntington Ferry.

At the end of Milford's Oronoque Road, near the present parkway bridge, in 1723 Zechariah Baldwin of Oronoque was given "liberty to set up a ferry at the said Oronoque, being about four miles northward of the ferry called Stratford Ferry." It remained popular in the late 1800s to row Oronoquers across to the flag stop at Baldwin Station on the Naugatuck Railroad.

On October 17, 1789 President Washington crossed the Housatonic for the seventh time. He never saw the bridge named for him—he died four years before it was built. He wrote, "The ferry is near half a mile, and sometimes much incommoded by winds and cross tides."

In 1795 the legislature rejected a petition for a bridge, when the town of Derby, newly made a port of entry in 1790, objected. But by October 1802 the pressure was so great that the General Assembly had to act. It granted rights to the Milford and Stratford Bridge Company to build a bridge, specifying "a suitable and convenient draw of the width of thirty-two feet for the passage of vessels, with piles eighty feet above and below the draw for tying up and warping through, two

The first Washington Bridge was built in 1803. Shipmasters complained about its narrow 32-foot draw, and celebrated when ice floes took it out in 1807.

lamps to be hung and lighted every night unless the moon shall give sufficient light," and a bridge tender to work the draw in response to signals from a horn or speaking trumpet. The company renamed itself the Washington Bridge Company and commenced construction. The 1824 Linsley map of Stratford shows the draw with two lift sections, located close to the Stratford shore, operated by block and tackle. The bridge was a low-budget affair, of wooden planking, supported on wooden pilings, without piers as such. It was built low to the water, and was often inundated at spring tides. Winters were severe, and the river was sometimes covered by a foot of ice, so it was no surprise that when the ice broke up and moved down river in February 1807 the bridge went out to sea with it. There was much rejoicing up the river in Derby. The town brought out the rum and brandy and celebrated. Colonel Tomlinson had 10 turkeys slaughtered, and at a jubilee he toasted "May the fishing and shipping interest of our river nevermore be disturbed by the intolerable nuisance of another bridge across the mouth of its waters."

When the bridge was rebuilt in 1810, the Assembly ruled that vessels come to a stop and warp through, and that carriages travel no faster than a walk. David Lacey, who built the bridge, was named bridgetender. He bought the inn that Captain Hepburn had run, on the Milford approach. Later called the Riverside Hotel, it remained until 1920.

Derby shippers continued to protest the bridge. One afternoon in 1812 the sloop *Delight* came sailing down the river with a cargo for New York. With ebbing current and heavy breeze, *Delight* was making good time when Captain Morris hauled down his sail and blew for the bridge. Before it could be opened, he drifted into it and damaged his bowsprit on the draw. He had to spend the night at anchor in the river in a heavy storm. His owners sued the bridge company. Because interested parties could not at that time testify in a lawsuit, the ship's boy—and cook—Willis Hotchkiss was the only witness. The shipowners were awarded only $8 in damages, but this was a landmark case; Judge Tomlinson ruled that bridges could not obstruct navigation.

In June 1824 the Revolutionary War hero Marquis de LaFayette returned to the United States on a triumphal tour. This time he was escorted with fanfare across a bridge named for his old commander. On Wednesday September 24 a little sidewheel steamboat tied up at the lower wharf in Stratford. On the following Sunday Captain Thomas Vose took the steamboat, named *General LaFayette*, upriver toward Derby. He knew the river, but the steamboat was new to him. When the tender finally raised the draw, Captain Vose, now in a bad humor, charged into the opening, slamming one of his paddleboxes into the pilings and splintering it. When the boat reached Derby, one young spectator observed "She's lost one of her ears!" Carpenter Truman Gillett and his apprentices were allowed to work on Sunday to ready the steamboat for a Monday departure.

As steamboats on the Sound grew larger, operators demanded that the draw be widened. In 1845 a bill to widen it to 60 feet passed the legislature. The company refused to comply. The Fairfield County state's attorney fought to revoke the bridge's charter, but the court ruled for the company on the basis that no vessel had actually been prevented from passing the draw. A committee of Derbyites, with the help of wealthy industrialist Anson Phelps, chartered the steamer *Salem* in New Jersey, loaded her with cargo, and headed her for Derby. They knew that she was 10 feet wider than the draw. With colors flying and an eager crowd watching, she was forced into the draw, remained wedged for two hours, then had to backtrack to the wharf. Phelps and company transferred the cargo to a sailing vessel and took it up to Derby, then sued the Washington Bridge Company for damages in Federal Court.

The problem solved itself. A clause in the company charter prohibited construction of another bridge within 6 miles. When the New York & New Haven Railroad came along in the mid-nineteenth century it found itself bound by this, although when written there had been no thought of railroads. The solution was for the railroad to buy the highway bridge, provide a 60-foot swing draw near the Milford shore, then return it to the Washington Bridge Company in exchange for permission to build a railroad bridge within 6 miles. This was done in 1848.

The railroad bridge—a covered bridge—was a marvel at the time. It was the longest covered bridge ever built in the state of Connecticut. It took a year to build and was completed in September 1848. The Bridgeport *Chronicle* reported:

In September 1848 the New York & New Haven Railroad completed this 1,293-foot-long single-track railroad bridge, the longest covered bridge in the state.

> The bridge across the Housatonic River at Milford is one of the finest specimens of masterly workmanship in this country, being 1,293 feet in length, stretching upon seven piers of the most substantial masonry, making the spans each 150 feet long, with a draw in the middle 134 feet in length, so excellently fitted and balanced that a mere boy of fourteen years of age can swing it open with perfect ease.

With a few patches and a little maintenance, the Washington Bridge that had opened in 1810 lasted 58 years. Then, on the morning of July 15, 1868, the draw suddenly collapsed on the sidewheel steamer *Monitor*, heading downriver on its way to New York. The *Monitor* was delayed for several days, but the bridge was out four years. Vehicles had to travel an extra 20 miles through Derby.

Finally in 1870 the legislature ordered the towns of Stratford, Milford, Bridgeport, and New Haven to build a new bridge, with an 80-foot wide draw. Again, the railroad came to the rescue. New York & New Haven Railroad president William Bishop decided to replace the old single track covered bridge across the Housatonic by a new, higher capacity twin-track cast iron Whipple truss bridge, designed by Francis C. Lowthrop and built by the Keystone Bridge Company in Pittsburgh. On January 10, 1872 the first regular train crossed the new bridge. In October the old wooden railroad draw structure, in use since 1848, was floated on a barge down

On July 15, 1868 Washington Bridge collapsed on the steamboat Monitor. *The steamer was held up for four days, but the bridge was out for four years.*

In 1872 when the Consolidated Railroad built a new iron bridge, they gave their old draw to the Washington Bridge Company to rebuild the highway bridge.

to the waiting gap in the highway bridge. It was set in place immediately, and on November 17 the bridge opened to traffic for 22 more years.

In 1884 heavier locomotives forced replacement of the 1872 railroad bridge by rugged wrought iron trusswork stretched from pier to pier. In 1905 a new four-track bascule bridge replaced that bridge. Captain Robert Culver, one of the most skilled boatmen on the river, towed the draw span into position. The bridge is still in use.

On March 31, 1894 a modern iron trusswork highway bridge opened for traffic. The dignitaries fortified themselves for the opening ceremony at Minor Smith's Shorehouse nearby. The railroad persuaded the legislature to dictate that the bridge be only 17 feet wide, so narrow that a trolley line on it was impractical. In 1898, however, the Milford Street Railway Company laid a single track across the bridge to connect with the Bridgeport Traction Company. When a trolley was crossing, other vehicles had to hug the south lane, and a skittery horse could easily cause the loss of a carriage wheel.

The final Washington Bridge was dedicated on Armistice Day, November 11, 1921. Men, women, and little boys and girls dressed up in their uniforms or best clothes to join in the big parades and celebration. At two o'clock, bands, marchers, and floats lined up at Academy Hill: another group formed in Devon Center. Promptly at 2:30 p.m. the two parades came face to face in the middle of Washington Bridge, then marched to Rivercliff on the Milford shore for a glorious picnic. The fifth bridge has been in use for more than 80 years, longer than any of its predecessors. In 1989 it was reconstructed at a cost of $12.3 million, for use into the foreseeable future.

Four miles up the river from Route 1, where the Oronoque ferry once ran, Stratford's second highway bridge opened on Labor Day in 1940. A 38-mile parkway now stretched from Greenwich to the Housatonic River, and that day's ceremony was to extend that parkway across the Housatonic. A thousand spectators attended. At 1:00 p.m. Louise Merritt, daughter of late congressman Schuyler Merritt, for whom the parkway to the west was named, and former governor Wilbur L. Cross, for whom the parkway to the east was named, cut the ribbon, and before the day was out 24,500 cars drove across the bridge. A tollgate on the Milford side collected 10¢ per car. Time, traffic, and corrosion have taken their toll on the parkway bridge, now named the Igor I. Sikorsky Memorial Bridge, so as of early 2002 its replacement was underway.

On January 2, 1958 observers watched a motorcade speeding east along a new white ribbon of divided highway across the Housatonic. Governor John Davis Lodge had cut a ribbon in Greenwich at 9:30 a.m. and the officials were en route to the other end of the Connecticut Turnpike (Interstate 95, the John Davis Lodge Highway) to cut another ribbon and formally open the new road. It was appropriate to name the new fixed bridge, located next to the railroad bridge, for the ferryman who had struggled so long ago to take travellers across the river, Moses Wheeler. As the twenty-first century begins, it too is being expanded to handle modern traffic.

An 1836 nautical chart shows the lighthouse at Stratford Point, 53 feet above sea level, flashing white every 45 seconds. The only other light at the time was a fixed beacon off Short Beach, in the middle of the channel. The old Milford channel was gone, and Knell's Island had melded into the marsh. Buoys lined the channel as far as Washington Bridge, but there were no other improvements. Steamboats grounded on the bar at the river's mouth: At low tide the depth was a mere 3 feet. On July 30, 1859, according to Lewis Russell's diary, "The Propeller got aground outside today & she cannot get in until 10 oclock tonight. We have got freight on her." The *Monitor*, onto which the bridge had dropped in 1868, returned in 1871 to hit the bar and sink in 7 feet of water. An 1855 chart shows depths of 3 feet at the mouth, 2 feet near Milford Point, and 3 feet approaching the bridge, with 7 to 16 feet between. Even in the Sound, shoal water was a hazard. The same chart's sailing directions say: "Approaching Stratford Pt. from the east keep the lead in hand. The bottom never changes from soft to hard, and the land should not be approached nearer than 3 fathoms, giving the Light a berth of 1 to 2 miles to clear the shoals making out from Stratford Pt."

Each year the channel shifted and changed its depth. A rugged stone outer breakwater, a vestigial inner breakwater, and a jetty at the riverbend were begun in 1890 and completed in 1911. For years contractor Thomas Anderson's tug *Evona* could be seen towing stone down from Derby in the old sloop *Commodore Jones*, converted to a barge.

In 1955 a new dredging project began, to widen the channel to 200 feet at 20-foot depth. The dredge *General* would set its spuds in place, then sweep the grinder head back and forth in the channel, sucking dredged material through its pump, to send sand and gravel rattling through a steel tube floated on pontoons across the river to a spoils area. A large amount was dumped on Short Beach. The year 1955 was a busy one, requiring moored boats to be moved and re-moved. It was also a year of disaster and flood. Two hurricanes struck, one on August 18–22 and the other on October 14–18. Torrential rains upstate brought floods that swept the valley clean. The tidal current did not change for four days.

Quoting harbormaster Fletcher Lewis:

> '55 was the worst flood I ever saw. That was quite a night. We were dredging the channel and the dredge had proceeded in from the mouth. The dredge was operated by steam and the fuel was oil, which required an oil barge to supply the fuel. The afternoon before the flood the oil barge had been brought alongside the dredge and the oil had been pumped from the barge to the dredge. There were sixty men aboard the dredge. When the rush of water came down, she was moored by her spuds. These spuds held the dredge broadside to this tremendous current and the operators of the dredge knew that they were in a bad fix so they tried to get the spuds up. They managed to get one spud up, but with one spud down that left her worse than ever. The tremendous current rolled her over. Everybody managed to get aboard the oil

barge. To complicate matters we had two derelict barges up above the powerhouse, moored on the bank of the river. One of them came down about one o'clock in the morning, fetched up on Short Beach, the oil barge was alongside of her, the dredge was on her side, oil was coming out of the barge and covering the river and the boats. We were in real trouble. The water was at least five feet higher than I ever saw it at the most abnormal high tide.

It took two years to remove the *General* and complete the dredging of the river. Today, heavy oil barges pushed by big Moran tugs again scrape their own channels. It is time to dredge once more. The Housatonic will always need man's help, but to tame the river requires a delicate balance between developing commerce and yachting, and protecting our riverine environment.

On August 14–18, 1955 hurricane-driven floods swept down the Housatonic valley destroying bridges, roads, and towns. The dredge General *tried to move, but with one spud down swung across the channel and flipped over on her side and sank. It took two years to clear the channel. (Al and Florence Farnworth.)*

2. Industry at the River

From the onset, boats were the only practical means of transport: there were no roads in colonial times. Indian trails led north, east, and west, but it would be years before they developed into highways. Trained shipwrights were uncommon but demand was great, so master carpenters set up yards along the river to build vessels for eager traders. In 1648 the General Court, granting ferry rights to Moses Wheeler, called him "ship carpenter." Shallops, pinks, and pinnaces slid down the ways, then larger sloops and schooners, as mariners took them to New York and Boston, then to the West Indies. The major shipyard was the one at Shipyard Point—at one time complete with ropewalk—run by Curtiss, Wheeler, Russell, White, and Bedell, in turn. Now it is known as Brewer's Stratford Marina. In the 1850s Peter White built two- and three-masted schooners in the yard. Later Bill Bedell launched steam-powered oyster boats there. During World War I the Housatonic Ship Building Company built five wooden freighters, 257 feet long and displacing 2,551 tons, on the river. From 1929 to 1941 Sikorsky flying boats rose from the river to pioneer commercial flight around the world. No boats are built in Stratford today, but the means remain.

The Yards at Shipyard Point

In 1670 when the town renewed the ferry lease with Moses Wheeler, they ordered him to "keep in repair . . . ye horse boat" and "ye skiffer." Joiners, cabinetmakers, and master carpenters all worked at building ships. Skilled shipwrights were titled "Master Carpenters," and moved from yard to yard to oversee construction.

The Connecticut General Court took the seaworthiness and safety of its ships very seriously. By the end of the colonial period, the Acts & Laws of 1784 included:

> An Act for regulating and inspecting the building of Ships and other Vessels.
>
> Be it enacted by the Governor, Council and Representatives, in General Court affembled, and by the authority of the fame, That when and so often as any Ship or Vessel of twenty Tons or upwards

is to be built or set up in any Town or Place within this State, before any Plank be brought on, the Builder or Owner shall repair to one of the Assistants within the same County who upon Request is hereby impowered to appoint and authorize one or more able Ship-Wrights to be Overseers and Surveyors of the said Building, and of all the Materials and Workmanship in and about the same, as often as the Builder or Owner sees Cause to call them thereto; who are to take Care that all the Materials be found sufficient and suitable for the Occasion, and that the Work be done and performed strong, substantial, and according to the Rules of the Ship-Wrights Art.

At every yard the sounds of saws and hammers were heard from dawn to dusk. Large timbers were whipsawed, one sawyer standing below in a pit, his eyes covered by crepe cloth to protect from sawdust. Wood also came from the sawmills at Wheeler's Mill or Farmill, where water power provided the muscle. Mauls and mallets rang as planking was nudged into place and eight-sided trunnels (tree nails) fastened it to frames. Resident blacksmiths moved about, tailoring ironwork to the ship.

Benjamin Beach was a "merchant and builder of vessels" before 1700. Joseph Prince and later owners of the lower wharf constructed sailing craft where Moses Wheeler first lived. And up at Wheeler's (Peck's) Mill was Samuel Wheeler's boatworks. Across the river in Milford, other Wheelers built boats at Wheeler's Farm. In Oronoque, James Bennett's shipyard launched vessels before 1700. And in Ripton, Leavenworth's yard launched many craft, while other yards thrived across the river in Derby. In 1918 the place near the ferry where Moses Wheeler built boats became a launching site for 2,500-ton merchantmen.

Where Ferry Creek empties into the Housatonic River, with three sides on the water, there has been a shipyard for more than 300 years. It was called Shipyard Point when Daniel Curtiss built his first craft there, and until Joel Curtisssold it to Samuel Wheeler Jr. in 1826 it was Daniel's Point or Curtiss Point.

When Daniel and Abigail Curtiss died in 1795, their children sold parts of the land to local shippers, who built warehouses and launching ways along the river bank. In 1795 the Wetmore Brothers joined Matthias Nicoll to purchase the ropewalk that David Osborn had built. Of the 12 or more vessels they owned, at least four were built in Stratford and of these, the 168-ton brig *Prosper* in 1793, the sloop *Governor*, and the 173-ton ship *Victoria* in 1794 were launched especially for the Wetmores. In 1795 ship carpenter John Ebenezer Coe put in seven days' work sheathing a vessel—probably the brig *Julius Caesar*—for the Wetmores at seven shillings a day. When their business in Bridgeport and New York began to crumble in 1795, the Wetmores sold their interest in the ropewalk to Matthias Nicoll, closing out their properties at Shipyard Point.

In 1797 David Brooks and William Booth built the sloop *Factor* on an acre Brooks owned at the southeast corner of the point, then sold his yard to John Stilman, who had been building ships there with his brother Ashbel since 1795.

That year John Coe worked some 80 days for them, at five shillings per day. In 1799 his account book shows constant employment in the shipyard or in the woods obtaining timber, culminating in "launching week" that October.

Matthias Nicoll, who took over Abel and Abijah Beach's trade in New York and their property in Stratford, registered several of his vessels in Stratford, though only a few were built here—his schooner *Randolph* in 1785, and the sloops *Violetta* in 1789 and *Julia* in 1790. In 1795 he began to buy land at Curtiss Point, and by October 1797 he controlled the whole riverbank at the point, from the Wetmore wharf lot north of New Lane to the Stilmans' yard at the tip of the point. But the Nicolls had bigger plans than Stratford. When the War of 1812 erupted and Matthias's son Samuel went privateering, they sold all their land at Curtiss Point to Captain Samuel Wheeler Jr.

Hagar Merriman's recollection of going to a launching (possibly of Samuel Wheeler's *Julia*, or *Julia Ann*) as a young slave child in 1808 or 1809 reminds us that launchings were great social events, but the hazards of the river were ever present:

> I remember going to a launching; the place where we had to cross over was not a real bridge, but beams driven down into the water and boards laid across for you to walk on. After a long time of persuasion, my lady consented to let me go, so I went, tickled and delighted to death. When

New Lane, now Broad Street, runs to Shipyard (Curtiss) Point, where coasters unloaded at the upper wharf and shipyards operated for more than 360 years. Captain Benjamin's sloop Adele *glides down Ferry Creek. (Attributed to Edward Lamson Henry.)*

As seen from the lower wharf, White's yard spreads out across Shipyard Point from Ferry Creek to the river. Two sets of ways lay on the river side and one on Ferry Creek.

I was crossing the boards, the woman who had promised to take care of me ran on before and left me to cross all alone: but looking to see them launch the ship, my foot slipped and down I went into the river. A great many following on saw me fall, and a gentleman jumped down and caught hold of my frock and pulled me out. It was a long time before they could bring me to; they then got into a carriage and took me to my lady's house. She gave a loud shriek and said, "My! What is the matter now?" [The doctor] told her to wrap me up warm, and give me some tea and put me to bed. I always thought I had enough of launching and from that day I never went to one again.

Captain Wheeler built many vessels at the yard for his own use. In 1813 he was master and owner of the 42-ton sloop *John*. In 1817 Waterman Eells built the 67-ton sloop *Toleration* for him in his yard. The Wheelers ran the shipyard at the point for 32 years, until the captain's son Levi sold it to Lewis Russell in 1844.

In 1789 the Leavenworth yards came within the bounds of Huntington, but most shipbuilding at the head of navigation moved across the river to Derby. The *Commodore*, first centerboarder on the river, was built at Sugar Street in Derby by Tallmadge Beardsley. Albert Sherwood describes a launching at Halleck Brothers' Yard there:

Oh, the excitement and exhilaration to us boys who were on board, not satisfied to see the launching from outside; and as the blows continued and the boat, with snapping and groaning of timbers, finally settled to her bed, she started very slowly down the incline, continually increasing speed and momentum, plunged into the Housatonic and glided across the river nearly to the opposite bank, brought up by the anchor, which had been dropped as her bow reached the water, and the ringing racket made by the paying out of chain as it gradually lessened her way was the sweetest music I ever heard.

After the 1708 Indian massacre at Haverhill, Massachusetts, ship's carpenter Jacob Sterling moved to Newfield and set up a shipyard at Gaspin's Point (at the end of Pembroke Street). Richard Nichols took over that yard, then built vessels near his store at the head of navigation in the Pequonnock. In 1782 Captain Stephen Burroughs protested that he "hath for many years past and still owns a shipyard on his farm, where he carried on the business of shipbuilding until William Pixlee erected a dam across the [Pequonnock] river about three quarters of a mile below his . . . shipyard, at the narrows, which obstructs navigation effectually up and down said river from his place." Burroughs lost: the dam at Berkshire Mills became the new head of navigation.

The Pequonnock River evolved into Newfield Harbor, then Bridgeport Harbor. Old Mill Creek became Pembroke Lake, then Yellow Mill Pond. On Mill Creek/Pembroke Lake, boats could sail all the way to Old Mill to load grain, until Joseph Walker dammed the creek and built the Yellow Mill in 1792. On a New England tour in October 1789, President and Mrs. Washington passed through Stratford on the Boston Post Road. As they rode up Mill Hill, the President spotted a nearly completed sloop in an open field, with no water in sight. It was the *Hunter*, 45 tons burthen, being built for Captain Alison Benjamin who lived across the highway. Curious, he dismounted, and asked the workmen how they intended to launch the vessel—and where. They described how they would set the craft onto a cradle with runners, and slide it down the hill when winter came, onto the ice on Yellow Mill Creek, a full quarter mile away, to await spring thaws. It must have worked, because Captain John Benjamin was sailing *Hunter* out of Newfield Harbor in 1794.

Newfield offered a protected harbor, lower currents than the Housatonic, and an undeveloped waterfront. Small wonder that Stratford merchants built new wharves and warehouses there. In 1821 Bridgeport became an independent town, the terminus of turnpikes from the interior, and eventually a railroad hub tapping the Naugatuck and Housatonic valleys, and a thriving coastal port. As its shipyards grew, those along the Housatonic shrank.

An expanding fleet of sailing craft based in Stratford required sails and rigging. Sailcloth (duck), rope, and cordage were at first imported, but soon local craftsmen were producing finished sails and rigging. Both flax and hemp grew in Stratford, and several ropewalks existed in the eighteenth century.

Preparing the fibers of either flax or hemp was a labor intensive process. The stems were laid out in the sun to dry, then retted in the water at Fresh or Selby's Pond, then dried again, and scutched to separate the fibers, then combed through a hatchel. In the late 1700s flax remained a local crop, but most hemp yarn came from Holland, or from southern colonies.

There are records of at least four Stratford ropewalks. In 1765 John Benjamin bequeathed his rope house and shop at South Parade to his sons John and George. In 1791 the legislature decreed that the highway between Benjamin's Bridge across Pembrook Creek and Newfield Bridge across the Pequonnock be made:

> a straight line . . . through Asa Benjamin's rope walk. Twenty rods of the south part thereof must be taken up and shifted to the north end, together with his wheel house, which is thirty feet in length, and subject him to the necessity of purchasing a lot of land of about seven acres at an extravagant price, beside the expense of taking up the rope walk.

The town paid Asa $330 and the ropewalk was rebuilt.

In 1792 Daniel and Abigail Curtiss leased to Abigail's brother David Osborn a strip of land along the river bank at their shipyard on the point "to have sufficient ground to place or erect a house for a rope walk 40 ft. square, and to occupy sd. ground for a ropewalk." The ropewalk was two rods wide and about a ship's cable–100 fathoms, or 600 feet–in length. Only the wheelhouse was sheltered: the walk itself stood in open air.

First Osborne, then Nicoll and the Wetmores, who bought the ropeworks in 1795, employed a skilled ropemaker, assisted by laborers, apprentices, and slaves. In 1794 Captain William Provoost of the brig *Sisters* signed a contract with Osborne to indenture to him an Irish laborer, William Walch of Cork, to work at the ropewalk for a period of five years. Provoost agreed "to pay for his [Walch's] passage & to find & allow him meat, drink, apparel & lodgings."

In 1800 another contract was recorded in the land records:

> This Indenture made between Andrew Dayton and John Dayton his son, both of Std. on the one part & Victory Wetmore, John Thompson, Sam'l. W Johnson & Matths Nicoll all of Std. Merchants in company under the name of Victory Wetmore & Co.of Std. on the other part Witnesseth—that the sd. Andrew Dayton hath put and placed & by these presents doth put & bind out his son John Dayton & the sd. John doth hereby put, place, & bind out himself as an apprentice to the sd. Victory Wetmore & Co. to learn the Art & Mistery of a Rope Maker—The sd. John Dayton to live with the sd. Victory Wetmore & Co. & to serve with them in manner of an apprentice from the Date hereof until Oct 15, 1804. . . . Victory Wetmore & Co. each of them on their pt. do hereby agree promise & covenant to teach & instruct the sd. apprentice or cause him to be instructed & taught in the Art, Trade, or

In 1800 ropemaker William Walch lays a rope at the Wetmores' ropewalk, feeding strands onto a cone-shaped "top," while in the wheelhouse apprentice John Dayton turns a wheel to twist three strands into a rope.

> Calling of a rope maker by the best way or means they can, also to teach and instruct the sd. apprentice or cause him to be instructed & taught to read & write & cypher as far as the rule of 3 if the sd. apprentice be capable of learning.

The Stratford ropewalks gradually shut down. By 1824 the only remaining ropemaker was James Jones, next door to Silas Burton's weaving shop, and by 1860 the only local walk was one operated by a man named Curtis near Esek Lane.

Early sailcloth was a strong, thick, handwoven cloth, lighter than canvas, called duck. Like rope, it was made of hemp or linen. In Colonial times it was nearly all imported as Osnaburg, Hollands duck, or Russia duck, depending on the source. In 1734 the General Assembly passed "An act for the encouragement of raising hemp, making canvas or duck, and also for making fine linen." In 1746, however, Parliament placed a duty on duck not woven in Great Britain, discouraging American production of sailcloth until the Revolution, when importation of English duck ended. President Washington's diary for October 17, 1789 states, "At Stratford they are establishing a manufactory of duck, and have lately turned out about 400 bolts."

Local joiners, cabinetmakers, and wheelwrights in the area were skilled at making spars, blocks, and deadeyes for Stratford ships. In the early nineteenth century the industry was self-contained, but local sources later dried up, and shipbuilders traveled to New York for sails, spars, and hardware, to be delivered by sound steamer or sailing packet.

In 1854 Lewis Russell sold the shipyard at the point to Peter Cornell White from Northport, Long Island. The Whites owned the yard for 50 years. The yard had ways for launching vessels of more than 300 tons—two large marine railways on the Housatonic, and a smaller railway on the Ferry Creek side. The large railways used wooden 12x12 timbers for rails, with side boards nailed to them to guide the ship cradle. At the top of each ramp was a horse-powered capstan to haul ships. To slide the vessels off the railway for long term work, more timbers lay at right angles to the ways, and heavy blocks and tackle were rigged to the cradles. Grease from the slaughterhouse across the creek covered everything, smeared over all the rail timbers. When a vessel became stuck on the ways, it was jacked up so grease could be injected, then sent on its way. The men were covered from head to toe with grease: some 300 gallons a year were used. The yard hauled and set masts with a large wooden crane. A steam box with a boiler next to it could steam 60-foot planks for bending into place.

With this equipment, White launched the 135-ton schooner *Helen Mar* on September 27, 1855, the 199-ton schooner *Josephine B. Small* on September 26,

When White, and then Bedell, ran the shipyard, the winter scene at Ferry Creek was crowded with stored boats. These houseboats provided quarters for bridge builders.

1861, the 333-ton schooner *Joseph Baxter* on September 13, 1866, the schooner *Jesse Knight* on July 17, 1867, and the 108-ton *Clarissa Allen* in 1867. When the *Margaret Kennedy* sank at Milford in a severe gale in 1869, White rebuilt it at the yard. The schooners *Chieftain*, 1853; *Henry B. Drew*, 1867; *Grace Darling*, 1882; and the sloops *J.C.R. Brown*, 1871; *Julia*, 1871; *Star*, 1873; and *Sarah Louisa*, 1874 were all Stratford built.

Launching these vessels was a time of risk, when anything might go wrong. When N.R. White tried to launch the schooner *Jesse Knight* on July 14, he "did not get her off," whether due to tide or poor planning is unknown, but it took him until the 17th to succeed.

The time it took to build the schooner *Clarissa Allen* is typical. On December 13, 1866 White spent the day in the woods with Nathan Wells spotting timber, and that night met with Captain Justus Hale and the other stockholders at Captain Parks's home. Construction took all spring and summer. On the morning of August 24, the masts were set and in the afternoon of September 2 the *Clarissa Allen* was launched. On September 18 Captain Hale took the new schooner to New York, and on December 21, 1867, a year from her inception, *Clarissa Allen* set out from New York toward Corpus Christie on her first paying voyage.

Faced with improved railroad and steamboat transport, White's orders for new coasting schooners dwindled. The Peter White Shipyard turned to building sail and steam powered oyster boats, possibly including the 147-ton *Ruel Rowe* in 1887. Master carpenter Moses Hart built several steam powered oyster dredges in Stratford, probably at John Bond's at the lower wharf. They included, in 1885 the 126-ton *Josephine*, in 1886 the 141-ton steamer *City Point* and the 77-ton *Mikado*, and in 1887 the 104-ton *Kate C. Stevens*. Nathan Wells's diary records on December 23, 1885, "Went to the lower dock to see the steamer *Josephine* launched. She slid off in fine style about 2 oclock pm." In 1897 an aging Peter White turned over operation of the yard to William Edward Bedell, master carpenter.

William Bedell, born on May 15, 1847 in Port Jefferson, Long Island, grew up working in his father's shipyard in Hempstead Harbor. When he leased White's shipyard in 1897, he advertised in the city directory:

> Wm. E. Bedell Marine Railway, Builder of All Kinds of Boats
> Gasolene Launches a Specialty
> Upper Dock, Foot East Broad Street Stratford, Conn.

The yard was busy from the start. Rapid changes were occurring in the oyster industry. As leased beds expanded, companies grew in size, and steam powered dredges replaced sailing craft. Oyster boats, once dugout canoes, then New Haven sharpies, diverged into two types. Sailing craft, still mandated for natural growth beds, increased in size and carried donkey engines to power winches. Leased beds used specially designed steam (and soon gasoline) powered vessels capable of carrying 3,000 to 4,000 bushels of oysters.

The *Rhoda E. Crane* was one of Bedell's first products. Oysterman Charles B. Crane had her built in early 1897, registered her in Bridgeport on April 24 as hailing from Stratford but, before the year was out, sold his home in Stratford and registered her at Greenport. *Rhoda E. Crane* grossed 14 tons. She had a long open deck and an aft pilot house. This arrangement, followed by most oyster boats, allowed the pilot to view all sides of the ship, his dredging post, and his dredges mounted near the bow, and to control all dredging and maneuvering operations from within. Oysters were piled on the deck as high as the pilot house windows. Her power plant was one of the first gasoline marine engines, an 18-horsepower Wolverine.

In 1904 William Edward Bedell bought the yard from the heirs of Peter White, and managed its operation until his death in 1924. Bedell built only wooden boats, for oystering, freight carrying, and harbor tugs. Howard Hyde, who worked in the yard and later managed it, said "Once the boats were built, they would never come back. They are still around. They built them good."

A complete record of Bedell-built boats does not exist, but Hyde, harking back to *c.* 1910, said: "In those days there were several Master Carpenters. Reuben Green was one. Moses Hart was also one. They would come in and build a boat and take credit, but it was built in that yard. Just the same down here at the town docks [Bond's Dock]—they would build right on the town docks and just slide them over. Reuben Green built a couple. Ash Bond built a couple, and there were others."

Fletch Lewis expands on Howard's statement in his story of the river:

> In the 1800s the Lower dock or Bond's dock was the scene of much boat building. Moses Hart made a specialty of building oyster steamers at this location. Some of the better known of these boats were the *Bond Currier* [launched July 1 1885], *Kate Stevens*, and the *Mikado*. Ashabel Bond, owner of the *Bond Currier*, married Mr. Currier's daughter and Mr. Currier furnished the money to build the *Bond Currier*.

Bedell's shipyard produced an estimated 90 boats between the time he took over the yard and the building of the last boat, *James Bond*. Among the largest of these was the *Comanche*, a New York City quarantine boat; the large oyster boats *Governor* and *Siva*; and the yachts *Rose A.* and *Sarah Vreeland*.

In 1909 Bedell built his largest boat to date, the 64-ton, 70-foot oyster steamer *Louis R.*, Reg. No. 206476. The boat was of classic design, deck forward, pilot house aft. *Louis R.* was the last steam powered oyster dredge built by Bedell, and kept her steam power until 1961, when it was replaced by diesel. In 1996 *Louis R.* still came up the Housatonic as a Tallmadge Brothers buyboat.

The Bedell shipyard remained a family operation for three generations. Son William Caniff Bedell, born in 1880, was listed in the city directory as an employee in 1899. His children in turn, Nina, William Edward, and Kenneth all helped operate the yard. The senior William Edward's sister married Captain

George Culver, and their son Irving spent years working in the yard when he wasn't oystering.

After old Bill Bedell died in 1924, William Caniff Bedell, master carpenter, took over the yard. His skill was just as great, but the oyster fisheries were shrinking, and in 1929 the great depression swept the land. After that, the only recorded order for an oyster boat was for the 26-ton *Grace P. Lowndes*, built for Lowndes Oyster Company of South Norwalk in 1931. In 1936 Bedells built the *James Bond* on speculation: It lay at the wharf for more than a year before the Andrew Radel Oyster Company in Bridgeport bought it. Third generation William E. Bedell constructed these last two boats, but because he had never been certified as a master carpenter, his father, then in his 60s, was registered as builder.

The hurricane in 1938 laid waste the coast, destroying boats, buildings, and beds. Oyster beds were buried in debris and silt by the storm. Processing plants located along the waterfront were damaged or lost entirely. It was the eve of World War II, and manpower to rebuild the industry had disappeared.

The demise of the oyster industry had a significant impact on Bedell's. The yard continued to haul the few remaining boats for painting and repair, but none were built, and major work was rare. The last oyster boat rebuilt at Bedell's was the 41-ton *Laurel*. To stay in business, Bedell's turned to maintaining yachts. Howard Hyde recalled the business at that time:

The oyster steamer Laurel *was the last oysterboat rebuilt at Bedell's. Built in 1891 by A.C. Brown in Tottenville, New York, the 110-year-old* Laurel *is still in use as a buyboat in 2001. (Robert Treat sketch.)*

The lower wharf in 1885 was home to boatbuilders, oystermen and shellermen, coasting vessels, and John Bond's saloon and prizefighter training camp. (Robert Treat sketch.)

Everything was all yachts then—big yachts. I don't mean little thirty footers. Most of these yachts were owned by big companies, all from the New England area. When the boat got there, the owner would simply walk away and the yard took care of everything—everything! When the guy called that he wanted his boat, he would give you a certain amount of time. That boat had to be overboard, ready to run when he walked on the dock. Of course they paid for it. It was an expensive yard. This was the only yard big enough to haul out the boats. All the cleaning, vacuuming, windows, and polishing was done. The customer stepped aboard like he just bought it. If there were any problems, no matter what, they would be fixed. Once it left the yard, there was not one complaint that ever came back. Cost didn't mean anything. The last two years I was manager, I remember Bill was on the phone with a new customer and he was talking about cost. Bill told him "Why don't you leave us a thousand dollars and when that runs out we will call you." That was the way business was.

After 1950, large company-owned yachts became scarce, and Bedell's had to turn to smaller pleasure boats. But it remained a top quality, top price yard. When a boat was hauled, its rigging was removed and its masts and woodwork were scraped to bare wood, then professional varnishers and painters laid on six to eight coats. By then, William C. Bedell was in his 70s, and his son William E. ran the yard. In 1956 Howard Hyde was named yard manager. Howard recognized the changing nature of the business, and pushed for yard modernization: lighter and more automated gear, and slips in place of moorings. The marine railway was now powered by a gasoline engine but the cumbersome hauling system was still in place, so, when given the green light, Howard ordered the first Travelift in the area, and drove the pilings and built the track for it himself with the yard's own crane. A hauling job that before had taken half a day now took 20 minutes.

On February 14, 1960 William Caniff Bedell died at age 80, and that year his children sold the yard to Richard Palmer as the Stratford Marina. From Palmer it passed to David Olsen, then in 1994 it became Brewer's Stratford Marina. In 1999 a clubhouse for visiting yachtsmen and a new waterfront restaurant were added, and the concrete block warehouse that Alfred Waklee had built early in the twentieth century gave way to a large new steel-girdered shop. As Curtiss's, Wheeler's, Russell's, White's and Bedell's, the yard saw more than 300 years of shipbuilding.

LIFE AT THE LOWER WHARF

Two miles up the Stratford channel, at a place called Waterside, the earliest wharves were built. By the end of the American Revolution, Waterside was a place of wharves and warehouses. LeGrand Cannon from New York, who lived over at Sandy Hollow, operated Cannon's Wharf, with his three sons Lewis, James, and LeGrand. The wharves above it and below it were gradually eclipsed, but their warehouses remained as their owners plied the shipping trade.

In 1784 Captain Nehemiah Gorham bought the land north of Cannon's Wharf from Ebenezer Thompson and partners, and settled in with his new bride Mary. The property already had a barn, a warehouse, and a dwelling, which Gorham expanded. A stone breakwater still visible in the 1920s indicates that he had his own wharf there.

Major exports to the West Indies were salt beef, pork, and leather goods. In 1784 widow Charity Kneeland conveyed her land north of Gorhams to Elijah Blakeman and his family, with dwelling house, weaver's shop, and slaughterhouse at the bend in the road known as Butchers' Flats. At the slaughterhouse, animal products were packed directly into hogsheads from Thomas Curtis's cooperage on Meetinghouse Hill, and hides were sent to Joseph Walker and Victory Wetmore's tannery to be tanned for shoes, pants, saddles, and harness for the export trade. The weaver's shop was a source of duck for sails.

Between the slaughterhouse and the wharf the Silbeys/Selbys lived. In 1795 John Selby Jr. married Betsy, who ran their business whenever he was out to sea. After Captain Selby was caught smuggling rum in 1797, he lost his appetite for going to sea. His last recorded voyage was as master of the schooner *Olivia* in September 1798. In their house at Waterside (now 627 Stratford Avenue) they spent the next 28 years running a small tavern, supplemented by whatever income they could gather, listed in their account book. In 1801 Lemuel Hubbell made a bedstead, a washing stool, and some "winder" hoops, and cut eight loads of wood, in trade for a musket and a shilling. Joseph Hubbell the shoemaker charged 3s 6p for making a pair of shoes for little Eliza and 2s 6p for mending a pair for Betsey; at another time he made a pair of shoes for 3s 6p, but Betsey made a jacket for him for the same amount. Samuel Wells was a good customer at the bar. His 1804 tab includes butts of rum, bowls of toddy, nips and pints and gills of rum, and ends up, appropriately for a drinking man, with payment of 3s 1p for "one pine board for coffin."

Captain Selby sold oysters by the bushel. Silas Hubbell, Joseph Thompson, William Fairchild, William Walker, Joseph Walker Esq., Samuel Lampson, and Ashabel "Baulding," each stopped in for a bushel or two. Asa Curtis once bought a half bushel, David Seeley bought nine at once, and Dr. Charles Tomlinson must have valued his Vitamin E—he bought seven bushels over a one-month period in 1803.

To supplement the bar, earnings from sale of food, lodging, sewing, oysters, and wood are listed. Other accounts show shad, onions, and potatoes changing hands. In 1815 Betsy earned £3 9s weaving cloth for John Thompson.

Some customers paid their drinking bills by labor. Abner Judson's pints of rum are balanced "by carting dung and plowing." In 1805 Matthew Rice sold Selby 322 bushels of shells for making wall plaster, and in 1802 Phinas Blackman charged him 3s for slaking lime. Others cleaned his well, brought him blackgrass, and carted flour from Yellow Mill. Selby bought spirits by the gallon and sold it by the glass. His David Brooks account shows Brooks as a wholesaler: "4 gal rum, 5 lofs sugar, 113 gal rum, 1 hhd rum (107 gal), 32 gal rum, 1 hhd. rum." His customer accounts include rum by the tot, the gill, or halfpint, and by the pint (9p); gin by the butt or button (apparently half a nip and worth 2p), and by the bot or bote; brandy by the bot, the gill, and the gallon; cider by the gallon; and stingers, slings, and toddies (9p).

Selby's only two nautical entries after 1798 are entered in 1804, to William Gorham, "for piloting the brig," and for "cash due from Dickinson for wages on board schooner *Salley*, £5 14s 3p." Pages sewn into the book in 1817 record the sale of oysters.

East of Selby were the house of Lemuel Curtis, and that of Ebenezer Allen, whose deed read "bordered east on the high water mark, or channel." In 1773 no public highway yet ran southward along the river.

After Peter Curtiss built a wharf at the end of New Lane (now Broad Street) in the 1790s, the wharf at Waterside became known as the lower wharf. When James Cannon sold it in 1796 to John Thompson and Matthias Nicoll, it became Thompson's Wharf again. Both Thompson and Nicoll were active shippers. Records for 1800 show the schooner *Rose* bringing Thompson salt from Exuma, probably for the slaughterhouse, to pack salt meat for export. Nicoll had shipping interests in New York, and owned Stratford lands and businesses inherited from his father Benjamin, who, with his brother William and his half-brother William Samuel Johnson, had foreclosed on Abel and Abijah Beach in 1766.

In 1804 the proprietors gave Captains William Booth and Nehemiah Gorham a stretch of waterfront south of Thompson's Wharf located between the highway and the channel (low water line) of the river, to build a wharf and store, which were completed by the end of January. This wharf and store are at the place where John Brooks had built in 1759 (now 19 Shore Road). That August, Nicoll and Thompson sold Thompson's Wharf to Booth.

In 1816 Nehemiah Gorham sold his third of the wharf to Booth's widow Mary Ann Booth, and in 1820 she and Booth's other heirs, daughter Mary Ann Walker and her husband Jonathan Otis Walker, sold 13/15 of the wharf to Curtis Chatfield. Jonathan Otis died at sea on his way to his West Indies business in 1821.

In 1806 19-year-old Lewis Chatfield Jr. was skippering the 17-ton sloop *Mary* out of Huntington. In 1819 he and his wife Clarisa bought the riverfront property north of Captain Gorham, together with its dwelling house (now 640 Stratford Avenue), slaughterhouse, and weaver's shop. In the 1870s white-haired Captain Chatfield was still rowing children around the harbor.

His brother Curtis Chatfield married Captain Selby's daughter Eliza and moved into the Selby home to help, operating their brother Lemuel's 20-ton sloop *Susan*. In 1814 he charged Lemuel 8s for a sloopload of shells, in 1815 he made David Chatfield pay him $5 for breaking *Susan's* boom, and in 1816 he bought *Susan* from Lemuel for $300. *Susan* was kept busy for the next few years shuttling along the coast: Weaver Silas Burton took passage to New York delivering rugs and Samuel William Johnson shipped freight.

Duck, twine, and rigging from New York came to David Brooks. Business was so good that in 1819 Chatfield and his father-in-law traded up to the 32-ton sloop *Castle*. In 1820 Curtis Chatfield sold the "slawter house" to Nathan Thorp

Some time before 1910 an unidentified oyster sloop waits to be hauled on the railway north of Waklee's old warehouse on Broad Street.

for $20 and bought the lower wharf from the heirs of William Booth. *Castle* was kept busy hauling all sorts of freight, including stone from Middletown and Portland, and meal from Berkshire Mill. An 1824 bill to Philo and Ezra Wakeley for ships' timber denotes busy shipyards. As Chatfield's business increased, it was time again for a larger sloop, and in 1825 *Eliza C.*, 42 tons, was registered. Robert Fairchild's journal on September 4, 1827 notes "My daughter Julia this day went to New York in the *Commodore Hull*, Capt. Chatfield" but does not say which Chatfield.

On Wednesday, September 22, 1824, the first steamboat, *General LaFayette*, arrived in the river from New York, and changed water travel forever. That year the wharf was extended toward the channel to accommodate the steamboats. With regularly scheduled arrivals, freight and passenger traffic expanded, and the lower wharf bustled with activity. A consortium of businessmen built a new large warehouse there. In 1828 Curtis Chatfield began to concentrate on oystering, bought several of the little oysterhouses built below the bank, and sold the wharf to John Andrews. It then went to Roger Humiston, and in 1832 to oysterman Isaac Smith. South of the lower wharf, little shacks were built, where oysters were prepared for market. By 1867 the Smiths had six or more of these stores, and by the close of the nineteenth century, some 15 oyster houses filled the area, 13 in a single row.

In 1844 Captain John Brooks's steamer *Nimrod* took the mail contract away from the stage line, and for several years Postmaster David Brooks came down to the wharf to pick up mail from New York. When Elias Wilcoxson's family emigrated west in 1846, they carted their possessions to the wharf and took passage on the *Naugatuck*.

After 1849 it became the fashion to "take the [railroad] cars" to Bridgeport, then go to New York by boat from that busy terminal. Aside from the occasional Derby steamboat docking at the lower wharf, schooners with lumber, stone, or brick made up the traffic. They brought coal from Perth Amboy to both the upper and the lower dock. But West Indies trade shrivelled, as large sailing vessels brought cargo into New York harbor for redistribution by Sound steamers and the railroads. Isaac Smith combined two homesteads into one large house at the corner, and deeded the house at present day 30 Shore Road to son Henry. When Isaac died in 1861, Henry inherited the whole operation.

By the time Henry Smith died, the busy days of shipping in Stratford were over. Passenger steamboats, bankrupted by the railroads, seldom ran to Derby, and the lower wharf stood empty. So in March 1883 the family sold the wharf to John C. Bond. Born in Commack, Long Island, on October 24, 1840, Captain Bond had worked as a ship's carpenter, commanded schooners out of Northport, sailed to California, then moved to Stratford and purchased several buildings at the dock.

Bond lost no time converting the warehouse on the dock into a combined convenience store, saloon, cafe, and prizefighters' training center. He added a platform on the roof, and built a veranda with upper deck around the building.

John and Julia Bond's house at 603 Stratford Avenue was home to boxers in training and to oystermen, shellermen, ship's carpenters, and seamen.

Downstairs was an arena, and upstairs were rooms for fighters in training. His home across the street provided more quarters. Meachen's two-story oyster house (now 19 Shore Road), his shed on pilings where an old wharf had stood, and a cottage built on pilings between 1882 and 1893 (later called Kate's Cottage), boarded others. Bond's enclave housed several activities: his boxers sparred on the outdoor deck where Wheeler's store had been, oystermen worked in the complex of stores and his brother Ashabel and others built boats in a shed on the wharf beyond the training quarters. Until his death in 1886, Albert Laing could be seen sitting at his upper window carving decoys, or entering into his account book 10¢ for beer at Bond's saloon. Beyond Bond's house, in two halves of the old Selby House, lived Maria Peck and her aunt Eliza Chatfield.

The daily routine at the training camp began at 6:30 a.m., unless an early riser who woke at 5:00 a.m. "starts in to unmercifully punish Capt. Bond's piano." Breakfast was of nourishing eggs, oatmeal, and cereals, fruits, and tea and milk. After this "light" meal, the boxers walked down to the center to pick up their mail and buy a newspaper, then to stroll leisurely back to camp. At 9:00 a.m. the group set out for a 6- or 7-mile run—the first joggers, in an era when most Stratford men got their exercise hoeing corn or tonging for oysters. On return, it was time to strip off their heavy sweaters, and take a cooling dip in the clear waters of the Housatonic, then to the rubdown room for an invigorating massage by their trainers. At noon, the dinner table would groan with bodybuilding meats and fish and vegetables, tempting to the men, who knew they had to restrain themselves to keep in trim. Free time ended at 3:00 p.m. A reporter wrote in 1914:

At 3:00 the boys attire themselves in their gymnasium suits and with the trainers keeping time they start in on their shadow boxing, rope jumping, body exercises, and bag punching. The day I was present K.O. Brown and [Battling] Levinski were in New York but there was my friend Bobby Reynolds, Johnny Howard, Joe Johnson, and George Manus to give me an idea how the boys went through their stunts. Howard was busy endeavoring to 'knock the stuffins out of KO's punch bag.' Bobby Reynolds was fighting for dear life, shadow boxing with an imaginary foe, whom he declared he must have licked, because there was nothing left of him when he was through. Manus was trying hard to beat another imaginary friend, whom he was chasing around the floor, but there seemed to be a dozen fighting him at once, for he was swinging in all directions. Johnson, who is about one size smaller than a house, was mixing it up with the post. After he grew disgusted with the post, who had no inclination to mix in, the big fellow went out chasing an imaginary foe.

During any day from April through September one could find Captain John and his wife Julia moving about the training quarters. A tall, strong, jovial man, sporting a handlebar mustache, Captain John pushed his fighters to their limits, with a regimen of strenuous roadwork, vigorous double rope jumping, and endless rounds of sparring, for boxers and trainers alike.

Bond's Training Quarters turned out some of the greatest boxers in America. "Terrible Terry" Mc Govern, who won the world championship featherweight crown by knocking out George Dixon in 1900, first put on his gloves in Stratford.

After a morning of running, rowing, chopping wood, and an afternoon of sparring, the boxers at Bond's pose with beer kegs, oars, and saloon patrons.

Larry Temple, Hugh McGovern, Joe Johnson, Stanley Ketchell, Young Corbett, Jack Britton, Tommy Ryan, Tommy Murphy, and Jack "the Duke" Diamond, all trained at Bond's. Battling Levinski was Barney Lebowitz in real life. When K.O. Brown put on a suit and tie, he was Valentine Braun (a name that may have caused him to take up fighting.) John L. Sullivan, who defeated Jake Kilrain in 75 rounds in the last bare-knuckle fight in America in 1889, was a frequent visitor.

The training camp also attracted every red-blooded young man in the area. Shang Wheeler, as a young and healthy oysterman, made an excellent sparring partner, and spent a lot of time there. J. Fletcher Lewis tells a story of events at the camp:

> It seems that Shang had a girl and Tommy Ryan had his eye on Shang's girl. Tommy was a heavyweight and so was Shang. Old John had a big woodpile out alongside of the old building and there were two axes, and he would send these strappers out to chop wood. One day after Tommy had been successful in stealing Shang's girl, Shang came down Stratford Avenue and saw Tommy outside of the training quarters, working on the woodpile. Shang made a wild dive for the other axe, alongside the door, and started for Tommy. Tommy threw down his axe and started for the dock. He dove off the dock. Shang marched up and down the dock with the axe on his shoulders and yelled "You come ashore and I'll cut your head off!" They finally had to collar Shang and then somebody dove overboard to save Tommy from drowning.

The author's father-in-law, Bill Beloin, also put in a few rounds as a youth. Lifelong Stratford resident and one-time welterweight boxer Michael Sterback spent much time at Bond's Dock as a youngster and later as a boxing trainer under Battling Levinsky. He recalled Wheeler and Ashabel Bond's son Edward as sparring partners, and remembered Terry McGovern as a rough, tough fighter. Sterback looked back on Bond's as the home of so many good boxers, and a great place to train.

Not all visitors to Bond's carried away great memories. Trainer Jack "the Duke" Diamond wrote to a friend in 1908, "launch capsized in terrific gale. Two children drowned." That morning, Decoration Day, Shelton residents Mr. and Mrs. James Raucher, their children John and Gertrude, and four relatives had come down to Bond's in their motor launch for a day's outing. When bad weather threatened, Mrs. Raucher wanted to take the children home on the trolley, but her husband insisted that they stay aboard, so she went on alone. At 5:50 p.m. rain erupted and a fierce wind sprang up. Seventy feet from shore the launch capsized, and the children disappeared, despite efforts of their father and his brothers. Another launch, belonging to Dr. Sharpe of Shelton, came alongside to aid the men in the water. Their cries were heard on shore, and several boxers and trainers dove into the turbulent water. Again and again they dove, searching for the children, but they could not find them. John and Gertrude Raucher drowned.

The golden period of Captain Bond's training camp lasted more than 30 years. In 1914 the captain could be seen seated in his armchair on the open deck, watching swallows skimming over the open water, smoking his Missouri meerschaum or a black cigar, and thinking of the good times past. On November 11, 1915 his heart failed, and an era ended. The following month Battling Levinsky, living in the cottage over the water at 31 Shore Road, took over the operation and ran it for several years. Finally the old quarters were abandoned, to become a depression period home for the Hotchkiss family, and Levinsky's operation moved to Bridgeport. But for a dwindling number of old-timers, the smell of brine and sawdust and the the sound of punching bag leather and canvas were still there.

In 1919 Julia Bond sold the property, comprising the dock and its two buildings, a row of oyster shacks north of Byron Romer's home (now 19 Shore Road), and her residence across the highway. In 1940 it passed to the town, and in 1943 Bond's house came down.

Commerce at the dock declined to nearly nothing. In the 1920s oystering activities predominated, and a sign on the cottage at 31 Shore Road proclaimed boats for rent. Citizens beached their boats beyond the cottage, and reached them at low tide along the cart path on the shore. The public highway on the bank now ended at 50 Shore Road.

Later, "Captain Joe" Slatcher sold bait and rented rowboats from a little scow tied up near the dock. The old dock rotted, and became a base for teenagers to swim across the river. When the ladies in rocking chairs at the Housatonic Boat Club complained of young men swimming nude across the river, the club's board of governors investigated and found that they were visible only through binoculars.

The dock was rebuilt in 1949, rebuilt again in 1977 after damage by the August 1976 Hurricane Belle, and once again in 1997. By 1966 the Housatonic Boat Club had raised the roadway on their property, and in 1975 Town Manager Venables had it oiled for them. In 1957 and 1960 Katharine Hepburn stayed at the little red cottage, then owned by the theater, and gave it its name, Kate's Cottage. Passing cars on the newly oiled road struck and damaged the cottage, and in 1990 arsonists gutted it. In 1993, after the DEP refused to allow its reuse on site, a group of enthusiasts disassembled it for use elsewhere as a duck decoy museum, which was never built.

Waterfront activities again picked up. Andy Brown opened a new boatyard, Brown Boat Works, north of the dock at 638 Stratford Avenue, which his son took over and his granddaughter owns today. Oystering revived, and oystermen kept their craft at Brown's and unloaded their catch at the launching ramp. Tallmadge Brothers placed pilings in the river, where their buyboats, the *Greenport* or the old Stratford-built *Louis R.*, loaded oysters from the fleet. As a new millennium begins, a new generation of Browns plans a seed oyster farm at the Boat Works.

But the majority of users are the people. Expectant fishermen dangle lines from the wharf year round. Hunters launch their duckboats at the ramp and motor across to Knell's Island with their dogs. Boaters launch their outboard boats from trailers. Kayakers practice rolling over and uprighting themselves, and canoeists launch their craft here. Bird watchers and bird feeders occupy the dock and launching area, spreading grain—or bread or bagels—for the ducks and swans and gulls. And on summer evenings, older citizens bring their own folding chairs, and congregate to enjoy the outdoor air, exchanging appetizers, cocktails, and news.

Bond's Dock has been in use for nearly four centuries. Its use has changed, but it remains a hub of waterfront activity, a resource of the town.

THE HOUSATONIC SHIP BUILDING COMPANY

In the first decade of the twentieth century, only 10 percent of American imports and exports was carried in American ships. When war broke out in Europe in 1914, foreign ships were diverted to the wartime needs of their own countries and suddenly coffee, tea, sugar, silk, and rubber were not arriving, and export products were sitting on American docks. The federal government established the Shipping Board, which sought to produce new ships.

To stretch scarce materials, ships were designed of low grade steel, concrete, or wood. The Hog Island freighters, made of steel, bore up well, and continued as tramp steamers for many postwar years. Concrete ships were heavy, and carried little cargo: most ended up being used as breakwaters. Wooden ship design was an

On December 31, 1918 crowds gathered on the Devon shore to watch the launching, as Fairfield *waited on the ways for a launching signal.*

A month after Fairfield *was launched,* Ganeri, *the second ship, was ready. Fantail filled with officials, she slid down the ways to the cheers of the crowd.*

ancient art and might have been successful, but because of inexperienced workers and the use of green wood, the vessels leaked, warped, and rotted.

Nationwide, the Shipping Board set up 160 new shipyards, one of which was in Stratford, where wooden ships had been built for 275 years. In late 1916 a company was organized and a contract was let for five 2,500-ton wooden steam ships. The company president was Frederick E. Morgan (brother of U.S. Treasurer Daniel Morgan), Carl Foster was secretary/treasurer, and Foster Hawkins was general manager. An ad in the City Directory for that year read:

The Housatonic Ship Building Co.
Foster L Hawkins, General Manager
Standard Designs for Sailing and Auxiliary Vessels
500, 1000, 2000 and 3000 Tons Dead Weight Capacity
Stratford, Conn. U.S.A.

North of the New Haven Railroad bridge the company bought riverfront land and built six parallel sets of launching rails and a wooden engineering building. Keels were laid and hulls began to take shape, but materials were scarce and progress was slow. The ships, designed by naval architect Theodore N. Ferris, were the largest ever built at Stratford, measuring 2,551 tons gross and 1,528 tons net, with lengths of 267.3 feet, 46-foot beams, and 23.9-foot drafts. Their Allis Chalmers reciprocating steam engines delivered 1,400 indicated horsepower, and they were to carry a crew of 41. Nationwide, some 400 examples of this ship design were built. The L.H. Shattuck yard in Newington, New Hampshire was one other nearby yard building them. Because the channel of the Housatonic was so shallow, the ships launched at Stratford were towed to Providence before their engines were installed. With no engines, the ships were light enough and therefore floated high enough to safely negotiate the channel.

Only *Fairfield* ever operated as a steamer. Delays and overruns haunted the program. Ships contracted at $300,000 ended up costing $425,000. Finally, the Emergency Fleet Corporation appointed Lawrence Bernard general manager, to make "sweeping changes."

The Armistice was signed on November 11, 1918. The first ship was launched on December 31. Ralph Goodsell recalled the event. Sightseers lined the Milford shore, and small boats had to be shooed down the river. Tug whistles blew and the *Fairfield* slid down the ways without a hitch. Five tugs eased her down the river and over to Bridgeport, on that last day of the year, just in time to meet a schedule and receive a payment. At 10:00 a.m. on January 30, 1919 a second engineless hull, *Ganeri*, followed down the ways, and on March 9 the Bridgeport *Herald* announced another, the *Portland*. Work continued on the rest, although the need had passed. On June 25, 1920 wooden scaffolding around one hull collapsed and injured several workers. Ephraim Wakelee, ship's carpenter since the launching of the four-master *Perry Setzer* in 1903, who had gone into house carpentry until the new shipyard opened, died from his injuries.

Portland and two others were finally completed but never had engines installed. *Portland* reappeared in Stratford in 1957, to help to right the overturned dredge *General*. Until then she had spent her life as a barge in the Tappan Zee carrying bricks.

In the 1920s, the site was occupied for awhile by Sunshine homes, builder of houses from concrete blocks, then by Simon Lake's last enterprise, Argonaut Salvage. In 1928, when Lake owed the Town more than $14,000 in back taxes, Town Attorney Ray Baldwin instituted foreclosure actions. The shipyard stood abandoned until after World War II, when Vincent Bendix bought the property to build his helicopter factory. The old wooden shipyard office and lofting building is gone now, and the new brick factory is home to Dresser Industries. Not many years ago the steel launching rails were still visible at the river's edge.

Igor Sikorsky and His Flying Boats

In the spring of 1929 Sikorsky Aviation Corporation moved into a new factory between the river and the road to Lordship, to build a new kind of airplane. Conventional shipbuilding was dying on the river, but this "new age" facility was to become a major element in the history of the river—and of international flight. The factory had 147,000 square feet of floorspace, and the property covered 36 acres. It was completed about mid July, just in time to start production on the new S-38 amphibion (Sikorsky always used the Greek spelling of the word).

Across the road, a new airport with 2,000-foot gravel runways had just been completed by pumping gravel onto the marsh, while excavating a new seaplane basin on the river. Between the river and the airport, the location was an ideal spot for testing both seaplanes and landplanes. On July 5, 1929 the new airport was dedicated, and soon the factory opened. On September 1 Sikorsky Aviation Corporation became a part of United Aircraft and Transport Corporation, a company that by the end of the year included Boeing, Chance Vought, Hamilton Standard, Northrop, Pratt & Whitney, Stearman, and three airlines.

Igor Ivanovich Sikorsky (1889–1972) had already had one aviation career and was in the midst of a second. A third, the development of the helicopter, was ten years in the future. After studying at the Kiev Polytechnical Institute in 1907 and in Paris in 1909, where he learned from early birdmen Louis Bleriot, Henri Farman, and Louis Ferber, Sikorsky went home to Kiev to build a helicopter, against all advice. After two failures in 1909 and 1910, he decided that "temporarily I must enter the fixed wing business." He went to work in charge of airplane design at the Russo-Baltic Wagon Company. In 1913 he designed and built the world's first four-engined aircraft, the 88-foot wingspan 9,000-pound bomber called Bolshoi Baltiiskii (The Grande). Seventy-three follow-on bombers were built, and Czar Nicholas personally congratulated the designer.

Then came the Russian Revolution. After a year of exile in France and his arrival in America in 1920, Sikorsky finally persuaded a few friends to finance him. On March 5, 1923, Sikorsky Aero Engineering Company was founded on Victor Utgoff's chicken farm on Long Island, where a small group of emigrés built aircraft for sale. Worker Nick Glad said, "During the week, we worked hard on the airplane outdoors, and the chickens ran around under our feet. On the weekend, we would kill and eat the chickens, and take the rivets from their crops, to use the following week."

In that time of few and primitive airfields, transport aircraft able to land without airports made sense for use around the world. In a small factory at College Point, Long Island, Sikorsky responded with airplanes with boat hulls, capable of landing on land or water. He and his workers built an S-34 and six S-36s. An enlarged and modified S-34, the S-36 (Navy XPS-1) amphibious sesquiplane—with a full upper wing and a half-length lower wing—had a boat hull, retractable landing gear, and two Wright Whirlwind J-5 engines, giving a cruise speed of 100 mph. Having proved the concept, the company decided to build ten amphibians of a new design, and advertised: "Land Where and When You Want."

The S-38, another sesquiplane, had a boat hull with seats for ten, and two outboard stabilizing floats on abbreviated lower wings. The 71-foot-span upper wing was high enough above the surface to avoid striking the water in a roll. Two Pratt and Whitney Wasp engines were hung from the wings high above the water. One wag described the aircraft as "a collection of airplane parts flying in formation."

Regardless of appearance, the S-38 was an instant success. From its first flight on June 25, 1928, it demonstrated performance and handling qualities as good as

The Sikorsky 10-person S-38 amphibian enabled Pan American Airways to launch overwater international flight in 1929. A total of 114 of the flying boats were built. (Igor Sikorsky Archives.)

any other aircraft its size. It cruised at 100 mph, had a top speed of nearly 130, and climbed a thousand feet a minute fully loaded. It water-taxied very well, and could crawl up onto a beach or ramp on its own landing gear. With nine passengers and a crew of two, its range was 750 miles. Sikorsky moved to Stratford to build the S-38 where land and water runways were both available.

The S-38 proved very popular. Explorers Martin and Osa Johnson flew a zebra-striped S-38 named *Osa's Ark* in Africa, along with their single-engined S-39. Howard Hughes bought one, and took delivery at night. With no way to tow it to the airport, he made a nighttime takeoff from the taxi strip and phoned the next day to complain about the price of fuel.

Juan Trippe launched Pan American Airways with the S-38, and international flight began. On February 4, 1929 Pan Am's consultant Charles Lindbergh flew the inaugural flight, 2,327 miles from Miami to Cristobal in the Canal Zone, and on the 13th he returned with the first air mail on the route. Igor Sikorsky began a long friendship with Lindbergh at this time. The launching ramp at the factory and the river channel itself grew busy with takeoffs and landings. Altogether, 114 S-38s were built.

In 1930 the company built the first four-seat S-39, designed by Michael Gluhareff, according to cousin Igor A. "Professor" Sikorsky. It was powered—underpowered, actually—by a pair of 100-horsepower Cirrhus engines, which were soon replaced by a single 300-horsepower Wasp Jr. engine. In 1931 20 were built for small air services and executive transport. The Johnsons bought one of these, painted with leopard spots, and named it the *Spirit of Africa*.

As soon as the S-38 was flying on Pan Am's routes, its president Juan Trippe, Sikorsky, and Lindbergh began to plan its successor. The result was the S-40 American Clipper, a 34,600 pound (three-and-a-half times the weight of the S-38) flying boat. As the S-40 design developed, fishermen on the Housatonic would often see a motorboat dashing by, towing a scale-model aircraft hull at 30 miles per hour from a towline tied to a kitchen scale. Tests made in rough water on the Sound showed the hull "as steady as a steam yacht."

Soon Sikorsky was making frequent trips to the Pan Am office in New York. "We'd hold conferences," Lindbergh said, "usually in Juan Trippe's office where there was a long table. Igor would lay his drawings out on the table and we'd gather around—Trippe, Andre Priester who headed Pan American's engineering, Igor, and myself." The S-40 looked like an overgrown S-38. Lindbergh described it as a flying forest and called for something more streamlined, but Sikorsky insisted that to meet a very tight schedule they must proceed with the unbeautiful but proven design, then in future produce a more advanced aircraft.

The S-40 was launched down the ramp into the river in the spring of 1931. Its sheer size was impressive: 114-foot wingspan and 77-foot hull length. It began as an amphibian, but later shed its wheels and became a pure flying boat. On October 12 it took off from the Housatonic and flew to Washington, D.C., where

With 150-mph cruise speed, 1,200-mile range, and 32-passenger cabin, the S-42 was far ahead of its time. On August 1, 1934, in a single eight-hour flight, it captured eight world records and made the United States the foremost holder of aviation records. Here it rounds Stratford Point Light. (Joseph Keogan painting.)

Mrs. Herbert Hoover christened it the *American Clipper*. It continued to Miami and began its first airline flight, to Havana, Jamaica, Colombia, and the Canal Zone, stopping nights for passengers to stay at hotels en route. Sikorsky was on the flight and consultant Lindbergh served as copilot.

Including the seats in the smoking lounge, the S-40 carried 40 passengers in luxury and comfort. Its spacious compartments had walnut paneling, upholstered chairs, and backgammon tables; a uniformed steward served hot meals from a small galley. It was the largest flying boat built to that date and the first of a long line of Pan American clippers.

In 1932 Housatonic River users were treated to the sight of a new aircraft being tested; the 12-passenger S-41 closely resembled the S-38, and with 310 more horsepower was intended to replace it, but the S-38's own success and the arrival of the great depression made this unlikely, and only seven were ever built. To bring in money, the company also built wings to Michael Gluhareff's advanced airfoil design for retrofit on other aircraft, and in 1932 and 1933 produced two amphibians that never had Sikorsky numbers, being U.S. Navy designs.

No sooner was the S-40 *American Clipper* on its first flight between the American continents than work on its successor was underway. In fact, Igor Sikorsky has said that on the inaugural flight, at evening meals en route, "Lindbergh and I would take the menu, turn it upside down and make sketches for a long-range flying boat. . . . At those dinners we laid down the basic principles around which to design a flying boat." In 1932 Pan American ordered three new flying boats from Sikorsky, and three from Martin Aircraft. Martin's offering was larger and more powerful than Sikorsky's design but the S-42 was much cheaper than the Martin M130 ($210,000 versus $417,000), and would be ready many months sooner (as it was).

The S-42 was a a four-engine all-metal high-wing flying boat. Everything about it was impressive. It was the largest airplane of its day, standing 21 feet, 9 inches tall and 69 feet long, with a 114-foot wingspan. Cruising at 150 mph, its four 750 horsepower Pratt & Whitney Hornet engines and its radically new Hamilton Standard variable pitch propellers (which gained Hamilton's Frank Caldwell the Collier Trophy, aviation's highest award) took it 1,200 miles with 32 passengers aboard. Its high wing loading with new variable wing flap for takeoff, clean cowls, and flush riveting gave it performance phenomenal for its time.

When the first S-42 was completed shortly after Christmas in 1933, solid ice covered the Housatonic, delaying rollout until March 29, 1934. As the aircraft was towed along the causeway to the launching ramp that day, onlookers gasped! It was the cleanest and most beautiful aircraft Sikorsky had ever produced. Chief Pilot Boris Sergievsky intended to conduct only water-taxi tests that day, but as the bird skimmed across the surface of the sound, using only half its 3,000 horsepower, suddenly it lifted, and was airborne. Sergievsky quickly throttled back and set it down, but Sikorsky, in the co-pilot's seat, decided it was ready for its first flight the following day. When flight tests showed that the S-42's combination of speed, range, and lift exceeded that of any other flying boat in the world, Sikorsky and the flight crew decided to include world record attempts in the test program.

At 9:24 a.m. on August 1, 1934 observers at Stratford Point lighthouse watched as the aircraft passed over at 2,000 feet, heading west. Sergievsky, Pan Am's Ed Musick, and Charles Lindbergh were its crew. Its course would take it 311 miles (a mile more than the 500 kilometers required), to the New Jersey end of the George Washington Bridge, down to Staten Island, up to Block Island and Point Judith, then back to Stratford.

At 5:18 p.m. that day the S-42 completed its fourth lap around the course, circled and landed in the river, and taxied up the ramp. In a single flight of eight hours and 1,200 miles it had captured eight world records and made the United States the foremost holder of aviation records.

The record-setting aircraft was immediately put into service as the *Brazilian Clipper* and reduced the time from New York to Buenos Aires from eight days to five. Its top speed was 188 mph., it cruised at 160, and had a range of 1,200 miles with 7,000 pounds payload, and 3,000 miles with 1,500 pounds. Transatlantic service was planned, but the aircraft was so advanced compared to British competitors that Great Britain would not allow its use until they caught up, so Juan Trippe made other plans.

Pan Am had planned to use its larger, longer range Martin M-130 clipper to develop its Pacific routes, but it was not ready on schedule, so the second S-42 was used instead. With extra fuel tanks to extend its range, on April 16, 1935 it left the Golden Gate and made the 2,400-mile flight to Hawaii in 18 hours and 37 minutes, to deliver the first Transpacific mail. Later, the larger Martin flying boats took over, with an S-42 run—the China Clipper—extending the route to Hong Kong.

Ten S-42s were built, all for Pan American Airways. Most were used in the Caribbean and Latin America. Their era ended on August 9, 1945 when the last clipper flew into Dinner Key at Miami from Jamaica and Puerto Rico.

On June 1, 1935, a new twin-engined amphibian took off from the river. The sleek S-43 was a modern 15-passenger candidate for the old S-38 market, with S-42 technology and 750-horsepower Hornet engines. It had a top speed of 182 mph and, with 400 gallons of fuel and a useful load of 6,000 pounds, an 800-mile range. Fifty-three were sold, three as flying boats and 50 as amphibians. Customers included the U.S. Navy, Pan Am (which used them to develop its Alaska routes) and island/coastal markets around the world.

Meanwhile, the U.S. Navy put out bids for a new four-engined flying boat to patrol the far reaches of the Pacific. Sikorsky's response was the 47,000/49,000 pound S-44, also known as the XPBS-1 patrol bomber, first flown from the Housatonic on August 13, 1937. When Sikorsky lost the Navy production contract to Consolidated Aircraft based on price, the company turned the VS-44 design (United Aircraft combined its Vought and Sikorsky divisions in 1939, thus the VS) into a commercial transatlantic passenger transport. American Export Airlines bought three of these and, under license to the Navy, operated them across the Atlantic all through World War II. The last flight was on October 22, 1945.

Powered by four Twin Wasp engines rated at 1,200 takeoff horsepower each, and cruising at 211 mph, the new ship could fly non-stop nearly 5,000 miles across the North and South Atlantic with a full load of 32 passengers in eight compartments, plus 1,600 pounds of mail.

It was a cold, clear day on January 17, 1942 when the first VS-44, the Flying Ace *Excalibur*, was rolled out. Mrs. Henry Wallace, wife of the U.S. vice president, swung a bottle of champagne against the plane's rubber nose and the bottle bounced. Again it bounced. And again. Finally, Eugene Wilson, president of the corporation, held a pipe against the nose. Success! In its newsreels, Fox Movietone News sped up the clip and the effect was that Wallace seemed to be beating the aircraft.

Excambian was delivered to American Export Airlines in May, followed by *Exeter*. *Excalibur* crashed in September 1942 on a bad takeoff at Gander, Newfoundland, but *Exeter* and *Excambian* continued to provide the only non-stop transatlantic service during the war, 3,329 miles from the United States to Foynes, Ireland, in 14 hours and 17 minutes. The comfortable quarters included cushioned seats for 32 VIP passengers, a galley, and berths.

Soon after the war, *Exeter* was lost in South America in 1947, leaving *Excambian* as the last of the flying boats. Rescued by Avalon Air Transport in 1957, for years it shuttled passengers the 12 miles to Catalina Island off the California coast, together with a fleet of Grumman Goose amphibians (they called it Mother Goose), then put in some time at Charles Blair's/Maureen O'Hara's Antilles

With a Navy development contract for a new patrol bomber, Sikorsky produced the XPBS-1. Here it lands in the Housatonic near the outer breakwater.

Air Boats operation in the Virgin Islands. After being holed and left to lie on the beach at Charlotte Amalie, *Excambian* found its way home to Stratford in 1987, where it was restored, and on June 18, 1997 was delivered to the New England Air Museum in Windsor Locks for display. It and a handful of other survivors are the last of the flying boats that helped establish international flight, developed at Stratford on the Housatonic.

Losing the Patrol Bomber production run, the company turned the XPBS design into a passenger plane. Three VS-44s (V for Vought)—Excalibur, Excambian, and Exeter— carried VIPs from the United States to Foynes, Ireland, the only nonstop transatlantic flights during World War II.

3. PATRIOTS AND PROFITEERS

From the founding of the town in 1639, its people were constantly called to defend themselves. Each generation faced its foes and each produced its heroes. Located at the shore, the town looked seaward to its threats, and developed men to handle ships and fight battles on the water. In the French and Indian Wars, landsman David Wooster fought at Louisbourg and militiaman Solomon Plant served on the St. Lawrence. In the Revolution sea-trained David Hawley followed General Arnold on Lake Champlain while Nathan Gorham both fought and traded with the Tories across the Sound. In the War of 1812 John Sterling learned to sail, and young Pulaski Benjamin, taken from his ship, was locked in Dartmoor Prison, while Captain Samuel Nicoll made a fortune as a privateer. Joshua Sands was a navy man for 50 years from 1812 to 1862. William Barrymore captured the Confederate blockade runner *Julia* and served aboard the monitor *Monadnock* in the Civil War. The seaside town of Stratford sent sons around the world to serve a maritime nation.

IN THE NAME OF WEALTH AND FREEDOM

From 1639 Stratford's settlers feared enemy attack from the sea. Until the Anglo-Dutch War ended in 1664, each sail on the horizon brought concern. But with the collapse of Nieuw Amsterdam in August 1664, Dutch threats ceased.

French threats were much more serious. In 1739, long before he became a general in the Continental Army, Stratford-born David Wooster commanded the 100-ton Connecticut sloop *Defence*. In 1745, when Massachusetts governor William Shirley organized an expedition against Louisbourg in French Acadia, Wooster, a captain in Colonel Aaron Burr's regiment, was there. The Yankees stormed the fort and took the town. Given charge of a cartel ship returning French soldiers to France, Wooster did well: King George II awarded him a regular captaincy with half pay for life.

The only practical way to cross America's interior was by water: The waterways were the highways. During General Jeffrey Amherst's 1760 campaign to drive the French from Canada, Connecticut militiamen paddling bateaus reached Fort Oswego on Lake Ontario. Militiaman Solomon Plant wrote:

Colonial military operations demanded versatility. In 1739 David Wooster commanded the Connecticut sloop Defense; *in 1745 he led militia in Governor Shirley's seaborne assault on French Louisbourg. (Yale University Art Gallery, Mabel Brady Garvan Collection.)*

July 12. Came a French Brig and a Scooner within about a mile, laying there Coast [course] toards fronten ack [Fort Frontenac, across the lake at St.Lawrence River] and in the afternoon there was a Scout sent out to an island about 30 miles.

July 15. Our two snows [brigs with a separate mast for the spanker. *Mohawk* and *Onondaiga* each carried 90 men and protected the fleet of bateaus, whaleboats, and row galleys.] came from Niagre [Ft. Niagara, at the west end of Ontario] and at night set out after the french Brig and Scooner.

July 22. Arrived here all the Connecticut forces. [and prepared for the 250-mile downriver trip to Montreal.]

Aug. 6. We received orders to be Ready at a minits warning to Imbark for Swgotcha [Oswagatchie, now Ogdensburg, New York. On August 10 the army crossed the lake to the St. Lawrence River.]

Aug. 17. One of the french vesels Came about five miles up the River from the fort and our Rogalles [row galleys] engaged her about two hours at which time the french vesel Struck to them with the loss of three killed and eleven wounded and about ten o'clock we pushed of and went to Swagotche old fort where we got plenty of green Corn and beens.

While gunboats captured the French brig and ran the schooner aground, the bateaus waited out of cannon shot along the bank then went downriver to a rocky island where 300 Frenchmen at Fort Levis delayed the Americans for two weeks. After this fort fell, the troops drifted down the river. Captain Baker's company and Solomon Plant were still eight days from Montreal when they learned of the city's surrender.

At the Cascades, which were falls above Montreal, 37 bateaus, 17 whaleboats, and one row galley were wrecked; 84 bodies were recovered. Travel on the river was more dangerous than battle. Amherst's army reached Montreal on the 6th, met the other English spearheads from east and south on the 7th, and took the city on the 8th. When French governor Vaudreuil surrendered all of Canada to the English armies, French influence ended in North America. Three hundred miles away, Stratford could now live without fear of French attack, and by November her soldier sons were home.

All changed, however, as actions of the British crown became more repressive. Minutes of a Stratford town meeting held on December 18, 1774 read:

> The meeting then took into serious consideration the unhappy circumstances of the poor people of Boston now suffering in ye common cause of American liberty under the oppressive acts of the British Parliament called the Boston Port Bill . . . and thereupon unanimously voted, that a subscription be immediately opened and collections be made and sent, for the relief of the poor sufferers in that town . . . and Messrs. Philip Nichols, Josiah Hubbell, David Hawley, Nathan Bennet, Stephen Burroughs, and LeGrand Cannon are appointed a committee to solicit, and transport to Boston such donations as they shall receive by any safe opportunity addressed to ye committee appointed to take care of and imploy the poor of that place.

It was no accident that every man named to the committee was a merchant, trader, or sea captain in the Boston trade.

On April 21, 1775, when postrider Ebenezer Hurd reported that British soldiers had fired on Colonials at Concord and the mother country was waging war on its colonies, sides were quickly chosen. King George III authorized British commanders of private ships to attack and seize Colonial ships wherever they were found, and the governor of Connecticut (and later the Continental Congress) issued letters of marque to American mariners to outfit vessels to capture British merchantmen. After the British occupied New York, loyalists fled from Connecticut to Long Island, and patriots fortified the Fairfield County coast to fend off Tory raids and attack by ships-of-war. Long Island Sound became a battlefield for the next eight years, its seaways alive with warships, raiders, merchant vessels, and privateers.

Ebenezer Coe, who had already lost an eye to British invaders at the Battle of Ridgefield, described typical raids: "In Stratford January 22d 1781 Lost twenty-seven sheep by the hands of the enemys of America to be caryed to Long Island from the Great Neck," and again, "May 13 1781 the Enemy Landed on the Great Neck and killed for me a valuable young horse of three years old."

Captain William Birdseye feared that if the British won the war he would lose his property on Main Street, so in 1779 he sailed to Long Island and joined the British army. He did lose his property—but to the patriots at home—and returned to find his house being auctioned. But his neighbors agreed not to bid—except for one Samuel Ufford, who came near to being mobbed—and Birdseye kept his home.

Captain John Barlow, Isaac Whippo, George Smith, and Silvanus Dickenson all came the other way and settled in Stratford: The latter two were pensioned after the war for serving as spies for General George Washington while living on the island. As supposed loyalists they had free access to New York, and were able to observe and report on enemy activities.

Immediately after the battle at Lexington, coaster captain John Brooks Sr. was chased in from sea by the *Asia*, first British warship to arrive. When *Asia* anchored off Stratford Point, the townsmen sent out a party under flag of truce to find out their intentions. Their intentions soon were known: They commissioned a young truce-party member named Chapman a leftenant, and signed up several others. They also topped off their stores with whatever food the residents would sell them, and trade was brisk.

In 1775, while trading in the West Indies, Captain Benjamin Brooks's vessel was captured by the 20-gun British ship *Levan*, and the crew taken prisoner.

By the winter of 1783, the war on land had quieted, but at sea the fight continued. On February 20 Amos Hubbell took his 70-ton sloop *Julius Caesar* out to attack a British privateer. A letter from a Colonel Tallmadge to General Washington describes the action:

> One of the last naval exploits of the Revolutionary War was the capture of the British privateer *Three Brothers*, commanded by Captain Johnstone, mounting eleven carriage guns, four swivels, and twenty-five small arms, and navigated by twenty-one men. This vessel was cruising on Long Island Sound, and was discovered near Stratford Point. About 2 o'clock in the afternoon troops were embarked in a fast sailing vessel prepared for this emergency and commanded by Captain Hubbell. At 4 o'clock they fell in with the *Three Brothers*, received a broadside from her, followed by her swivels and musketry (our troops being concealed) until both vessels met, when the troops arose, gave the enemy one discharge of musketry, and then boarded the *Three Brothers* with fixed bayonets. The captain of the privateer was killed and three or four of his crew were wounded, two of them mortally. While Captain Hubbell's vessel was much damaged in hull, spars, and rigging, not a man on board was killed or wounded.

Stratford provided scores of seamen to man state and private vessels. The schooner *Swallow*, with 10 guns and 60 men, commanded by James Hovey and owned by Pierpont Edwards and Company of New Haven, was commissioned on March 9, 1780. On her first cruise *Swallow* was captured by the British Letter of Marque *Annapolis Rover*, and on November 9 was libeled at Halifax.

In 1779 Joseph Hull of Ripton (now Shelton) was appointed to "annoy the enemy" with a fleet of whaleboats in the Sound. His prizes, sent in to New Haven, include the British *Bethesba* loaded with provisions, taken on December 3, 1782 and libeled January 2, 1783; a British boat with cargo commanded by a Captain Barlow, taken on March 29; a schooner commanded by Thomas Bird, taken on April 6; and a recaptured British prize on its way to New York, libeled June 10.

Knowing that the British loaded wood for New York at an inlet near Throg's Neck, Hull ran in one night at midnight with about 50 men, captured a firewood supply boat, concealed 20 of his men aboard, and approached a British schooner. When the sentry on deck hailed him with "Have a care" not to collide, he shouted "No, no, room enough!" and proceeded to run under the schooner's bow and draw close alongside. His men leaped aboard. The British commander, roused from sleep below, rushed on deck and was shot to death. With his own boat hoisted aboard the schooner and the British woodboat alongside, Hull sailed for Black Rock harbor, passing three unsuspecting British vessels off Eaton's Neck. One of Hull's crew was David Blakeman of New Stratford (now Monroe). In boarding, Blakeman was slashed across the abdomen by a cutlass, and while the battle raged he lay on deck holding in his bowels. He was sewn up by a captured British surgeon and recovered to live a long life, but as a result of damaged vocal chords was ever after known as "squeaking David."

Nathan Gorham played all parts in the revolution: patriot, hero, loyalist, smuggler, opportunist. In 1776 he was at Washington's evacuation of Long Island, and wrote:

> The Stratford Company was the last to leave, and just as the last boat was leaving the British Lighthorse were coming down upon it, and it was so loaded that three men were left—John Benjamin, myself, and another. We ran up the river where the Navy Yard now is, and finding a small boat, although dried and leaky, we launched it and jumped in and with pieces of a rail rowed for the New York shore, bailing with our hats. We drifted with the tide up to a place called Corlear's Hook and almost to where the British had commenced crossing, our boat sinking under us as we struck the shore.

Later in the war, Gorham signed on as mate and sailmaker to his friend John Barlow, who had agreed to command a privateer out of Boston. To reach Boston, they bought an old nag for $7 and set out, Barlow riding on ahead and Gorham walking. After several miles, Barlow would leave the horse tied to graze, and walk on. When Gorham found the horse, he would mount and ride past Barlow, repeating the process. At Boston, they turned the poor thing loose.

At sea in search of British merchantmen, Gorham and Barlow sighted a vessel and set out in pursuit. Overhauling the ship, they commanded her to strike, and were surprised when she opened her ports and showed herself to be a man-of-war. Barlow and Gorham were taken to New York and put aboard the infamous prison ship *Jersey*. When dysentery broke out aboard the overcrowded hulk, 10 to 15 prisoners died each day. Gorham, being relatively healthy and a good oarsman, was assigned to take the dead ashore and bury them in mass graves, where the Brooklyn Navy Yard was later located. Becoming ill himself, Gorham decided to join the British navy to avoid certain death, and was soon aboard a ship and sailing south. In an encounter with an American privateer armed with long 32-pounders, the British ship was severely damaged, and put in at the Spanish port of St. Augustine, Florida, for repairs. From there, Gorham escaped in a stolen canoe, and headed north toward home.

John Brooks Jr. reported:

> As the war progressed Stratford became notorious for what was called illicit trade in boats with the British, who had possession of Long Island, which made it very convenient for those engaged in it, to export small articles, such as hams, cheese, butter, eggs, and small stock of all kinds. Some of these boats were captured by the guard. One of the boats, however, was not so fortunate, being hailed by the sentinel as she was rowing out of the harbor laden as above, and not paying any attention to the challenge, was fired upon, by which two men were killed, on which the boat surrendered.

Gorham was active in this trade. One bright winter day in March, he and a sailor named Crowell were hired by John Thompson, William Southworth, William Beers, and others, to cross with them to trade for corduroy cloth. They went over in the night, did their trading in the forenoon, and came back in the afternoon near evening. Arriving near the Connecticut shore of the Sound, they saw a government boat beating at the mouth of Stratford harbor, and therefore kept off in the Sound waiting to run in under cover of darkness. But a snow squall came up and they were compelled to run before it, the wind blowing very hard, the sea high and frequently breaking into the boat.

Crowell and Gorham were clothed in heavy pea jackets and sat in the stern of the boat breaking off much of the sea, each holding an oar to steer the boat. They soon became coated with ice, which kept them warm, while the others bailed the boat and suffered with the cold.

Gorham's grandson Nathan McEwen described the scene:

> They scud the boat nearly to the east end of Long Island, where they run ashore. Some of them went for a light and on returning found Beers

frozen to death. Crowell's and Gorham's pea jackets were so frozen that it was necessary to get out of and leave them where they sat. The snow having become deep there were only two of them able to reach a house, where they found a gang of men on a carouse, who at once went and helped bring in the others, although some had frozen hands, except Beers, who was dead.

In 1748 Captain Thomas Ivers of New York began to buy property in Stratford near the lower wharf, and by 1762 he owned a quarter of the wharf itself. Ivers became a prominent merchant, with his home and warehouses on the river adjacent to the wharf, and his trading sloops moored in the stream nearby. Jack Arabas was his slave.

Not much is known about Jack Arabas—not even his real name—but he made a mark in history. His service records in the Revolution spelled his name Aribas, Arrabas, and Arabas, and he could not write at all. He probably could not pronounce it, either, but owners customarily called their servants by the family name, and Jack, likely born in Africa and sold to Ivers in some tropical slave market, could not say Ivers—it came out Arabas.

Before the Revolution, shipmasters who traded in the West Indies commonly rounded out their crews by buying slaves at markets in the islands. Others hired

While Nathan Gorham was imprisoned in the contagion-ridden British hulk Jersey *on Wallabout Bay, he was assigned to row the dead ashore each day for burial in a mass grave. (Collection of the New York Historical Society.)*

Trade with Loyalists on Long Island was illegal but lucrative. Whaleboats like this one crossed the Sound at night with provisions, and returned before dawn with contraband from England.

free black men as seamen. Such seamen, lacking formal education, became skilled deck hands, ship handlers, seacooks, navigators, even sailmakers. Crispus Attucks, a 47-year-old martyr of the Boston Massacre, was such a sailor. Nero Hawley of Stratford was another. The postwar 1790 Stratford census includes 49 free "nonwhites" and 99 slaves, and judging from the family names—Hubbell, McEwen, Nicoll, Gorham, Hawley, Lewis—a number of them were hands aboard the ships of local sea captains. Arabas probably lived aboard one of Captain Ivers's vessels, and learned his skills in coasting trips on the Sound or voyages to the islands.

At the outset of the Revolution, General Washington, a slaveholder himself, opposed having blacks in his army, but changed his mind in 1775: "It has been presented to me, that the free negroes, who have served in this army, are very much dissatisfied at being discarded. As it is to be apprehended, that they may seek employ in the ministerial [British] army. I have presumed to depart from the resolution, and have given license for their being enlisted."

In 1777 Captain Ivers's son William turned 18 and became subject to induction in the Continental Army. However, it was legitimate to purchase a replacement, and that is what is believed the Iverses did. Captain Ivers offered Jack in place of William. The town paid a bounty of £10 for the enlistment, which the captain pocketed.

In October 1777 Jack Arabas was sent to Fishkill, where he was enlisted in November for the duration of the war as a private in Captain Ely's Company, 6th

Regiment, Connecticut Line. He may have seen action in the American storming of the British fort at Stony Point in July 1779.

In 1781 Arabas was serving in Connecticut's 4th Regiment under Colonel Butler as member of the state's first black company. Mustered out in 1783, he returned to Stratford with a $600 bonus and, having heard the rhetoric of the Revolution, he fully expected to be freed.

Captain Ivers had other plans. He didn't intend to give up his property, which was worth $1,000 or more. But Jack had learned that only free black men could be enlisted, and saw his fellow soldiers Cesar Edwards and shipping merchant Aaron Hawley's man Nero—probably also a deckhand—manumitted. The captain had violated an agreement. So Jack the sailor fled, toward New Haven.

When Ivers discovered Arabas was gone, he put out word of a runaway slave that must have reached New Haven shortly after Jack arrived. He was caught next day and clapped in jail.

By luck, Jack was able to challenge his imprisonment and, with a local lawyer, obtain a writ of habeas corpus, requiring Ivers to justify keeping him in jail. A hearing was scheduled immediately. Jack was fortunate to be represented by a brilliant young Yale graduate, Chauncey Goodrich. Just starting his practice and eager to prove himself, he was described as "unshaken in his principles, cool and determined in his conduct."

The judge was James Wadsworth, another Yale graduate, veteran state legislator, veteran of two wars, and now a respected jurist. His Yale biography claimed he had "a peculiar dignity of manner," and "an antique strictness of morals."

Goodrich argued that Arabas, having fulfilled his agreement with Ivers by serving in the army for six years, should be free. His argument in the court record was: "Sometime in the year 1777, being then a slave for life to the said Ivers [Jack] was by his said master's leave and consent duly enlisted as a soldier into the Continental Army for and during the war . . . and that at said time of enlistment his said master received the bounty for said enlistment . . . and that he the said Jack faithfully performed the duties of a soldier during ye war at the close thereof was honorably discharged."

Judge Wadsworth, after hearing the arguments, ruled, "This court are of opinion . . . that as none but freemen could by legislation of the Congress be enlisted into the Continental Army . . . the consent of said master to such enlistment in judgement of law amounts to a manumission."

This landmark ruling recognized that only freemen could serve in the army, and that by serving they were free. It was a small but important step toward equal rights for blacks. Jack's case served as prior law for the rights of some 300 soldiers from Connecticut.

In 1787 Arabas was still in New Haven, producing coins as a stampman in a copper mill. There his record ends, but he probably returned to a seaman's life. Port records of the young nation show that a large percentage of ship hands were African-American. In Philadelphia in 1800, 20 percent of seamen were black. On whaling vessels it was closer to 40 percent. The life was hard for sailors before the mast, black or white, but nearer to equal than ashore, and the mobility of seamen brought new awareness to black Americans ashore, and did its part in ending slavery.

To many in Stratford, the American Revolution brought opportunities to profit and to gather wealth through overpricing, smuggling, and privateering, but to them and others it also brought the opportunity to join the fight for freedom from absentee government, the freedom to choose their own destiny.

THE DEEDS OF DAVID HAWLEY

On September 4, 1775 Captain David Hawley, in search of powder and muskets for the towns of Fairfield and Stratford, sailed his sloop *Sally* from Stratford to New Providence in the Bahamas with a cargo of salt meat and grain to trade. After visiting several islands, *Sally* returned in December with a mere hundredweight of gunpowder, 1,305 bushels of salt, and 18 hogsheads of sugar.

On Hawley's arrival home, far from being grateful, the General Assembly charged him with violating its embargo on exports, imposed a few days before he sailed. But after hearing his story, the Assembly freed him and allowed him to "dispose of said powder equally between the towns of Fairfield and Stratford," which he did.

On March 16 Hawley took *Sally* to sea again, as a privateer commissioned by Governor Jonathan Trumbull (called Brother Jonathan by George Washington), but within four days was captured by the British privateer brig *Bellona*, then put aboard HMS *Rose*, Captain James Wallace, at Newport. *Rose's* journal dated March 21 reads:

> AM Weigh'd and came to sail, as did the Squadn Steering down the River. Fresh Breezes with Sleet at times at 1PM Brot too Join'd *Fortune* T[ende]r at 2 past 3 saw 2 sail SE. gave Chace at 2 past 4 saw 2 in the SW made the *Glascow's* Sigl to Chace as did the *Fortune* tender. At 6 Join'd the *Glascow*, *Hawke* T[ende]r and the sloop *Sally*, David Hawley Master from Newhaven with Flax Rye Indian Corn, Flour, Beef and Pork which the *Hawke* had Seiz'd. At 8 lost sight of the Chace In 2d Reef T Sails.

Hawley and his captive crew were transferred to the *Glasgow*. On April 6 Commodore Esek Hopkins and the Continental fleet hove into sight, returning from a raid on Nassau, New Providence. Hopkins's fleet attacked *Glasgow*, which retreated into Newport Harbor. Hawley was offered five shillings a day, a good cabin aboard, payment for his vessel when the war ended, and a good plantation anywhere on the continent, if he would only act as their pilot; he turned them down. As a result he was separated from his men and taken with the fleet to Halifax, Nova Scotia. Escaping with eight other men in a small boat, Hawley sailed south and reached Old York in Maine, thence on to Hartford. The

Captain David Hawley served as Connecticut naval officer, privateer, and merchant captain. He began the war by bringing salt and gunpowder home from the Bahamas.

Connecticut *Gazette* of May 20, 1776, reported:

> Captain David Hawley, who came to Hartford last Saturday from Halifax, where he had been prisoner and where he left on April 14, 1776, was captured with his sloop by the British armed schooner *Bellona* on March 17, 1776 when he sailed out of Stratford. He was plundered and damned, together with his crew and his country. About 10 o'clock at night they joined the *Rose*, *Glasgow* and *Swan*, Men-of-War, and went on board the *Rose*. He and his crew were prisoners on the *Glasgow* and were taken to Halifax, April 10, 1776. Captain Hawley, with eight others made his escape in a small boat and came to New [*sic*] York.

On July 11, 1776 the Connecticut Council of Safety appointed David Hawley Second Lieutenant of the ship being built for the Connecticut Navy at Saybrook (now Essex), to be named *Oliver Cromwell*. But long before the ship was completed, Hawley was ordered to raise a "Company of Seamen" to report to Colonel Benedict Arnold on Lake Champlain. Between August 9 and 25 he signed up 26 local men, and set out for Ticonderoga.

All winter Arnold's small force had been laying siege to Quebec, but when British General John Burgoyne brought reinforcements from England in May,

Arnold's force, shrunken by smallpox and lack of food, retreated down Lake Champlain. Fortunately, in 1775 Arnold had captured two vessels at St. Johns, one of these the 70-ton schooner *Royal Savage*, mounting four 6-pound and eight 4-pound guns. Arnold was also rushing to complete a small fleet of 3-gun gondolas and 10-gun row galleys being built at Skenesborough (Whitehall) on the lake. (Arnold's background included experience as a shipping merchant and shipmaster.) In June he had written to the Continental Congress, "to augment our navy on the lake appears to me of the utmost importance." Congress responded on July 3 by sending ship carpenters, riggers, and seamen to the lake, and Hawley's men were among these. The gondolas were flat-bottomed open rowing craft, 54 feet long and 15 wide, with square sails to sail before the wind. (One of these, *Philadelphia*, has been raised from her grave and is on view at the Smithsonian. A replica now sails on Lake Champlain.) They were patterned after the gundalows used on Long Island Sound. Each had a 12-pound bow gun and two 9-pounders pointed thwartships. They were packed with 44-man crews. The galleys—only three were completed—were 72 feet long, with a pair of lateen sails, eight to ten carriage guns, and crews of 80 men.

The British plan was for Sir William Howe to sweep up the Hudson from New York while Governor Sir Guy Carleton led Burgoyne's forces south from Canada

The 24-gun frigate Rose—*a sixth rater—spent the last night of 1777 in a 14-vessel convoy at anchor in the Sound observing Stratford and New Haven. In 2001 a replica sailed the Sound. (HMS* Rose *Foundation and Kay Williams.)*

to join him, to cut the colonies in half along the Lake Champlain-Hudson River corridor, and end the war. It nearly worked.

In desperation, Arnold took his makeshift little navy of eight gondolas, three row galleys, two schooners, a cutter, and a sloop northward, and reached the northern end of the lake on September 1. He pleaded with General Gates at Ticonderoga to send more seamen and more completed galleys, and on the 21st wrote, "I have sent Two Boats to sound round the island Valcouer who report that it is an exceeding fine, Secure harbour." On the 23rd he headed to Valcour Island, south of present day Plattsburg, and anchored his fleet in the narrow bay between Valcour and the New York shore, to wait for Carleton's large fleet to appear. On the 28th Hawley and his men arrived at Valcour. He was put in command of *Royal Savage*, which served as Arnold's flagship.

Burgoyne's fleet under Sir Guy Carleton and Captain Thomas Pringle moved slowly south, a fresh north wind behind them. They discovered Arnold's vessels—they nearly sailed past them—on the morning of October 11. The British fleet included the 180-ton three-masted ship *Inflexible*, with eighteen 12-pounders; the gun platform *Thunderer*; the schooner *Carleton*; 670 sailors, 400 bateaux with 4,000 British regulars and German auxiliaries, and 650 war-painted Indians in canoes. The Americans had some 700 militiamen, Hawley's sailors,

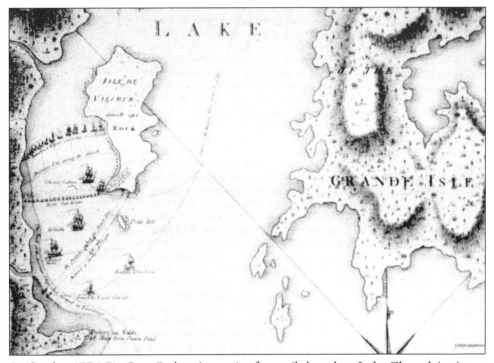

In October 1776 Sir Guy Carleton's massive force sailed south to Lake Champlain, intent on splitting New England from the other colonies. But Benedict Arnold's little American fleet delayed their plan and salvaged the Revolution.

and 15 "gunboats, galleys, and schooners." Bayze Wells, a cousin of the Stratford Wells family, wrote in his journal: "About eight AM the Guard boat Came in and fired an Alarm and brought News of the Near Aproch of our Enemy about 10 AM a twenty two Gun Ship hove in Sight and two Sixteen Gun Schooners and two Sloops and one floteing Battery which mounted twenty Six Guns Six twenty four Pounders and A Large number of boats. They soon gave us battle. We Returnd the Same to them."

The British fleet ran down the eastern side of Valcour Island, then rounded up to struggle back to windward toward the Americans. Arnold ordered *Royal Savage* and the three galleys underway, to lure the British into his cul-de-sac:

> The Gallies & *Royal Savage* were ordered Underway, the rest of our fleet lay at an Anchor at 11 OClock. They ran under the Lee of Valcouer & began the attack. The schooner by some bad Management fell to Leward & was first attacked. One of her Masts was wounded & her Rigging Shott away. Capt [Hawley] thought prudent to run her on the Point of Valcouer, where all the Men were saved, the Enemy Boarded her & at night set fire to her.

Under direct fire from the British schooner *Carleton*, with twelve 6-pounders, Hawley had been beating to windward to return to the bay when, in an unfamiliar vessel known to be a poor sailer and with insufficient room to tack, he grounded her on rocky Valcour Island. After Hawley ordered his crew to abandon the stranded *Royal Savage*, a boat crew from the enemy schooner *Maria* boarded her, fired her, and blew her up. Arnold wrote:

> At half past 11 [a.m.] the engagement became General and very warm. Some of the Enemies Ships & all their Gondolas beat & rowed up within musket Shott of us. They Continued a very hot fire with Round & Grape Shott untill five OClock When they thought proper to retire to about Six or Seven hundred Yards distance & continued to fire, untill Dark — the *Congress* and *Washington* have Suffered greatly. The latter Lost her first Lieut killed, & Capt & Master wounded, the *New York* lost all her Officers except her Captain. The *Philadelphia* was hulled in so many Places that She Sank.

Sixty Americans were killed or wounded. In the fog of the night, Arnold took his crippled fleet south in single file, with Hawley and his crew aboard Colonel Waterbury's battered galley *Washington*, bringing up the rear. In the morning, after receiving a few broadsides from the pursuing enemy, *Washington* struck her colors and Hawley was again a prisoner. The balance of the American fleet was run ashore and lost.

A few days later the British delivered the prisoners to Fort Ticonderoga under a flag of truce, paroling them in a gesture of generosity. Hawley returned to Stratford.

The rout on Lake Champlain reads like a disaster for the American cause, but this first fleet action ever fought by Americans halted Burgoyne's move south that year, prevented the colonies from being split, and ultimately won the war.

The following April, Connecticut Governor Trumbull commissioned Hawley captain of the Connecticut sloop-of-war *Schuyler*, mounting six carriage guns and with a crew of 40 men. In June and July he captured 11 prizes, all merchant vessels. On November 4 agent Shaw wrote to the Marine Committee that the conscriptions of Hawley's crew were up, and Hawley "has brot the sloop into this Port [New Haven] with all her Stores and Deliver'd her up & chooses not to go in her any more finding that he Ranks only as a Lt & being a Capt on ye Lake &c."

On December 9, as part of General Israel Putnam's plan to cut off supplies to the British in New York, *Schuyler* was sent across the Sound with the schooners *Spy* and *Mifflin* to protect a convoy of four transports full of troops. The plan was to cross the Sound from Norwalk to attack Setauket. At dawn the expedition found itself within two miles of the British frigate *Falcon*. *Schuyler* was driven onto the Long Island shore at Old Field Point, and surrendered, along with Colonel Ely, Colonel Webb, and 62 of their men. In spite of this, the attack succeeded. It is unclear whether Hawley or a Lieutenant Carr from the Continental ship *Cabot* was in command of *Schuyler* at the time, but it is thought that it was Hawley and that he was jailed in Newport again.

One of the few trained seamen available to General Arnold, David Hawley was put in charge of Arnold's flagship the Royal Savage.

As the British approached down Lake Champlain, Arnold positioned his little fleet inside Valcour Bay, upwind of the entrance. Hawley's Royal Savage, *the largest vessel, is centered in front of the fleet. (C. Randle painting, National Archives of Canada.)*

In 1779 the Council of Safety purchased the captured British sloop *Mars*, renamed her *Guilford*, added her to the Connecticut navy, and sent her cruising under William Nott. On June 18 David Hawley was appointed to replace Nott, but on arriving in New Haven found that many of the crew had deserted, and he had to get replacements. Hawley rounded up a crew of 41 men, including a few who had served on *Royal Savage*, but he never got to sea. On the Fourth of July a British fleet of 48 ships and 2,600 troops attacked New Haven harbor. Hawley abandoned *Guilford*, saving anchors, ammunition, sails, and stores, but the British burned her at the wharf. At a Court of Inquiry on September 13, Hawley was acquitted "without the least blame or misconduct."

Hawley was soon at sea again. On May 1, 1779, a whaleboat full of British and Tories had landed at Fairfield, kidnapped militia General Gold Selleck Silliman, and taken him to New York. Since Connecticut did not have a prisoner of equal rank to exchange for the general, the solution was obvious: capture one. The selected victim was Judge Thomas Jones of Southhampton, Long Island, a judge of the Ministerial Supreme Court of the Crown, and an old Yale classmate of the general. Hawley agreed to go get him.

On a bleak November evening in 1779, Hawley and 20 volunteers crossed the Sound in a whaleboat, dragged the boat up on the beach and hid it in the underbrush. Travelling some miles overland at night, they reached the judge's home, burst open the door, grabbed the magistrate and one other prisoner, and set out for their boat. Because the alarm was out, they had to hide for two days, but reached their whaleboat on the third night and set out for home. The swap was soon made, but not too soon for Mrs. Silliman, who boarded the judge and had to listen to his loud complaints.

Through the winter Captain Hawley stayed in port, but in the spring of 1780 he put out into the Sound again, in search of British booty. On April 6, in an armed whaleboat, he and his crew captured the 30-ton Tory sloop *Sally*, with a cargo of molasses, rum, beef, and pork. On April 20 he led three armed whaleboats from Fairfield to the south shore of Long Island, where he took 11 prizes. Seven of these were ransomed or destroyed, the other four he took to Fairfield for libel. In October 1780, with Ebenezer Jones of Stamford, he took the schooners *Fly* and *Sally* and the sloop *Dorset*.

At Hartford Admiralty Court on June 13, 1780 a spokesman for Hawley contested the claim of Gideon Olmstead, commander of the privateer *Hawke*, to a British sloop. The records read:

> In behalf of David Hawley Commander of the whaleboats *Retaliation* and *Restoration* duly commissioned and authorized to Cruise against & Capture the Vessels and Property of the Subjects of the King of Great Britain . . . said Hawley and his Crew did on or about the 5th day of April AD 1780 in the South Bay . . . make prize of said Sloop . . . and said Sloop . . . continued in the possession of the Claimants Nine Days . . . . till they fell in with the sd privateer *Hawke* . . . under English Colors, when supposing them to be a Brittish Privateer . . . came to anchor . . . entirely under the Command of his Guns . . . Capt. Hawley then Hail'd said Privateer and demanded who she was . . . but no answer was returned but an order to go immediately on board, with Hawley not complying with it received sundry Shot under English Colors . . . Quitted said Sloop and fled to the Shore.

The court ruled in favor of Captain Olmstead, but this statement seems to prove that Hawley was commissioned by Governor Trumbull to command the two state gunboats in 1780, and that two of his three whaleboats on the scene were indeed the *Retaliation* and the *Restoration*.

On March 16, 1781, he was commissioned again to command the two gunboats, one gun and eight men each, to prevent illicit trade between Long Island and Connecticut. At the same time, he had to be on the lookout for British patrols. One event on August 25, 1781 proved fortunate for salvage master Hawley. Stratfordite Nathan McEwen related, "a small gun which in derision was called the 'Clister pipe' was taken down the Neck to oppose the landing of the British. While there, a squall came up sudden and struck the [British] brig *Kingfisher*, which immediately sank. Her masts being out of water, the crew took refuge in the rigging." Another account says, "2 Sloops & a Brig having taken a Guard at West Haven, coming off by Stratford point, the Brig overset and the Hatches being open, immediately sunk; 2 of the Prisoners were drowned with some of the hands. Capt. David Hawley took her Strands & Rigging off—her Masts were seen some time at low water till an easterly storm took them away."

In September Hawley reported that he had landed on Long Island four times that summer, and had captured a large quantity of supplies. At the same time, he was busy exporting grain to the patriots at Rhode Island, as shown on permits for flour, wheat, rye, corn, and flax. The first permit says "in ye schooner *Sally*," which raises the question "which Sally?". Did he buy the one he captured last, did he recover his own, or was it a different boat? Regardless, In 1797 the Hawleys were still shipping in a schooner named *Sally*.

Hawley's last commission was issued in Massachusetts on May 13, 1782, to command the sloop *Seaflower*, 4 guns and 30 men, owned by him and others. After the war, he continued to conduct his West Indies trade from his brick house near the wharves in the borough of Bridgeport until his death in 1807. Despite his imprisonments by the British, despite the times he lost his vessel by capture or by running it aground, David Hawley at Valcour Island and in Long Island Sound so slowed the enemy's advance and blocked his operations as to play a vital part in his nation's history.

THE PRIVATEERS

After the Revolution our young nation had only such freedom as it could defend. In 1798 Ezekiel Hubbell's ship *Citizen* was taken into Halifax by an English cruiser. In 1799 Captain Wilson Hubbell was captured and killed by a French privateer. Seaman Abijah Beardsley was abducted from Samuel Hawley's Antigua-bound brig by a British press gang, and in 1807 Captain Isaac Chauncey, on leave from the navy and bound to India and China as master of a merchant ship, threw a British press gang officer overboard. Jefferson's 1807–1808 embargo hurt American shippers more than foreigners. Finally, on June 18, 1812 Congress was driven to declare a state of war.

The war spelled economic disaster for Yankee shipowners. British blockaders bottled up the coast. The New England states threatened to secede, and Nantucket Island declared itself neutral. The only paying business on the sea was privateering, and that not in American waters. Adam and Noah Brown built the noted *General Armstrong* and *Prince de Neufchatel* in New York for use in European waters. In Philadelphia Andrew Currier applied to the Collector of the Port for a Commission of Letter of Marque and Reprisal for his "14-gun" brig *Rattle Snake*.

On Sunday, May 23, 1813 Captain Samuel Charles Nicoll's privateer schooner *Scourge* lay in New York harbor, armed, provisioned, and manned to cross the Atlantic to attack British shipping. Nicoll was well prepared to be a privateer. Born on May 13, 1782, he was the second son of General Matthias Nicoll, a prominent shipping merchant of Stratford and New York.

Although Matthias was listed as master of the 31-ton sloop *Julia* in 1800, it is likely that 18-year-old Samuel was actually in command. In 1809, when the effects of Jefferson's embargo were being felt by all American shippers, Matthias mortgaged all his Stratford property to Samuel, probably to protect it from other creditors. By 1813 Samuel had both extensive shiphandling skills and business experience.

Who owned the *Scourge*? The request for a Letter of Marque was signed by New York merchants Peter Schenck and Frederick Jenkins. It read:

To the Honorable James Monroe, Secretary of State for the United States of America.

The petition and application of Peter N. Schenck and Frederic Jenkins of the City of New York humbly sheweth—

That your Petitioners are Citizens of the United States of America and owners of the schooner called the *Scourge* of the burthen of two hundred & forty eight 38/95 Tons, whereof Samuel C. Nicoll is Master, having equipped and furnished and provided said vessel as a Privateer (the said vessel being manned with one hundred men and carrying fifteen guns with small arms) humbly Solicit that a Commission or Licence may be granted to them for the said vessel for the purpose of Cruising against the Shipping of the Enemies of the United States during the present War. And your petitioners &c.

Peter N. Schenck, Fred Jenkins, New York 8th May 1813

Schenck's counting house stood near the East River docks on Maiden Lane. Together, Schenck and Nicoll's brother Francis Holland Nicoll owned the 18-gun privateer brig *Anaconda*, commanded by Nathaniel Shaler. It was *Anaconda* that mistook the schooner *Commodore Hull* for the Halifax privateer *Liverpool Packet* and shot her up. Nicoll's cousin Edward Holland Nicoll was a partner in

In 1780 Hawley and his whaleboat crew captured Tory Charles Penny's sloop Sally *on the Sound, laden with rum, molasses, beef, and pork. (Fairfield Historical Society.)*

nearby Smith & Nicoll. Jenkins was partner to Rensalaer Havens, owner of the privateer brig *General Armstrong*, Captain Samuel Chester Reid, noted for standing up to the British ship-of-the-line *Plantagenet* and two others in Fayal harbor in the Azores in 1814. Havens's brother was Congressman Jonathan Nicoll Havens, hinting at another family connection. Old papers might show that these merchants and others all owned shares in all of these privateers, in agreements made at the Tontine Coffee House.

As to the builders, the East River shipyards near Corlear's Hook north of the counting houses are candidates. Christian Bergh's yard, C. Bergh & Co., at the foot of Scammel Street, is known to have built a number of sharp little schooners and brigs, some of which were privateers. Adam & Noah Brown, at the foot of Stanton Street since 1807, also built some fast privateers, and later built Black Ball packets for other area houses.

Scourge grossed 248.4 tons and carried 15 guns—a mid deck 24-pound cannon, eight 9-pound long range cannon, and six smaller cannon—and lots of musketry. Captain Nicoll and his officers, First Lieutenant J. Doane, Second Lieutenant Robert L. Perry, and Third Lieutenant Nathaniel Nagel, commanded a crew of 110 men.

Also in New York harbor was the ad hoc squadron of Stephen Decatur, comprising the frigate *United States*, 44 guns; the *Macedonian*, 38 guns, (now part of the U.S. Navy); and the 20-gun sloop-of-war *Hornet*. Bottled up by a British blockade squadron, Commodore Decatur decided to escape to sea through Long Island Sound, so on Monday, May 24 the squadron, accompanied by *Scourge*, left Kip's Bay and approached Hell Gate. *United States* drew 23.5 feet astern and the channel was sharp with rocks. (It would be 1885 before Flood Rock was blasted out of Hell Gate passage.) Master's Mate William Striddy, aboard the *Hornet*, wrote: "We sailed in company with the Frigate *Macedonian*, Capt. Jones, & the U. S., Commodore Stephen Decatur; there was also a privateer of 18 [sic] guns, called the *Scourge*, Capt. Samuel Nichols [sic]. We sailed through Hellgate in a thunder squall. The *United States* touched bottom was struck by lightening at the same moment, but received no injury."

Decatur anchored for the night off Riker's Island, then drove his ships down the Sound toward the Race, *Hornet* (and undoubtedly *Scourge*) in the van, but hesitated to break out into the Atlantic until the 1st of June: "We duly dallied for several days, in Long Island Sound instead of going to sea immediately, as did the privateer. This gave the enemy time to go from Sandy Hook and as we were going out by Montauk Point; we met the seventy-four frigate, and another ship. They gave chase and we made for New London (the wind ahead) our ship sailing very dull, the English frigate neared us so as to open her fire on us."

United States and *Macedonian*, driven into New London, sailed up the Thames and were bottled up for the duration of the war, their cannon removed and used along the shoreline for coastal defense.

But not the *Scourge*. Nicoll must have sailed out through the Race on Wednesday the 26th, before Captain Robert Oliver's British squadron arrived

When Samuel Nicoll met a frigate off the North Cape, he thought it was the United States, *which he had left in Long Island Sound, but it was her twin, the* President, *Commodore Rodgers commanding. (Courtesy the Mariners' Museum, Newport News, VA.)*

from New York. He would have followed the northeast flow of the Gulf Stream across the Atlantic. The next report of *Scourge* appears in a Norwegian shipping document:

> The first of the caper [privateer] ships that appeared by the coast was the *Scourge* from New York owned by two businessmen from New York. On Saturday night, July 3rd, 1813 at 7 o'clock a.m. one saw the vessel sailing into Hammarfest for the first time, as one had seen a British naval vessel there four years prior. One saw that the *Scourge* was not a merchant ship. Lt. Westbye on Hammarfest's fort called the alarm to be ready for enemy attack. The ship sent a longboat with an officer asking for fresh water. As Lt. Westbye was not knowledgeable of the English language, he asked Christie, a businessman from Kristiansund who happened to be in town, to go on board to check the vessel's papers. Christie was very well received and was shown the ship's papers and was convinced of the ship nationality and purpose in coming into port. Just in case, though, they anchored the ship right under the fort's cannons so as to keep the ship under a watchful eye. As the ship had been to sea for 40 days, it left NY at the end of May. Lt. Westbye permitted by request the crew in small parties to go on land to stretch their legs. The Americans behaved well, and the following Tuesday after they stocked water, they left Hammarfest.

This painting is believed to show Scourge *and* Rattle Snake *attacking the British merchantman* Brutus *in the North Sea. They captured 4,505 tons that summer. (Courtesy South Street Seaport Museum, New York.)*

Even before arriving in Hammerfest, *Scourge* had taken its first prize on June 29, the British bark *Concord* of 187 tons and 2 guns, from London for Archangel under ballast, sent in to Trondheim; then, after leaving Hammerfest, on July 14 the ship *Liberty* of 253 tons and 8 guns, from Liverpool for Archangel in ballast, sent in to Hammerfest.

Again Nicoll fell in with a U.S. frigate, this time on July 19-22 off the North Cape, and again escaped the British because of their concentration on the warship. Ironically, the frigate was the USS *President*, under Commodore John Rodgers, sister ship to the *United States.* Commodore Rodgers reported: "At the time of meeting with the Enemies two ships, the privateer schooner *Scourge* of New York, which I had fallen in with the day before, was in company; but their attention was so much engrossed by the *President* that they permitted the *Scourge* to escape without appearing to take any notice of her."

Lloyd's List of Shipping on Aug 13, 1813 reported that the frigate *Alexandria* and sloop-of-war *Spitfire* had chased and lost the *President* on July 23, when "she was accompanied by a fast sailing Privateer of 16 guns, and 200 men . . ."

On July 27 *Scourge* sighted the American privateer brig *Rattle Snake*, 297 tons, 16 (not 14) guns, and 130 men, off the Norway coast. The two captains agreed to work together, dividing the spoils two thirds to *Rattle Snake*, one third to *Scourge*. During the whole month of August, the two caper vessels sailed together outside North Cape and took 19 English vessels that, as they were taken, were sent down to "Drontheim" (Trondheim) where almost all of them arrived.

Scourge and *Rattle Snake* worked together off the North Cape all summer. The two Americans sent 23 vessels—4,505 tons of shipping and 60 guns—into Norwegian ports for adjudication that summer, then sailed south to Trondheim. There, both vessels fitted out, and *Scourge* was converted into a brig. They set sail again on October 29, but due to a leak and bad weather, *Scourge* returned to port after ten fruitless days off the coast of Scotland. On November 20, *Niles Weekly* reported:

> The *Scourge* privateer is still doing a great business off the North Cape [of Norway]. Not a vessel for Archangel escapes her, says a letter from Lisbon. "Everything taken is sure of being saved, as three hours sail will send them in behind a chain of islands, and on the one at the entrance the privateer has supplied an old battery, strong enough to keep off small cruisers. The Danes take possession of them immediately, and conduct them to Drontheim, so that the crew of the *Scourge* remains complete, as Danes are hired to man the fortress they have erected."

While refitting in Trondheim, about 40 of the crew, their terms up, received permission to take the captured *Liberty* home, and set sail in December. Damaged at sea, *Liberty* put into Stromness in January and the crew were detained.

When *Scourge* was ready to return to sea, Captain Nicoll decided to remain at Trondheim, where he could oversee the sale of ships and goods brought in. He kept the ship's purser (who was in poor health anyway) to help him, and put his senior lieutenant, Robert Perry, in command of *Scourge*. Perry was a good choice. He took two months to reach America and captured 15 more prizes on the way.

Captain George Coggeshall, born in Milford and a privateer and trader himself, wrote:

> During this cruise, *Scourge* made 420 prisoners and arrived at Chatham, Cape Cod, in May [1814], after having been absent from the United States about a year. This vessel was very appropriately named, for she was, in truth, a severe scourge to the enemy. She inflicted a chastisement upon the commerce of Great Britain that will cause her name to be remembered for several generations.

In 1905, naval historian Alfred Thayer Mahan noted that:

> Although individual American vessels sometimes made numerous seizures in rapid succession, they seldom, if ever, effected the capture or destruction of a large convoy at a single blow. . . . In 1813 two privateers, the *Scourge* and *Rattlesnake*, passed the summer in the North Sea, and there made a number of prizes . . . which being reported together gave the impression of a single encounter . . . [but] were spread over a period of two months. . . . The *Scourge* appears to have been singularly

fortunate, for on her homeward trip she took, sent in, or destroyed, [fifteen] more enemy's vessels: and in an absence extending a little over a year had taken four hundred and twenty prisoners—more than the crew of a 38-gun frigate.

Scourge was indeed a threat to English pride and pocketbooks: American privateers in the War of 1812 captured 1,344 English ships and of these, *Scourge* alone took 27, more than any other out of New York. With Napoleon defeated and our young republic nearly on its knees—its armies driven back from Canada, its ports sealed by blockade, and Washington burned—Britain could easily have continued the war. But with the Royal Navy spread around the world, the privateers were literally destroying British commerce at its threshold. Insurance rates exceeded 15 percent.

Merchants in Liverpool, Bristol, and Glasgow held meetings and petitioned Parliament to stop the war against "that Power, whose maritime strength we have impolitically held in contempt." The resulting Treaty of Ghent, signed on December 24, 1814, gave liberal terms, freed up our lands beyond the mountains, and set the stage for American growth and empire. The impact of the privateers extended far beyond their dreams.

And privateering made them rich. When Captain Nicoll returned home, he bought from William Samuel Johnson 23 acres "near Long Beach at place called Lordship" and added to it until he owned a 150-acre estate. From the farm, called Lordship Manor, the captain could view all across the Sound.

That year Elvira Benjamin was paying particular attention to Samuel Nicoll. In the spring she wrote to her sister "The captain has returned from Amelia [Island, Florida] several weeks since and has been on to Washington since then: he is now in New York for a week or two on business. I expect, nay, hope! he will spend the summer in Stratford. He offered me his heart and hand before he went to Amelia last fall . . . and ever since his return his attentions have been increasing."

On February 23, 1820 Elvira became Mrs. Samuel Nicoll. A letter to her sister suggests that Nicoll had been overseeing construction of a new steamship at Amelia Island, stating, "He is going to South America in April to take a steamboat out there in which expedition if he is successful he will probably make something very handsome, and if he is not he will at least make an advantageous voyage—not to sail it there by steam, but to take it out to run in their waters. He went to New York last evening to make some arrangements for a few days. When he returns I am going down with him to stay until he sails."

In the 1830s Nicoll built on Elm Street a magnificent Greek Revival mansion, where he lived until his death on May 1, 1850. The house is now the office of the Stratford Festival Theatre.

While Nicoll was wreaking havoc on Great Britain in the North Sea in 1813–1814 and Stratford's sailing sons were scattered round the globe, their families at home lived in terror of attack from the sea. Pulaski Benjamin's sister Elvira—the future Mrs. Nicoll—penned this letter in the spring of 1814:

Samuel Nicoll's brother Francis Holland Nicoll, shown here, and Peter Schenk owned the privateer Anaconda *together, and Schenk registered* Scourge, *so the Nicolls were probably co-owners of that vessel as well.*

Last Friday evening this town and Bridgeport were thrown into great consternation by the appearance of a British Frigate at anchor between here and Bridgeport. Just before dark they got out their boats and sounded along the shore. It was supposed they would at least burn the shipping if they spared the towns. There are several ships and brigs at Stratford, brought there from New York since the war, which it was believed would induce them to come in. Gen. Foote ordered out the Regt. Of Militia and in less than 24 hours I am told there were nearly six hundred troops in Bridgeport. As the night drew excessively dark and the wind blew violently, they did not attempt anything, and the next day they were back again to the eastward. Out militia were all out parading the streets all the next day; it had been the most warlike appearance of anything I have seen. We, however, like a soldier's family, were not at all alarmed—and William lamented deeply his not being large enough to accompany the militia down to the beach the night they lay off there."

The fleet had probably never intended to attack the town, but was buying fresh provisions from Yankee opportunists under cover of darkness. Rumor had it that the manager of Johnson's tide mill in West Stratford, one Garlick, carried on extensive contraband traffic with the British, buying sheep and cattle for resale to their naval officers.

The real threat to Stratford was not the Royal Navy; it was instead the privateers from Canada and the provinces who sailed under the red jack of Britain. Foremost of these was the schooner *Liverpool Packet*. She was a former slaver, bought at

Converted from a slaver by Captain Enos Collins in Nova Scotia, the lean-lined Liverpool Packet, *with undercut stem, raking keel, swept back masts, and the speed of a Baltimore clipper, was the ideal Loyalist privateer. (Courtesy Mr. Windsor Wood.)*

auction in 1811 in Halifax, Nova Scotia, by Enos Collins of nearby Liverpool, ostensibly for use as a sailing packet between the towns. The *Packet* measured 54 tons, 53 feet, 4 inches stem to stern, and was described as "a lean lined thing . . . with bold bows, undercut stem and raking keel, and two taut spars, longer than she was, slanting back so sharply they seemed to be falling over her narrow stern. . . . She had all the signs of one of those Virginia pilot boats which were coming into fashion as Baltimore clippers."

Owner Collins was one of the first to learn that the United States had declared war, and immediately fitted out the schooner with five guns—a 6 pounder, two 4s, and two 12s—a 45-man crew, 200 rounds of cannister and 300 of roundshot in her magazine, 400 weight of gunpowder, 25 muskets, 40 cutlasses, and 60 days' provisions. He had a commission from the governor for "apprehending, seizing, and taking the ships, goods, and vessels belonging to France &c"—all the governor was yet allowed to authorize. Trusting that the "&c" covered whomever she would encounter, the *Liverpool Packet* put to sea on the last day of August 1812. Within the 60 days his provisions would allow, Captain Joseph Barss Jr. made three lucrative cruises, and on the third he took four schooners in five days between Cape Cod and Cape Ann.

The largest of these was the 79-ton Bridgeport schooner *Little Joe*. This must have pleased his prizemaster Thomas Freeman, who had been a prisoner aboard Derby captain Isaac Hull's USS *Constitution* when she sank the *Guerrierre*, and who had vowed revenge. Freeman must have encouraged Barss to raid Hull's neighbors in the Sound, and his revenge included £530 prize money with which he was able to buy the privateer schooner *Retaliation*. Captain James Fayerweather of the *Little Joe* was surely just as unhappy at losing his fat cargo of corn, flour, leather goods, duck, and drygoods. A note in the Fairfield County Customs records reads, "The within license [*Little Joe's*] was taken away by force by John Sherman [sic] commander of the *Liverpool Packet* one of his Majesties Privateers as appears by the protest of sd Fayerweather Dated Egertin [sic] Mass Oct 19 1812."

With a new letter of marque, the *Liverpool Packet* set out again from Nova Scotia to harry shipping between Boston and New York. Another entry in the Customs Office records, alongside the registry of the sloop *Minerva*, 43 tons, on February 7, 1814, master Eliada Baldwin, includes the note, "Proof has been exhibited at this office the within vessel was taken by a boat belonging to the British schooner called the *Liverpool Packet* and her papers detained on the 11th day of August 1814. Collector Walter Bradley." The sloop was recovered, and again registered to Captain Baldwin on October 10, 1815.

On another occasion, on an afternoon in 1814, the men at the little fort at Welles Tongue [Seaside Park], guarding the entrance to Bridgeport harbor with a single cannon, probably borrowed from the laid-up frigate *United States*, saw three sails rapidly approaching the harbor mouth. They turned out to be two local coasters being chased by the *Liverpool Packet*. The first, a sloop, made it into the harbor, but poor Captain Lewis Hart ran his schooner *Nancy* hard aground on the outer bar. The crew of the *Packet* boarded *Nancy* and would have burned her to the waterline, but Captain Hart had had the presence of mind to toss his tinder box over the side. A volley of shots from Captain James Allen's company at the fort and a few balls from Captain Samuel Hawley's single cannon drove off the attackers.

The *Liverpool Packet* and many American privateers operated right up to the signing of the peace on Christmas Eve, 1814. This was the last war in which the town of Stratford had to fear the predations of privateers.

FIFTY YEARS TO ADMIRAL

The life of Joshua Sands is the history of the U.S. Navy. He served for 50 years, from his appointment as midshipman on June 18, 1812—the day that Congress declared war on England and began the War of 1812—to his retirement on July 16, 1862, when the country was in Civil War. Young Sands reported to Sacketts Harbor on Lake Ontario on September 7, 1812, a month before his commodore arrived.

Commodore Isaac Chauncey was himself a Black Rock native, great-great grandson of Stratford's second minister, Israel Chauncey. He had been in the Navy ever since there was a navy, from 1798, and had served in Tripoli under Commodore Edward Preble. When the war broke out, President James Madison appointed him to the command of the Great Lakes.

In November Sands cruised Lake Ontario aboard Chauncey's only naval vessel, the gun brig *Oneida*, 16 guns. After taking a few prizes and testing the batteries at Kingston, Chauncey settled down for the winter to expand his squadron. The *Madison*, 24 guns, and the *General Pike*, 15 guns, were built that winter, and seven schooners armed. As soon as Madison was ready that April, Chauncey took her across the lake and, with General Dearborn's forces, captured York (Toronto). When the fleet returned to Sackett's Harbor, with the dying General Zebulon Pike aboard, they found British General Prevost and Admiral Sir James Yeo advancing against Chauncey's base, and drove them off. This was Midshipman Sands's baptism under fire.

Sands was on the *General Pike* that August when Chauncey and Yeo met again. Chauncey's fleet was armed with long guns for distance fire, whereas Yeo's sturdy vessels carried carronades for close encounters. Chauncey's fighting technique was to "edge away," in hope that Yeo would follow him. In the final encounter on September 28, called by the Americans the "Burlington Races," Yeo's flagship *Wolfe* was mauled by the *Pike's* long guns, and raced away downwind.

Sands's indoctrination to battle on Lake Ontario was a lesson in extreme caution. While Chauncey's second-in-command, Oliver Hazard Perry, made the lakes famous in the Battle of Lake Erie—"We have met the enemy and he is ours!"—Ontario remained serene. Sands served aboard the new frigate *Superior*.

After the war, in March, 1815 President Madison ordered a squadron under Decatur to the Mediterranean to protect American merchant ships. Even after the Bey of Tripoli capitulated, the U.S. maintained a presence there. In 1816 Ensign Sands went aboard the USS *Washington*, completed in October 1815, on Mediterranean patrol. *Washington* was one of three 74-gun ships-of-the-line laid down during the War of 1812. She grossed 2,200 tons, and carried 30 long guns, 33 mediums, and 20 carronades—all 32 pounders. During her two-year cruise, Sands was promoted to Lieutenant.

In 1819 and 1820, U.S. squadrons continued to patrol against maverick states in the Mediterranean. As lieutenant aboard the sloop-of-war *Hornet*, Sands saw service in Spain, the Mediterranean, Africa, and the West Indies. Off Africa the Navy apprehended slavers, now designated pirates by act of Congress.

From 1821 to 1824 Lieutenant Sands saw the south seas as an officer on the 74-gun "liner" *Franklin*, sister ship to *Washington*, protecting ships from pirates in Sunda Strait and the Gaspar Straits. *Franklin* must have spoken New York ships in the China trade manned by Stratford skippers—*Ajax*, Hubbell; *China* and *Superior*, Dowdall; and *Nimrod* and *Splendid*, Sterling.

Lieutenant Sands spent the next four years at the New York Navy Yard. Since the War of 1812, the Navy's job was to protect the American merchant marine around the world. Funds were limited and few new ships were built. In October 1828 he went aboard the sloop-of-war *Vandalia*, launched that year, to the Brazilian Squadron until September 1830. *Vandalia* was one of several ships built to replace the older sloops-of-war, now in bad shape—in fact, Sands's old ship *Hornet* went down with all hands off Tampico in 1829.

Joshua Sands's career was typical for a naval officer of the period. Advancements were rare. He remained a lieutenant, stationed aboard the *Rendezvous* at the New York yard for many years, and was finally promoted to Commander on February 23, 1840.

In 1847 came a chance for action. In 1836 Texas had declared its independence from Mexico: Mexican leader Santa Anna moved to crush the rebellion, but the Texans won their war. In 1845 the United States annexed the Republic of Texas. In 1846 President Polk ordered General Zachary Taylor into action against Mexico, and on May 13 Congress declared war. On March 9, 1847 American troops under General Winfield Scott hit the beaches at Vera Cruz in the first amphibious assault in the nation's history. Commander Sands was there.

Raphael Semmes, then flag lieutenant to Commodore David Conner of the Gulf Squadron, reported the action: "Commodore Conner had previously directed the two steamers, *Spitfire*, Commander Tatnall, and *Vixen*, Commander Sands, with five gun schooners, to anchor in line, abreast of the beach, to cover the landing, in case any opposition should be made. This part of the movement had already been hansomely executed." *Spitfire* and *Vixen* were 241-ton steam schooners, capable of seven knots. Each carried an 8-inch 68-pounder shell gun on the bow and two 32-pounder carronades aft.

On March 21 Commodore Matthew Perry, a steam advocate himself, succeeded Conner, and on the 25th he ordered the gunboats to bombard Castillo San Juan de Ulloa. Within 80 yards of the castle, Tatnall's flotilla, *Spitfire*, *Vixen*, and five schooners, ignored Perry's retirement signal and pounded the fort for half an hour until Perry sent a boat with orders to retreat.

Midshipman Joshua Sands cut his teeth in the Battle of Lake Ontario under Commodore Isaac Chauncey, and began a 50-year career in the Navy. (Courtesy the Mariners' Museum, Newport News, VA.)

In the Mexican War, Commander Sands served under Captain Raphael Semmes as captain of the little steam gunboat Vixen *in the first amphibious assault in American history, at Vera Cruz in 1847. (Courtesy the Mariners' Museum, Newport News, VA.)*

In June Perry launched an expedition to seize the town of Tabasco, 70 miles up the Tabasco River. This was another job for the steam gunboats. Four of them, *Spitfire*, Sands's *Vixen*, *Scorpion*, and *Scourge*, towed barges upriver filled with 1,064 seamen and marines from the larger ships. When Perry reached the town, David Porter in the lead boat, *Spitfire*, had already taken Tabasco.

Texas and California became parts of the United States. Peace and naval quiet returned. Sands returned to the Navy Yard, commanding the *New York* receiving ship in 1849. In 1853 he was commander of the war-sloop *Allegheny* in the East India Squadron. His promotion to captain came on February 25, 1854, followed by assignment to the big sidewheel frigate *Susquehanna*, Franklin Buchanan's old command, in the Mediterranean Squadron.

In July 1857 Sands and *Susquehanna* were ordered to serve as escort to the USS *Niagara* and the HMS *Agamemnon*, assigned to Cyrus Field in his first attempt to lay a telegraph cable across the Atlantic. Field had obtained subsidies to lay the cable from the British and American governments, though not without opposition. One congressman wrote that he did not want "anything to do with England or Englishmen," and Henry David Thoreau wrote "perchance the first news that will leak through into the broad, flapping, American ear will be that Princess Adelaide has the whooping cough."

Cable was loaded onto both *Niagara* and *Agamemnon*, the idea being that when the first had paid out her whole 1,250 miles of cable in mid Atlantic, the other would attach to it and complete the job.

Cable laying began on August 6 at Valentia Bay in Ireland, when *Niagara* began to pay out cable from the coils in her hold. After only 5 miles the cable snapped, and *Niagara* had to begin again. All went well for four more days, 335 miles out to sea, until on August 11, in 2,000 fathoms, the brake on the paying-out apparatus was applied too suddenly and the cable snapped again.

The attempt was abandoned until the following spring, but in 1858 Joshua Sands was not there to help: he and *Susquehanna* were laid up in the West Indies with yellow fever aboard. When *Susquehanna* returned to New York, the Board of Health let her sit in quarantine at Staten Island for three months without being disinfected. The resulting outbreak of yellow fever created a riot, and the mob burned down the quarantine station. (Meanwhile, the cable-laying job was completed and the cable functioned until it went dead in September). An operable Atlantic cable was finally laid in 1866 by Isambard Kingdom Brunel's great ship, *Great Eastern*.

In 1859 Captain Sands was again en route to Montevideo, this time as Flag Officer (Commodore) of the Brazil Squadron. Lewis Russell's diary, home in Stratford, says, "Wed Aug 3 1859. Captain Sands is going away to Rio Janeiro in 2 or 3 days in the frigate *Congress*." Sands's squadron included his flagship the 1,867-ton USS *Congress*, "rebuilt"—a term used by the Navy to finance new vessels using maintenance funds—in 1841, the steamer *Pulaski*, and three brigs. A fast sailer, built in the Portsmouth Navy Yard, *Congress* was the last sailing frigate designed for the navy.

When Cyrus Field first attempted to lay the Atlantic cable in 1857, Joshua Sands was there in command of the sidewheel frigate Susquehanna, *on the left edge of the picture. (Robert Dudley painting.)*

There was little action on the Brazil Station, except to cruise back and forth from Montevideo and Buenos Aires to Rio de Janiero, assisting American merchantmen. In 1861 each mail brought more alarming news from home. On April 13 Fort Sumter fell to the Confederates, but Sands did not hear of it for two months. Finally in June he was ordered home to Boston with the *Congress*. His Stratford neighbor Captain Truman Hotchkiss, in Montevideo harbor at the time, watched the navy's preparations to depart. On June 19 Hotchkiss boarded *Pulaski* to hand the commodore a letter for Mrs. Hotchkiss in Stratford, and on the 20th visited *Congress* to say goodbye.

It was an end and a beginning. Picture four men in *Congress's* wardroom. The old flag officer would be promoted to admiral, then banished to lighthouse service. The flagship *Congress* would be sent to Hampton Roads to her destruction by the ironclad CSS *Virginia*, formerly the USS *Merrimack*. The commodore's neighbor and subordinate, Ensign Barrymore, would command small steamboats in Admiral DuPont's blockade, and capture Confederate blockade runners. Hotchkiss would scour the Atlantic for nonexistent cargos. And the commodore's young aide, just out of the Naval Academy, Ensign Mahan, would carve a niche in naval history.

On June 21 *Congress* sailed for Boston. The trip took 62 days. As Sands passed through the West Indies, his old navy superior Raphael Semmes, now commanding the Confederate raider CSS *Sumter*, was attacking Union shipping close at hand.

After refitting, *Congress* was dispatched to Hampton Roads to blockade the port of Norfolk and on March 8, 1862 was sunk and burned to the water's edge by former U.S. Navy captain Franklin Buchanan, now captain of the Confederate ironclad CSS *Virginia*.

Joshua Sands, now in his 60s, made the retired list on July 16, 1862, and served as lighthouse inspector until 1866. He appears as a rear admiral on the retired list, July 25, 1866, and shows up as Port Admiral in Norfolk in 1870.

Truman Hotchkiss went on to search for cargo for his schooner *Coast Pilot*, but shippers shunned Yankee shipping, fearing capture and loss to Confederate raiders. Union merchant ships nearly disappeared from international waters, presaging the end of American commercial sail.

In 1861 Montevideo harbor was host to Commodore Sands's Brazil Squadron and to American commercial ships in search of cargo. Truman Hotchkiss's schooner Coast Pilot *was one of these. (Courtesy Peabody Essex Museum, Salem, MA.)*

Captain Sands was commodore of the Brazil Squadron in 1861 when word came to return to Boston; the South was in rebellion. On June 21 his flagship Congress *headed north. (Courtesy Peabody Essex Museum, Salem, MA.)*

Master's Mate Barrymore remained in the navy through 1868. His experience aboard *Pulaski* prepared him for command of steam tugs, and he received medals for capturing blockade runners while serving under Admiral DuPont. After his discharge, he spent his life commanding pilot tugs in Bridgeport harbor and Long Island Sound.

The commodore's aide learned much about the old navy from Captain Sands, and went on to become an admiral himself, and the greatest naval historian and tactician of all time. His name was Alfred Thayer Mahan.

In his book *From Sail to Steam*, Mahan described his life as aide to Sands. He recognized Sands as an officer of the old school, who had fought three duels and in his last had killed his man. Mahan accompanied the commodore ashore on a visit to the scene of his last duel, on an island in the harbor of Rio de Janeiro. Solemnly reminiscent, the flag officer paced off the field, meditated a few moments in silence and then marched back to his barge. For hours on end Mahan watched him measure the quarter-deck with mincing steps, a queer little slouching figure beside the towering bulk of Captain Goldsborough. At night Mahan trailed the flag officer down the gun deck, carefully picking his way, like Sands, among the men sprawled in sleep between the guns.

One day as he was about to go ashore, the Commodore noticed that Mahan was wearing a handsome necktie his mother had given him. "Humph!" he growled. "Don't wear a thing like that with me. You look like a privateersman!"

Commodore Sands was noted even among his hard-fighting contemporaries for his personal courage. Duelling was so common it excited no comment in the naval circles of the day, and the commodore had had his share. The customs and manners of naval officers in the British, French, Dutch, and American navies had many points of resemblance. He had been brought up by captains like Decatur, Morris, and Oliver H. Perry, who in turn had served under men like Commodore Preble. There had been little change in the characteristics of ships during the two centuries before the War of 1812, and the character of their officers had changed scarcely more than the ships. In Commodore Sands young Mahan had a living model of the better-than-average officer of the sailing ship era.

In Stratford, Sands lived in the mansion built by Captain Dowdall. Sands Place in town is named for him. He later settled in the Norfolk area. Truman Hotchkiss on a trip to Norfolk recorded, "Friday 22 May 1874. Visited Rear Admiral Sands. Found him and family well."

STEAMBOATER IN THE UNION NAVY

Captain Truman Hotchkiss's journal of the schooner *Coast Pilot*, in Montevideo Harbor on June 19, 1861, says, "Mr. Barrymore came on board and spent an hour with us." William Barrymore was then serving under his neighbor Commodore Joshua Sands, Flag Officer of the Brazil Squadron, probably aboard the steamer USS *Pulaski*.

On June 21 Commodore Sands and his flagship *Congress* headed home to Boston, and Barrymore must have returned with them. He soon went south again, to join the blockading fleet sent south from Fortress Monroe. Julia Curtis's account book says "U.S. Navy Nov 12, 1861—went to Port Royal as master's mate—gone 10 months." Navy records confirm his next assignment: "The abovenamed man was appointed an Acting Master's Mate Nov 8, 1861 and ordered to report to the Commandant, Navy Yd. New York: assigned to duty on the Propellor *Henry Andrew* November 11: he also served on the USS *Mercury* in the S A Blockading Squadron and, October 7, 1862, reported his arrival at New York as a passenger in the prize bark *Fanny Lewis*." Barrymore actually arrived in New York earlier: on the 5th he appeared at the Curtis family doorstep, and stayed until the 22nd. (Julia charged him $12.50 board.)

By now, Barrymore's career was set. Now 25, he was fully indoctrinated in Navy ways—trained by crusty old Commodore Sands—and thoroughly familiar with sidewheel and propeller driven steam tugs and their engines. After his leave in Stratford, he was ordered to Port Royal, South Carolina, headquarters of Admiral DuPont's South Atlantic Blockading Squadron. The Navy's task was to blockade the Confederacy's 3,549-mile-long coast.

Barrymore's first command was the U.S. steam tug *Dandelion*, a 111-ton wooden steamer purchased November 21, 1862 as the USS *Antietam*. Appointed ensign and given command in January, Will wasted no time in following Captain Sands's example—appointing his neighbors—and on March 2 Admiral DuPont confirmed the appointment of Benjamin Russell of Stratford as Acting Master's Mate on *Dandelion*, to commence February 20, 1863.

Barrymore's record includes an award for "gallantry under fire" during Admiral DuPont's disastrous April 7 attack on Forts Sumter and Moultrie in Charleston harbor. When the flagship *New Ironsides* and eight monitors moved forward, the monitors found heavy obstructions in the channel and halted before the flagship itself could come within range of the forts. From the forts came withering fire. *Nantucket* was hit 51 times, *Nahant's* turret and pilothouse were so weakened that they were in danger of collapse "for want of bolts to hold them together," and *Keokuk*, forced to pass ahead of *Weehawken*, took more than 90 hits. "Riddled like a colander," she had jagged holes at her waterline and her captain, Commander Rhind, shouted that he didn't know if he could keep her afloat. At 5:00 p.m. DuPont gave orders to withdraw. Next morning, looking at his crippled fleet, the admiral announced "I have decided not to renew the attack."

At daylight, Commander Rhind signalled from his position, still within the line of fire from the fort, that *Keokuk* would soon go down. The flagship sent *Dandelion* in to try to tow her out. Barrymore tossed a line to the monitor, and tried to pull her out of danger, but it was too late.

At 7:30 a.m., April 8, *Keokuk* sank to the top of her smokestack in shallow water. Rhind's report described it: "On the arrival of the tug *Dandelion* the anchor was weighed and an ineffectual effort made to tow her stern around to the swell, the fractures in the bow being much larger; she began to fill forward; in a few minutes she went down, the tug coming alongside just in time to save the crew."

Dandelion, Barrymore, and his 21-man crew spent the following week at Port Royal with the flagship *Wabash*. On May 6, concerned that the Confederates might attack his vessels off Charleston, Commodore Turner wrote "I am very much worried about the little *Dandelion*."

But the tug remained busy. On July 6 Admiral Dahlgren relieved Admiral DuPont, and on the 7th Dahlgren ordered Captain Rowan of *New Ironsides*, "You will send in charge of Lt. Mackenzie, from the vessels of Charleston, in tow of the tug *Dandelion*, a sufficient number of boats manned to carry, in addition to their crews, between 200 and 250 men [to Folly River]."

A message from Captain Rowan cautioned Commander Shufelat not to receive the French consul if he came out to them from Charleston, for fear that might indicate recognition of the Confederacy, and ordered him to supply crewmen from his monitor to help take the island forts. "*Dandelion* will take your boats in tow tonight. Man them lightly. Don't fire on her as she approaches you." Barrymore remained busy towing boats up the Folly River. From the USS *Nantucket* at anchor in the Stone River on the 10th, "At 6 tug *Dandelion* arrived with *Pawnee's* launch in tow. On the 24th, from *Nantucket*, "At 5:30 a.m. went to quarters. At 5:30 tug *Dandelion* brought us a pilot."

On July 23 Barrymore was promoted to Acting Master. On August 17 he was in action again, in an assault on the island forts along the approach to Charleston. USS *Catskill* reported "At 8:20 p.m. a shot struck the top of the pilot house, shivering the inner plate and detaching three fragments of iron 3 by 5 inches in size, which, striking Captain G W Rodgers and [etc.] the tug *Dandelion* met us and we transferred the dead and wounded to her and then returned to station . . ."

On April 20, 1864 Captain S.C. Rowan, commander of the Charleston blockaders, assigned Will Barrymore to command the large blockade gunboat USS *Acacia*, a 300-ton schooner-rigged screw steamer purchased as the *Vicksburg* at Boston in 1862. Rowan's blockaders had a busy summer in 1864, encountering a constant stream of blockade runners off Charleston. Barrymore's abstract log of September 5 relates:

> At 9:15 p.m. anchored near the channel buoy. Blowing very heavy. Veered to 30 fathoms. At 10:45 saw a blockade runner coming out Maffitt's Channel; slipped, beat to quarters, and commenced firing rapidly at her. Several shots struck her. Finding the vessels closing in on her, she tacked, and ran back. Made signal to fleet "Blockade runner going in," the *Azalea* and *Sweet Brier*, close inshore, firing at her. At 11pm steamer ran ashore, then backed off and stood for Charleston Harbor.

A message from Captain De Camp of the flag steamer *Philadelphia* recorded the event to Senior Officer Captain Joseph Green, explaining why the blockade runner had escaped:

> First Capt. Barrymore of the *Acacia* states that at the time the signal was observed from the *Sangamon* he was on his station, just turning the Swash Channel buoy; steamed rapidly in for Breach Inlet, saw the *Azalea* close in under the land, but saw no blockade runner . . . *Azalea* saw nothing of any blockade runner . . . *Sweet Brier* saw no blockade runner. . . . the captain of the *Acacia* states that his vessel is about 10 knots, but she draws more than 11 feet of water, and is therefore not very efficient as a blockader amidst the shoals of Breach Inlet and Swash Channel buoy.

Deep-draft *Acacia* revealed her vulnerability on the 14th, first reported by Winona, "Discovered the *Acacia* aground within range of Breach Inlet batteries, which were firing on her, but shortly got off." Then by the flag steamer *Harvest Moon*, "Battery Marshall (on Breach Inlet) is very heavy and nearly destroyed the steamer *Acacia* a day or so since, when she grounded about 1300 yards from it."

By November 21, seven blockade runners were reported to have gone into Charleston at the last dark moon. One of these was the 117-ton sidewheeler *Julia*, from Glasgow. On Christmas day Will Barrymore was able to give the Union a fine Christmas present:

> Sir: I have the honor to report the capture at the mouth of Alligator Creek, South Carolina, of the blockade runner *Julia* of Glasgow. She

has a valuable cargo of cotton, and was captured under the following circumstances:

On the morning of the 23d instant, while on my way from Charleston Bar to Georgetown, with provisions for the USS *Canandagua*, after passing Cape Romaine Shoal, I altered my course to N by E, when two white smokestacks close inshore were reported from the masthead. A steamer was apparently blowing off steam. I immediately altered my course, and on closing toward the bar, discovered her to be a side-wheel steamer of perhaps 400 tons. No colors could be seen. As we approached nearer, her decks appeared crowded with men, her boats were lowered, and apparently preparations were made to abandon her. I ran in as near as the depth of water would admit (which was about 2 miles distant) and fired a shell over her. At the same time I hoisted the American ensign. As this met with no response, I lowered the only two serviceable boats I had, and armed them for boarding. I fired another shell and a solid shot over my boats, when the steamer displayed white flags at her masthead and in the fore-rigging, and I ceased firing. My boats were now rapidly nearing her, the gig in charge of Acting Ensign HT Blake, with Acting Second Assistant Engineer Thomas D Crosby, Acting Assistant Paymaster Joseph Foster, Acting Master's Mate William J McFadden, and 8 men: the third cutter in charge of Acting Master's

William Barrymore was appointed Acting Master's Mate on November 18 1861, and served in the Navy for over seven years, commanding gunboats, tugs, and monitors.

Mate Fuller, with 6 men. The last boat was seen pulling from the steamer when my boats were not a quarter of a mile distant. The boats boarded simultaneously and took possession of the steamer without opposition, not a soul remaining on board. The American ensign was hoisted at the fore at 12:20 pm. As soon as I saw this I went on board myself in my dingey, taking with me Acting Third Assistant Engineer JK Wright, who afterwards rendered efficient service in his department. I found the steamer aground, but believing that she could be got off, I ordered the attempt made by kedging.

Acting Second Assistant Engineer Thomas D Crosby now reported to me that her engine had been purposely disabled by her engineers (see his accompanying report.) I requested him to repair them if possible. He set about this task with an energy which insured success, and he was ably assisted by Acting Third Assistant Engineer J K Wright.

The attempt to kedge her off proved partially successful under the active superintendence of Acting Ensign H T Blake, and she was moved about one eighth of a mile. At 4pm temporary repairs were completed, enabling the engines to be worked, but the falling of the tide prevented her from coming off. Finding it useless to try to get her afloat at that stage of the tide, I sent my gig to the ship in charge of Acting Ensign H

This fleet of Union steamers includes tugs and gunboats. The wooden steam tug Dandelion *(formerly USS* Antietam*) was Barrymore's first command. She measured 90 feet, drew 8 feet, and made 9 knots. His 300-ton screw steamer* Acacia, *formerly* Vicksburg, *captured the blockade runner* Julia, *which Barrymore took to Boston for adjudication.*

T Blake, with instructions to send me more men, more muskets, and ammunition, and arranged with him concerted signals by which I could call assistance if attacked.

The boat returned in charge of Acting Ensign A S Rounds, who sounded the channel on his way in. When he arrived on board, I rigged boarding nettings and armed the men to resist any attack that might be made from the shore. I also sent in two boats to reconnoiter, and if possible to capture the *Julia's* boats, but in this they were unsuccessful, as they had been taken up Alligator Creek. At 1am on the 24th, it being half tide, the Julia floated, and I got underway and stood out to the ship and anchored. I now returned to my vessel, leaving Acting Ensign A S Rounds in charge of the *Julia* with a prize crew.

At daylight on the 24th I towed the prize farther offshore, that I might leave her with safety, and proceeded to Georgetown . . . On my return to the *Julia* at 4pm, finding the necessary repairs not completed, and my officers and men worn out by their constant and unusual exertions, I came to anchor for the night for the purpose of giving them rest and completing the repairs.

At daylight on the morning of the 25th I got underway, *Acacia* taking the *Julia* in tow, as there was much difficulty in starting her engines. At 8am cast off the hawser from the *Acacia* and proceeded toward Charleston Bar, the *Acacia* keeping within hailing distance to render any assistance that might be required. Arrived off Charleston Bar at 11:30am and reported the capture to the senior officer.

From papers found on board I judge that the *Julia* left Charleston on the 20th instant. Her topgallant forecastle and forward bulwarks were stove in, indicating that she had met with heavy weather and had put into the mouth of Alligator Creek for a harbor: also for fuel, for her decks were strewn with wood, which had apparently just come on board. The ship's log of a previous voyage was found on board; also the chief officer's log from August 30 to November 3, 1864. The latter shows that she sailed from Glasgow September 3 and arrived at Nassau October 22, 1864, where she took on board Captain Swan—Captain Embleton, who had brought her out, returning to England. She took in a cargo on the 29th of October and sailed about November 1 to run the blockade.

The *Julia* is an iron vessel, of 117 tons, English measurement. She was built at Renfrew, Scotland, in 1863. Her draft, when loaded, is 8 feet aft and 7 feet forward. Her engines are new and powerful. The greatest speed indicated in her log is 12 knots. I found on her two English ensigns, a burgee, with the name *Julia*, and a Confederate States flag.

The engine room journal of Thomas D. Crosby, Acting Assistant Engineer in Charge from the *Julia*, December 23, 1864, gives this account: "Boarded the

Blockade-runner *Julia* in Alligator Creek at 12:20pm, found no one on board, the safety valves were both blowing off with 5 lbs. of steam per gauge and all the blow valves open. The injection pipe broken and the port bilge pump outboard delivery pipe cut. all the handling & reversing gear broken."

After patching up the sabotaged parts—wrapping the bilge pump pipe with canvas and lashing a new crossbar to the starting levers—*Julia* headed down the coast past Cape Romain to Charleston, and headed in on Christmas day. She lay off Morris Island, with the donkey engine running the bilge pump continuously all the following day.

In 1861 Navy Secretary Gideon Welles had instructed the flag officers of the blockading squadrons, "You will please send a fair proportion of the prizes that may be captured to Boston for adjudication," so on December 28, 1864 Acting Master Barrymore was ordered to take *Julia* north for adjudication, and that's where *Julia* went. Out of coal and needing repair, *Julia* left Charleston at 10:30 a.m. on the 27th, with fires out, towed by Barrymore's *Acacia*, and reached Port Royal on the evening of the 28th.

There water wheels, ruptured pipes, and throttle were all repaired, and with Barrymore on the bridge the steamboat took on coal for the trip north, under her own power. On January 7 at 8:00 a.m. she passed the outer marks and headed north at full speed, engines at 29 RPM. At 1:45 she stopped off Charleston to repack the steam trunnions, and sometime after midnight stopped again to haul the fires and reinstall three grate bars in the forward furnace. At 4:20 a.m. she stopped again to repair the starboard water wheel. At 10:45 a.m. on January 8 *Julia* joined the fleet at Fort Fisher.

At 4:15 the steamer set out again, rolling heavily in a quartering sea. The evening of the 9th found her in Beaufort harbor, alongside the coaling vessel. "Took in 33 tons of bituminous coal from the brig *Tittania*." This was an opportunity to disassemble the starboard cutoff and repair it.

It was January 11 before *Julia* put to sea again. "Started at 11:15 a.m. At 11:50 struck heavy coming over the bar." But the ship was soon running full speed at sea, burning mixed anthracite and bituminous coal. On the 12th, at Hampton Roads at 3:10 p.m., then into Norfolk Navy Yard at 4:35, for 50 more tons of anthracite. Departing Norfolk at 7:00 p.m. on January 13, *Julia* plowed through heavy seas and reached New York Harbor on January 15 at 4:00 a.m. There Captain Barrymore laid her alongside the USS *Newbern* at the Navy Yard and took the train to Stratford. On the 18th, with 25 more tons of coal aboard, he cast off at 8:30 a.m. on the last leg to Boston, and at 2:00 p.m. on the 19th reached Boston Harbor.

On January 29, 1865 William Barrymore was married to Susan Curtis by the Reverend Charpiot in the Congregational Church at Stratford. He returned to duty on *Acacia* just in time to take part in Squadron Commander Captain Scott's February 18 foray into Charleston Harbor to draw Confederate fire and find out if the forts were occupied.

On April 9 Confederate General Robert E. Lee surrendered at Appomattox, on April 14 President Lincoln was assassinated, and in May Barrymore was detached and ordered to New York to report to Commodore C.H. Bell and take command of the USS *Naubuc*. Detached again on July 22, with a two-month leave of absence, he was to be honorably discharged if no longer needed. He was not discharged, but instead was ordered to Philadelphia, to duty on the monitor *Monadnock*, Captain Bunce, bound for the Brazil station under Commodore Rodgers.

Will Barrymore was familiar with both the station and the ship. He had been in Rio de Janiero under Commodore Sands and, while commanding *Dandelion* and *Acacia*, had observed *Monadnock* in action. A twin-turret monitor of 1,250 tons, *Monadnock* was among the best of the monitors. When the Emperor of Brazil inspected her in January 1866 Barrymore's job was to make sure her "Internal Rules and Regulations," which covered everything from language and lucifers to colors and clotheslines, were followed to a tee.

Detached from *Monadnock* on August 2, 1866, Will was ordered aboard *Pensacola*, then in two weeks to the receiving ship *Vermont*, at the New York Navy Yard. He is also listed as Acting Master on the USS *North Carolina*. After more than seven years of active duty, Acting Master William Barrymore was honorably discharged from the Navy.

From his service, Captain Barrymore built a career. In the early 1870s he captained tugboats in Bridgeport harbor. It must have been demanding work, because we find a receipt from 1871 showing that the captain bought from a New York merchant five gallons of Gaff Bourbon Whiskey (a taste acquired from his blockade days in the South?) for $14. In November 1874 he was appointed a pilot

Julia *was a 117-ton (English measurement) 12-knot steamer similar to this, built in 1863 in Scotland. In Nassau, Confederate Captain Swan took over from English Captain Embleton.*

of tugs in New York, and was employed as a Master of Tugs for the rest of his life. In a letter home on September 25, 1879 he wrote:

> I don't think I can get away before the 15:15 train Saturday for Sam is on watch but will try and start off if not home on that train will take the 9 express. Hope you are all well dear and baby is in good health. I have another nice picture for you. A sea scene a Man of War by moonlight which will go with the other one in the dining room. I think you will like it to match the other one. I have to get the "supply" out ready for the *Tallapasic* to tow to Philadelphia. . . . And now hoping to see you soon shall not be able to get away before 9 express tomorrow. With kisses to you and baby boy and with love.

The baby was their fourth child, Willie, born June 7, 1879. None of the children lived to maturity. Barrymore himself had suffered from violent attacks of headache ever since the war, and died of cerebral meningitis on January 24, 1890. At his funeral service at the Congregational Church bunting draped his casket; his pallbearers were sailors from the Brooklyn Navy Yard.

He was a master of both paddlewheel and screw steamboats, and a dedicated citizen of his town. One of the first Republicans, he was active in outings and torchlight parades and in community affairs. According to *Stratford's 250th Anniversary*, "Capt. Barrymore rendered conspicuous aid to his country during the dark days of the war while in the naval service of the Government, and at the time of his death was a member of the US Grant Post No. 327, GAR, of Brooklyn, NY."

In October 1865, Will returned to the Brazil station as a deck officer on the twin-turret monitor Monadnock *under Captain Bunce.*

4. New York, Boston, and the Tropic Isles

The dangers of the ocean were great: many Stratford seamen perished or disappeared at sea. But the rewards of commerce were greater. After the Revolution, British colonial restrictions ended, and local merchants sent out larger vessels, farther from Stratford, Newfield (Bridgeport), and Huntington Landing. Stratford's coasting sloops and schooners took grain, onions, apples, and oysters to New York and Boston, to Maine for lumber and granite, and southward to deliver shoes, straw hats, and clothing to the plantations. They returned with fish, manufactures, and imported goods. A month's trip to New Providence, Exuma, or Antigua sold grain, horses, shoes, duck, and barrel staves, and brought home salt, sugar, rum, molasses, tropical fruits, and woods. Soon the merchants became the wealthiest citizens. The fleet increased in size until sound steamboats and the railroads took over. Larger vessels—topsail schooners and brigs—traded to South America for hides and beef, and crossed the Atlantic to Portugal and Spain for wines. Worldwide commerce had begun.

Those in Peril on the Sea

"Throw out the lifeline, throw out the lifeline, someone is drifting away," wrote Reverend Edward Ufford, composing his hymn "Throw Out the Lifeline" in 1888. As a boy, Ufford had spent many summers with his grandparents at the family's ancestral Stratford home and had learned from the town's mariners the dangers of the sea. Old gravestones around town affirm those perils:

> Capt. John Barlow who died May the 4th 1786 in the 37th year of his age
> Tho' Boreas' Blasts and Neptune's waves Have tossed me too and fro
> In spite of Death by God's Decree I harbor here below
> Where I do now at anchor ride, With many of our fleet,
> Yet once again I must make sail, Our admiral Christ to meet.

> Capt. Birdseye Brooks who with his crew was lost at sea Sept 1789
> In the 22d year of his Age
> Stern Neptune nods, the billows rise

In vain the Seamen raise their cries
Each in a moment know their doom
And share alike their watery tomb.

Benjamin Curtis, died at Sea Sept 1789 AE 19

Reuben Curtis died at Sea Feb 8th 1802 AE 23

In memory of Capt Phinehas Lovejoy, Junr. who departed this life Sept 26,1803 AEt 41
Death like an overflowing stream, Sweeps us away, our life's a dream,
An empty tale a morning flower, Cut down and withered in an hour.

In memory of Capt. Abijah Blakeman, who was lost at sea on his passage
from Bermuda to New providence in August 1807, aged 29 years.

In memory of Capt William Booth aged 45 yrs and his son David Booth aged 17 years
and of Isaac Booth aged 27 years who were all drowned in Boston Bay
on the 18th day of Oct AD 1810.

In memory of Capt William Thompson,
who died at sea. Dec 14, 1812, aged 47 years.

1815 August Josiah Clarke lost at sea.

Early records list vicious storms and hurricanes but weather predicting was an imperfect art, so ships went out to face unknown conditions, summer and winter. Many simply disappeared.

Died in Canton, in China, on the first day of November 1829 where his remains are interred George Robert Dowdall, son-in-law of Gen'l Matthias Nicoll, in the 47th year of his age. Commander of the ship *Ajax*. In his profession he was inferior to none, And in the discharge of all Social duties as Husband, Father, Friend and Citizen, few excelled him. Also died at Canton, on the 27th of October, 1829, in the 31st year of his age, Edward Nicoll, First officer of the ship *Ajax*, And Son of Gen'l Matthias Nicoll. He was beloved by all who knew him.

Luckier New England seamen died in bed. One Cape Cod gravestone reads:

Captain Thomas Coffin Born Jan 7, 1792 Died Jan 10, 1842 He has finished catching cod And has gone to meet his God.

Most of Stratford's earliest settlers were landsmen, terrified by the sea. The ships they crossed in were stubby merchant ships, whose sailing qualities left much to be desired. The *Arabella (Eagle)*,1630; *Lyon*, 1632; *Francis*,1634; and *Elizabeth and Ann, Hopewell, Plaine Joan, Planter*, and *True Love* of 1635, all shared the characteristics of the *Mayflower*. The voyages were uncomfortable at best, dangerous at worst. When ships were not fighting gales and storms, they slatted about in windless seas. The ship *Lyon* out of London in the summer of 1632 carried Stratford settlers Curtis and Uffoot. *Lyon* reached Boston on September 16 after a voyage of eight weeks from Landsend, although the passengers had been aboard for 12 weeks. They had five days of east wind and fog, but no disaster. There were 123 passengers, of whom 50 were children.

Captain Samuel Wakelee, who shuttled new immigrants from Europe in the days before the Revolution, was once becalmed so long that his ship ran out of provisions, and the crew were reduced to near-starvation before they found relief.

Disappearances were common. In January 1646 New Haven Colony's 150-ton *Great Shippe* set sail from New Haven and was never seen again. Captain Jebediah Wells was lost at sea in 1758. In 1799 Captain Abel Wakelee drowned when Amos Hubbell's brig *Julius Caesar* went down on her way home from the West Indies. Except for the captain and a slave named Ned, the crew escaped in the longboat. In about 1800, Captain Benjamin Wheeler took a clipper-built schooner out of New York and vanished. In November 1810 Stephen Summers Jr. set out from Bridgeport for New Providence on a run he had done many times before; his brig *William* was never seen again.

On October 8, 1815 Captain Daniel Lewis and Josiah Clark drowned at sea. In January 1827 John Burritt and Stephen Danforth drowned when the brig *Henry Johnson* went down in the West Indies. David Peet was reported drowned in April 1830.

Sickness and disease took many Stratford mariners. Captain Abraham Hubbell succumbed to smallpox in Boston. His grandson Amos Hubbell Jr. died of fever in Havana in 1798. In 1830 Anson Hubbell succumbed to smallpox aboard Captain Sterling's *Sabina*, en route to Manila.

But storms and sickness were not the only hazards of the sea. Foreign men-of-war and pirates took their toll. In 1799 Wilson Hubbell's sloop, bound homeward from Havana, was captured by a French privateer. Hubbell's whole crew was replaced by a prizemaster and two men, except for Hubbell himself, who was bound in his cabin, along with steersman Samuel Cable, and the cook. Freeing himself, Hubbell was able to recapture the ship. On a promise of good behavior, the French officer was freed and given the run of the ship. After dinner one night, the Frenchman dropped his cigar near Wilson's feet and, stooping to pick it up, grabbed Wilson by the ankles and tossed him overboard. A strong swimmer, he swam after the ship, but was not brought back aboard, and drowned. He was 26.

In 1805 young Abijah Beardsley was in Antigua as a seaman aboard Samuel Hawley's brig, when he was impressed to serve aboard a British man-o-war. Later freed by the intervention of American businessmen Sylvanus Sterling and Robert Southworth, Abijah was taken to North Carolina aboard a British brig. There, Sterling Sherman wrote:

> I was then employed in a schooner of which my brother David Sherman was master. Both vessels being at anchor at Ocracock Bar, we went on board the brig. The captain said "I have a countryman of yours in board, I will call him and see if you know him." Soon a poor ragged sailor boy came into the cabin and, although we were intimate with him at home, we could not recognize him because his sufferings had been so great, they having been on allowance of a potato a day for a number of days. We brought him home, to the great joy of his widowed mother."

Beardsley's troubles weren't over. In September 1808 he shipped aboard one of the Prindle brothers' schooners out of Newfield. Heavily laden with livestock, and with the scuppers under water, Captain Mordecai Prindle headed for the West Indies, but ran into a hurricane off Cape Hatteras. The seven-man crew all perished in the storm. The Prindles lost two of their three vessels in that storm, and went out of business soon afterwards.

In 1848 Lewis Barnum's journal aboard the ship *Lebanon* describes both weather and enemy troubles, when *Lebanon* found the ship *Houqua* dismasted near Timor in the East Indies, then within a week prepared to repel native canoes.

Even in the Housatonic and in Newfield harbor, disaster struck. William Rose was owner of a fishing weir in Newfield before the Revolution. With his dog Lyon, he would tend his weir in a little dory, but one day fell overboard and nearly drowned. When Lyon swam to him, he grasped the dog by the tail, and directed him to head for shore. When near the shore, the dog turned and began to head out to sea. "Tudder way, Lyon," William gasped. The dog turned again, and towed him straight to shore.

The lower wharf was home to fishing, boating, and swimming. Accidents and drownings in the river were common. Nathan Wells's diary notes, in a statement that might have come out of *Huckleberry Finn*, if not for the tragic ending, "Feb

24, 1866. Rainy and foggy yesterday and today. This AM a son of Henry C. Smith aged six years fell off the wharf near his father's residence and drowned." Wells' diary for March 1 says, "This morning Henry C Smith caused a cannon to be fired to raise his boy who was drowned the other day, but to no purpose." The diary continues:

Apr 14 Henry C Smiths son was found by Mr David Bennett and buried today.

1867 May 27 A colored boy son of George Morris fell in to the river from Washington bridge and come verry near drowning rescued by Burr W Cosier.

Oct 4 Frederick Peck son of Charles H Peck is missing supposed to have fallen off the railroad bridge and drowned.

Oct 6 The body of Frederick Peck was fished up under the railroad bridge today.

1868 Aug 15 One of Mr Sedgewicks boys named John Schieteringe was drowned this evening near the shipyard while bathing.

Dec 14 Capt Wm A Lewis found a drowned man today near Eagles Nest which proved to be a man by the name of Fagan.

1869 Nov 17 A severe gale of wind from the SE. The schr *Margaret Kennedy* sunk this AM at 5oclock in Milford roads.

Early steamboats faced new hazards like boiler explosions and fires. At 3 a.m. on the icy night of January 13, 1840 the Sound steamer Lexington *went down ablaze, while Captain Brooks's* Nimrod *stood by, unable to help. The lives of 120 people were lost. (Courtesy the Mariners' Museum, Newport News, VA.)*

When the Sound froze over in February 1920, pilot William Staples drove the steamboat
Maine *through packed ice onto Execution Rock, and broke her back.*

1870 Nov 4 Mr Charles Gilbert received news of the loss of his daughter
and son-in-law Frank Hitchcock by the wreck of the steamer *Verona*.

1871 Mar 26 near the railroad bridge was met by constable McEwen and
summoned to act as jury on a drowned man found nearby Sep 14 Wm
Savage was drowned this AM at the RR bridge by falling from the
deck of the sloop *Wasp* where he was employed as cook.

1881 Jan 29 Israel Chichester frozen to death on a bar off the harbor.

Aug 14 The body of Wm H Rowland the mate of the steamer *Vulcan*
who was lost overboard some 2 weeks ago was found today by Wm
McDonald at Knees and Paws.

1886 Jun 14 George Green drowned in Housatonic River below
lower dock.

Steamboats were not exempt from disaster. On the wintry night of January 13,
1840, lightkeeper Samuel Buddington saw an orange glow across the Sound off
Eaton's Neck. It was the fast steamer *Lexington* afire. By 3:00 a.m. the vessel sank
and the icy waters were strewn with bodies. Other ships arrived, but too late. The
steamer *Nimrod*, Captain John Brooks, stood by. Captain Meeker of the Westport
sloop *Merchant* rescued the pilot but 120 lives were lost. Only four survived.

On October 13, 1899, the Bridgeport steamer *Nutmeg State*, built in 1890, was
also destroyed by fire, off Sands' Point, with great loss of life.

Transatlantic steamers took their toll on Stratfordites. In the 1850s E.K. Collins's American line of steamships outdid Cunard in size, speed, and comfort. But bad luck dogged the line. In 1854 a French steamer stove in Collins's ship *Arctic* in foggy waters off Newfoundland and sent her to the bottom. Then in January 1856, the 2,856-ton sidewheeler *Pacific* left Liverpool for New York and was never seen again. Among the 54 passengers lost—not many sailed in January—was Stratford businessman Samuel William Fairchild.

Years later, war brought disaster to Cunard. In 1915, Hollister Heights in Stratford was home to many immigrants from England, among them Jane Anne Mae Farquhar and her daughter Grace. Hearing that her stepmother was very ill in Scotland, Mrs. Farquhar decided to visit in spite of Britain's war with Germany, and took passage on the *Lusitania*. On Friday, May 7, a day before landing, the passengers were packing and had just finished lunch when a German torpedo struck the ship, and *Lusitania* went down. Mrs. Farquhar recalled, "People were crying and screaming. The boat was sinking quite fast, and the waves were dashing over the decks. My daughter slipped on the deck, and she was knocked against the rail, only to be saved from being washed overboard by one of the ship's crew." Close to 1,500 lives were lost, but the Farquhars were helped into a lifeboat, and returned to Stratford with an unexpected story.

The winter of 1920 was one of the coldest on record. On February 4 the steamer *Maine* left New York at 3:02 p.m. and headed toward the Sound and very heavy ice. At 8:30 p.m., wedged in the ice near Execution Rock, pilot Captain William Staples of Stratford stopped the engine, hoping that other boats would be able to open a path. None came, so at 9:25 p.m., hearing Execution's horn close aboard, Captain Staples put on full speed, and slowly worked ahead. At 10:32 p.m. the *Maine* struck Execution Rock. Deeply holed, *Maine* swung around and settled in 12 feet of water, anchor out. At 1:00 a.m. they sent up rockets, and at 3:00 a.m. the quartermaster was able to send Morse Code blinker signals to the *Charles W. Chapin*, which was about a half mile off. He sent "Did you report us?" The answer came back that *Chapin* had reported the *Maine* at 1:00 a.m., then asked "Are you the *Maine* and did you bust anything?" *Maine* answered "Yes. Two holds full of water and fires out, four passengers all well, send help." *Chapin* answered "I'm doing it now, goodbye."

On Thursday, February 5 the tug *Transfer #9* tried to reach the *Maine*, but ended up lying a quarter mile away. On the 6th the tug sent four men across the ice towing a skiff, but their mission was to borrow food. On the 7th Captain Staples watched the tug *Boston* with three barges drift aground between Execution and Hart Island, and the tug *Portchester* with one barge drift past with the flow of the ice. At 6:00 a.m. a sudden jar indicated that the *Maine* was starting to break in two. That morning men from the wrecker *Chapman Bros.* landed at Execution Rock and walked to the *Maine* across the ice, rigged lines, and took the passengers to shore, then in a lifeboat to their wrecker. At 6:20 p.m. the quartermaster walked across the ice to take food to the lightkeepers. Shortly afterwards, a loud report came from below, as the Maine continued to break up amidships. On Sunday the 8th, 12 crew members crossed the ice, and left aboard the *Chapman Bros.* The wrecking barge *Addie* came alongside and took off 19 horses. On Monday *Addie* returned and took all the freight to Bridgeport. Pilot Staples also went to Bridgeport aboard *Tug #9*, and returned next morning, but could not get aboard until Wednesday because of the ice. That evening Captain Hancort and six more crew members left the steamboat. On Thursday, February 12, more freight and more crew were removed, the fires were drawn on the donkey engine, pilot Staples paid off the crew, and the few remaining men stayed aboard to remove rugs, furniture, and coal, and to wait.

William Staples received his first Pilot's License in 1906, and his Master's License in 1909. In 1924 he was still piloting, aboard the steamers *Richard Peck*, *Lowell*, *Mohawk*, *Providence*, and *City of Taunton*.

Captain Robert Sherman was another Stratford seaman familiar with the hazards of the sea. The skills he learned aboard his father's oyster sloop led to pilot's papers in 1914 and a Master's License in 1915. On April 24, 1930, the freighter *Thames*, under his command, burned and sank off Sound Beach in Long Island Sound. Sixteen lives were lost and ten were saved. On October 27, 1931 his freighter *City of Stamford* was lost in Hell Gate channel. Sherman continued to serve as master and pilot until 1952. His son Richard followed in his footsteps.

In port, on sound or river, across the world's great oceans, for more than three and a half centuries, men from Stratford have challenged the perils of the sea. Some have won, many have lost.

Coasters and the Island Trade

After the Revolution, when British warships and privateers departed from American waters, the sound of hammers resounded in our shipyards, and sloops and schooners slid down the ways to engage in seaborne trade. With highways undeveloped, most trade and travel was by water. On October 2, 1787, Columbia College President William Samuel Johnson, a signer of the Constitution, wrote to his son Charles in Stratford, "Mamma is resolute to return with Capt. Coit who proposes to sail Thursday or Friday and in that case will leave me behind as I cannot probably leave New York before next week."

When the British Navigation Acts of 1783 closed the British West Indies to American ships, they headed for French and Spanish island ports. Dutch and Danish islands became smuggler's waystops to the British possessions. Piracy remained a problem in the islands, and American shipmasters carried arms on even the smallest vessels. One such was Captain Bartholemew, "Bartemy," of Derby, who carried two small deck cannon loaded with spikes, iron scrap, and chain to repel boarders. Captain Bartemy's first opportunity to use his cannon came not in the tropics but in the Housatonic.

Washington Bridge was recently built, and condemned as a nuisance by sailing skippers. Captain Bartemy was returning from the Caribbean with a cargo of rum, sugar, coffee, and molasses. After a tiring passage up the winding channel, the

When bridgetender David Lacey refused to open the draw for testy Captain Bartemy, the deck cannon, still loaded from the trip, changed the tender's mind. (Leo Fagan.)

captain dutifully blew his horn to have the draw swung open. Nothing happened. Then Lacey the bridgetender asked to see his papers. Enraged, the fiery little captain ordered his men ashore to open the bridge. When they were unable to work it, he became even more furious. He lit the fuse and fired away. Splinters flew in all directions. Lacey got the message, and within seconds the captain was able to warp through and sail on. He was never bothered again.

Bartemy's cargo from the islands was typical. Mrs. Thomas Clinton once said, "Trade with the West Indies began at an early date, and many homes had tables made of San Domingo mahogany. Mahogany, sugar, and rum made up a large part of each ship's cargo. My father used to chuckle at the number of deacons in Stratford who suddenly developed a taste for a fish dinner when word was passed that a packet was due to come up the Sound."

Stratford's primary export to the West Indies was grain—corn, wheat, and rye. The trade begun before the Revolution now grew rapidly, unfettered by colonial restrictions. Some 1797–1798 return manifests show the types of cargo entering the town:

> Schooner *Olivia* of Newfield, Master Peleg Thompson, from Turks
> Island for Newfield: 2400 barrels of salt, 2 baskets of salt, 100 wt.
> of cotton.

Brig *Louisa* of Newfield, Master & Owner Benj. Wheeler, from St. Martins: 2000 basket salt, 1000 oranges, 1 barrel lemons.

In 1725 Edward Hinman built a tide mill at a knoll called Eagle's Nest, on the east side of Nessumpaws Creek. After the mill had passed through several owners, Samuel William Johnson, son of our drafter of the Constitution, bought an interest in it in 1791, and soon became sole owner of the mill and a large amount of land along the creek, renamed Johnson's Creek. In 1800 when a flash flood destroyed Johnson's mill, he built a 40 foot by 60 foot, four-and-a-half story grist mill on the west side of the creek, with storage for hogsheads of ground corn. Sloops and schooners warped up directly to the mill, where Johnson and his partner William A. Tomlinson shipped grain to the islands. Johnson's son Edwards continued the business until the mill succumbed to fire in 1851.

In 1792 Joseph Walker received a town permit to build a dam and mill at Benjamin's Bridge across the mouth of Old Mill Creek, and in 1795 the State Assembly granted him "the exclusive privilege of a certain Salt Water Creek or Arm of the Sea on the Easterly side of New Field Harbor . . . and Liberty is hereby granted to the Petitioner . . . to erect and build a dam across said . . . Creek . . . in such a manner as to use . . . the Mill or Mills that may be erected there to the greatest Advantage." His four-story tide mill with six runs of millstones gave the name Yellow Mill to the bridge and the creek. From that time ships took

Coasters bound for the southern states and the islands loaded grain at the six-wheel tide mill known as Yellow Mill in Newfield Harbor. (George Lovell painting.)

on grain directly from a wharf at the mill. *Sally* and *Anna* were two of Robert Walker's sloops. Cornmeal and wheat ground at the mill made up the manifest of schooners bound toward the south and the West Indies, until it burned in 1884.

Samuel, fifth generation Wheeler, along with his sons operated Wheeler's (later Peck's) Mill. In 1797 the miller owned a 10-ton sloop named *Flying Fish*. In 1799 he registered his new 35.3-ton sloop appropriately named *Miller*. Son Samuel Junior, born in 1777, learned to sail on his father's sloops, owned the 16.8-ton sloop *Mary* with William Morehouse of Fairfield, then in 1808 bought the 13.8-ton sloop *Julia*. After sailing it for two years, Wheeler sold *Julia* in New London and replaced it with the 33.3-ton sloop *Julia Ann*, named for his little daughter. In 1819 he owned the 32.3-ton sloop *Castle*, Curtiss Chatfield master.

As owner of the shipyard at Curtis Point, Samuel Wheeler Jr. built, owned, and operated his own coasters. In 1817 Samuel registered *Toleration*, but the following year he turned her over to his son Levi, who commanded her for 18 years. Through 1835 *Toleration* beat up and down the coast, carrying any cargo available. In 1826 Robert Fairchild shipped his flax, 96 pounds of brown and 135 pounds of white, to be sold in Boston. Levi lived on New Lane, across Ferry Creek from his father's shipyard at the upper wharf, and kept the *Toleration* there. In 1835 his brother Isaac signed on as her skipper, while Levi helped his aging father at the yard. *Toleration* disappeared from the records after Samuel Wheeler registered the larger 96.1-ton schooner *Lexington*. In 1836 father and son registered the *Lexington* together. Then Levi moved on to other work, and in 1839 became master of the sloop *China*, owned by Major Brooks in Stratford. In 1844 Levi Wheeler sold the yard to Lewis Russell and bought a quarter of the sloop *Commodore Jones*. He appears on no more registers, although he lived until 1870. His father Samuel had died in 1858.

Isaac Wheeler lived across New Lane from his brother Levi. He, too, spent his life in the shipyard and at sea, commanding *Lexington* and others of the family boats. Isaac also owned *Parthenia* with Edward Curtis and skippered it until 1857. In 1843 Curtis sold his half to LeGrand Wells. The bill of sale says that *Parthenia* was a square sterned sloop built in Nyack, New York in 1823, enrolled at New Haven.

Year-round, in any weather, Captain Wheeler kept *Parthenia* at sea, between Derby and New York. Like his ancestor Moses, he was a rugged man. On one return trip from New York a severe storm sent water surging across the deck, and one savage wave swept young crewman Edward Kneeland overboard. Without hesitation, the captain had his coat and boots off, and was in the water swimming to the struggling boy. The crew thought they would never be able to reach the sloop, but the sturdy Wheeler climbed back aboard with his burden.

One night in February 1840 the alarm sounded: Charles Curtis's carriage shop on Bridgeport Road was burning. *Parthenia* was in port that night, so Captain Wheeler and his crew rushed over to the fire to help save the shop. Their strength and agility made the difference, and many a newly built carriage was shipped on *Parthenia* after that.

By 1858 *Parthenia* was aging, and so was the captain: he was 58. On January 25, 1858 Wheeler registered another schooner, *E.P. Burton*, as master and owner. The same size as *Parthenia*, (71.5 tons) she was 26 years younger, built in Stratford in 1849. Wheeler spent eight years on the water aboard the *Burton*, then in 1866 he and Louis Wheeler bought the 62.8-ton schooner *Falcon* from Josiah Stagg and put son Everett in command. Ill health finally brought Isaac Wheeler ashore: he died in August 1867.

When Wakeman Hubbell brought the sloop *Julius Caesar* home on May 11, 1795, her manifest listed: "67 hogsheads molasses, 3 tierces and 11 barrels, for a total of 7350 gallons; 28 barrels brown sugar (5520 lbs); 7 pots & 1 bag brown sugar (250 lbs); 5 small bags cotton & some loose cotton; 2 bags coffee (226 lbs); 375 lbs old iron; 1 barrel lime; 1 case gin; 11 straws of drinking glasses; 3 raw hides." Listed as sea stores—items allegedly for use aboard ship and thus not subject to import duty—were "4 gallons rum in keg, 4 gallons claret wine, 2 bottles of gin, 10 lb brown sugar, and 15 lb pot sugar."

On February 15, 1793 Richard and Amos Hubbell's brig *Junius Brutus* cleared for Martinique with 99 barrels and 113 half-barrels of salt beef, seven barrels of pork, and four barrels and three half-barrels of fish aboard. On October 10, 1793 the Hubbell brothers' ship *Fair American*, Captain Nathan Silliman, arrived in New York.

After 1795 their partnership dissolved. Arriving vessels, the sloop *Victress* and the ship *Superior*, steered for Richard Hubbell and Son. Amos built the "yellow store" above the lottery bridge in Newfield, and ran his own West Indies trade until his death in 1801.

On July 5, 1797 the brig *Independence*, Captain Thaddeus Hubbell, arrived in Newfield from St. John and Antigua with rum, molasses, sugar, and fruit, for P. Lyon, duty $1,856. On October 1 *Independence* arrived again, this time from Exuma with salt and fruit for D. Sterling. In 1801 she came to the new borough of Bridgeport from New Providence via New York and cleared as a coaster, with only five kegs of nails subject to duty. The next trip from New Providence on April 3 listed 2,778 lbs. nails, 770 of sugar, and rawhides and sheepskins, for D. Sterling; on November 20 from Exuma with salt, metals, glass bottles, and hides.

Independence's registry in Bridgeport in 1802 says "88 tons, built at Stratford in 1800, owned by Thaddeus Hubbell, David Sterling, Jas. E. Beach, Silas Sherman and Daniel Fayerweather, merchants. Master, Thaddeus Hubbell."

On March 17, 1805 Hubbell, master and part owner of the 100-ton brig *William*, arrived from New Providence via New York, and again on July 8 and October 24, 1806. After the Embargo of 1807 took effect, Hubbell willingly turned *Independence* over to Captain Anthony Stone, and it was he who was arrested and "seized for violating the Embargo Act. Ordered by the district court to deliver over to the claimants this cargo, the duties being first paid, 83 gals. 3d proof rum 112 pineapples, 573 lbs. sugar, 15 firkins butter; duties $44.73."

By 1809 the embargo was over, and Thaddeus Hubbell again took charge of *William*, arriving from Exuma on July 29, and from St. Bartholemew on

December 18. *William* was last registered at the Fairfield Customs Office in 1810, and her last arrival was on October 12 from Antigua. On November 10 *William* cleared Bridgeport for New Providence under command of Captain Stephen Summers and was never seen again. In 1811 Hubbell took command of the sloop *Volusia*, owned by Stephen Burroughs Jr. and Daniel Lewis, and on October 22 he returned from St. Barts with a cargo for himself.

The War of 1812 destroyed American foreign trade. No vessels were registered in Bridgeport that year; nevertheless, Hubbell brought home the schooner *Sally* on June 15, from Figurao, Portugal, carrying salt and fruit. The register of March 3, 1813 lists *Sally Ann* as a 107-ton schooner built in Derby in 1811. Her long list of owners—Hubbell, David Minot, Nathaniel Wade, Daniel Fayerweather, Curtiss Blakeman, Charles B. Hubbell—reflects a means of spreading wartime risks.

In 1815 Thaddeus was part owner (with Stephen Burroughs Jr.) and master of the 158-ton brig *Leopard*, built in Bridgeport in 1812. On May 13 he left Bridgeport with a manifest written in the hand of Customs inspector Salmon Hubbell:

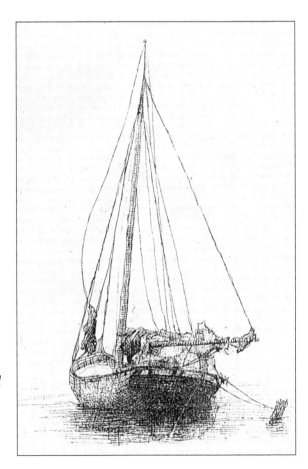

In the early 1800s the sloop Commodore, *Captain Kneeland Curtis, plied between Derby and New York, calling at Stratford for freight and passengers. (J.J. Wooding etching.)*

Invoice of merchandise shipped by Stephen Burroughs Jr. on board the brig *Leopard*, Thaddeus Hubbell master, bound for Lisbon, consigned to the master and being on account and risk of Stephen Burroughs Jr., merchant, Bridge Port, Conn.:

5,200 corn @ $1.00	$5,200
630 staves @ $1.00	$630
7 bbls. beef @ $12.00	$84
5 bbls. mess pork @ $24.00	$120
69 bbls. beans @ $4.40	$276
3, 000 ft. whit pine boards @ $22.00	$66
	$6,436

On August 13 *Leopard's* return cargo from "Martinico" via New York consisted of 4,065 gallons of 2nd proof rum, 1,719 gallons of 3rd proof rum, 3,258 gallons of molasses, 22,242 pounds of sugar, 237 pounds of coffee, 59 pounds of cocoa, 300 coconuts, four kegs and four jars of tamarinds, and a box of cigars.

On December 10, 1824 Thaddeus Hubbell registered the first steamboat in Fairfield Custom House records, the *General LaFayette*, together with Captain Vose. He died on November 30, 1849, age 85.

The seas were full of Captains Hubbell. While Thaddeus was skippering the *William*, William Hubbell commanded the 40-ton sloop *Harmony*, built in Derby in 1800. Ezra Hubbell, owner and master of the sloop *Experiment*, was lost at sea in September 1801, but another Ezra was sailing the sloop *Factor* in September 1803. Asa Hubbell commanded the sloop *Packet* from 1795 to 1800. Gersham Hubbell's career spanned at least 21 years, from the 45-ton sloop *Hannah Ann* in 1814 through the schooners *Mary* and *Decatur* and the sloops *Belle* and *Eagle*, to the 93-ton schooner *Virginius* in 1835.

Three of Amos Hubbell's sons and his daughter's husband went to sea. Young Amos's grave marker says he "died at the Havannah on the 15th day of October, 1798, by a malignant fever, aged 18 years." Wilson was killed by a French seaman in the undeclared war of 1799, as noted elsewhere. Charles Berry Hubbell was master and part owner of the 66-ton sloop *Victress* in 1814; then of the 67-ton sloop *Bridgeport*; and part owner of the sloops *Intrepid*, 21 tons; *Lapwing*, 46 tons; and the 93-ton schooner *Ann Maria*. He ran a drygoods business with his brother-in-law John Thompson in the yellow store until 1842.

In 1795 a second *Julius Caesar*, a 106.2-ton brig, was built for the Wetmores and Joseph Squire, and registered in Newfield. Captain Squire commanded her, relieved occasionally by Burr Thorp or Thaddeus Hubbell. In 1804 the name was used a third time, when William Hallock, MC, built a 150.8-ton brig in Stratford for Samuel Hawley and David Brooks.

The second *Julius Caesar* was part of the fleet of Prosper Wetmore & Brothers of Stratford, Newfield, and New York. The fleet included the sloops *Friendship*, *Governor*, *Huldah*, *Jenny*, *Nancy*, and *Peggy*, the brigs *Prosper* and *Sally & Betsy*,

Coasting schooner Louisa Polleys *waits for cargo at the decrepit Broad Street wharf, where the cutter* Caution *rests in her final berth.*

the schooner *St. Joseph*, and the ship *Victoria*. The Wetmores were three of Rev. Israhiah Wetmore's twelve children. Prosper entered the West Indies trade soon after the Revolution, operating from New York City; Robert lived in Newfield by 1798; and Victory had his home in Stratford where Front Street crossed the road to the lower wharf, and served as postmaster from 1793 to 1803. In 1794 the brothers built a store and wharf north of the Newfield Harbor bridge. "They conducted the West Indies trade, carrying provisions, cattle and horses to the different islands."

The schooner *St. Joseph* was theirs when it was seized in 1795. Old court and Customs records, newspaper accounts, and Captain John Selby's account book tell a story of the federal government's early efforts of control.

When John Selby married Betsy in 1795 he was already commanding vessels in the Caribbean trade, perhaps already in trouble with the law. A January 8, 1795 journal entry says: "Shipt on board Sloop *Peggy* as Master for Custommery wagers which is 30 doll. p month Ladend at the port of New York — Arrived at New London 24 day of May." Four days after his wedding, the page records: Shipt on board Schooner *St. Joseph* for 18 dollars p month as master," then "Arrived at Newfield 28 and discharged October 1st 1795."

In early October Selby sold oranges, limes, and sugar to his customers. His October 10 entry says, "Prosper Witmore and brothers, bot of John Selby Jr 6 hhd of rum containing 701 gallons, 15 gall out, £205/16/0 to be paid in 90 days at 6 shilling lawful money a gallon." On October 21 he entered, "Bound to New York, Land taxes [i.e. port entry fees] post hast. Taken in cash 42 dollars." His rush trip to New York to pay the overdue entry fees did no good. His account book has no November entries, but the United States District Court at New Haven does, dated November 23:

> On or about the 25th day of September last past, there was imported into said district of Connecticut from Antigua, one of the West India islands and a foreign port, 15 hogsheads rum of the growth and manufacture of some of the West India islands, in a schooner called *St. Joseph* 63 tons, whereof was the master John Selbie, Jr., of Stratford, in the county of Fairfield in said district, and that afterwards on the 28th day of September the said 15 hogsheads of rum were in said district unladened and delivered from the schooner *St. Joseph* in the district of Fairfield Conecticut, to wit., at Stratford in said district of Fairfield, without a permit from the collector of said district of Fairfield for such unladen and delivery, and that the value of said 15 hogsheads of rum at the time did amount to more than $400, all of which is contrary to the act of congress of the said United States in such case made and provided, and by force of said act the said schooner, *St. Joseph*, her tackle, apparel and furniture have become liable to seizure and the said schooner was on the 24th day of October, at said Stratford, seized in the harbor

Built in South Norwalk in 1863, the schooner Lizzie A. Tolles *was familiar to sailors all along the Sound, until she went down east and became the* Alice Wentworth. *(Courtesy Mystic Seaport, Mystic, CT.)*

of Stratford, in waters navigable for vessels of ten tons burthen and upwards by Samuel Smedley of Fairfield, collector of the customs, and was there holden by him for trial and that said schooner has by force of said act become forfeited to said United States.

The court went on to stipulate that on November 23 a hearing would be held at the statehouse at New Haven. (Connecticut then had two capitals, Hartford and New Haven.) On that day Pierrepont Edwards, then practicing law in New Haven, represented the government and Jonathan Ingersoll appeared for the owners. Ingersoll asked for a delay and was granted four hours, but no owners showed up from Stratford to contest the seizure.

As a result, *St. Joseph* was auctioned off at Newfield together with the sloop *Lady*, seized by collector Smedley for the same reason. Court records show that the U.S. Marshall on the 10th of December sold the *St. Joseph* "with her tackle, apparel, etc., at public venue to Prosper Wetmore, he being the highest bidder." Together the two vessels netted the government $602 over costs, but the rum brought $1,990. The buyer of *Lady* is unrecorded, but on December 31 John Thompson and Matthias Nicoll enrolled *St. Joseph* as owners, and on December 23 Thompson and John Benjamin enrolled *Lady*. In November, after *St. Joseph* was seized, Nicoll and Thompson sold the ropewalk at Curtiss Point to Wetmores. A month later they owned *St. Joseph*. Was there an agreement to swap the ropewalk for *St. Joseph* at the bidders price?

Meanwhile, there was more bad news for the Wetmores. A letter to collector Smedley from the United States district attorney in New York, dated January 16, 1796, advised him that the *Sally & Betsy* was condemned there and was to be auctioned off. Smedley sent his deputy Samuel Rowland to New York to observe the auction, but Rowland embarrassed Smedley by winning the bid himself for $1,750, outbidding the highest private bidder by $125.

Smedley then wrote to New York asking that the vessel be sold to Prosper Wetmore for his bid of $1,625, but agent Giles replied "We are sorry that it is out of our power to comply with your request in giving up the ship *Sally & Betsy* to Mr. Wetmore for we made sale of her to Capt. E. Hubbell of Newfield last Saturday." Ezekiel Hubbell, starting to build up his own shipping business after working for his uncles, must have gone down to New York to the auction, declined to bid when he saw Wetmore, the old owner, bidding, then made an offer after collector Rowland withdrew his winning bid. Hubbell sailed *Sally & Betsy* to the islands until she was captured by the French in the undeclared war of 1799.

From the foregoing, we can put together what probably occurred. The new federal government, only six years old, imposed entry fees and import duties that were unpopular with merchants and shipowners. It was fair game to avoid the duties whenever possible, to keep their rum "from collector Smedley's voracious maw," as one of them put it. To counter this the Congress enacted the seizure law, paying informers half the profit from the auction of confiscated vessels and their cargo.

Shipowners avoided the unpopular law by bypassing customs—smuggling. If they succeeded, they profited.

If they were discovered, the informer profited and the customs officers and other federal officials were paid to seize and auction off the vessels. Merchants were reluctant to bid on their neighbors' ships, and seemed to have a tacit agreement to let the owner recover his vessel.

We don't know what punishment was meted out to whom, but the minister's sons don't seem to have been called to account for anything. The financial shock of the confiscations, though, must have been severe. In 1796 they turned over their share of the grist mill at Benjamin's Bridge to Robert Walker, and in 1798 Prosper Wetmore & Bros. slid into bankruptcy and turned over all its assets to trustees. Robert moved to New York, where he and Prosper carried on in shipping. Together with New Yorker Garet Keteltas, they owned the brigantine *Letitia* and the ship *Eleven Sons*. In 1817 Prosper took passage for France on one of his own ships and disappeared at sea. Victory remained in Stratford, as postmaster, state representative, and local businessman.

As to Captain Selby, his account book contains no entries between January 10, 1796 and March 25, 1797, when he records, "Shipt on board sloop *Polly* as master for Frenchman's Bay. David & John Deforest owners."

Had he been in jail for the year? It is noteworthy that he is now carefully listing the ship owners he sails for, and that the next entry is "Arived from Frenchman's Bay and left the sloop the same day on the voige no. 1," showing that on April 31 [*sic*] he gave up responsibility for the vessel. The May 5, 1797 entry reads, "Shipt on board sloop *Polly* for Frenchman's Bay Voige No. 2." He was home again on June 7, a round-trip time of five weeks. On December 11 the entries read, "in New York on board of the schooner *Oliva*—as master at 25 dollars pr month and half of the commons." This is his last entry to mention command of a ship.

Just what happened to change John Selby's life is not recorded, but years later Nathan McEwen told this story:

> He commanded a brig built all of mahogany in the West Indies, with which he came into and went up the Housatonic River to Friar's Head [now Ryder's Lane], where in the night he unloaded some casks of rum and put them into a building to save the tariff or duties. A young man being near, courting late in the night, discovered the transaction and complained to the authorities that he might get the reward, which was half the vessel and half the cargo, The vessel was seized by the government, condemned and sold. Capt. Selby was fined and imprisoned. After lying in prison a long time, his wife smuggled a saw in to him with which he broke jail and went pirating, and was gone several years. Finally, becoming tired of the business, and desiring to see his family, he, through agents, made a compromise with the government and was pardoned by paying nine thousand dollars."

Not all Stratford seamen went into sail. Captain Alfred Blakeman commanded ocean steamboats between New York and Richmond. Here he poses (right) on his steamer Old Dominion, *with two Stratford friends.*

McEwen was known for weaving yarns, but Selby's low wages for commanding *St. Joseph* and his subsequent sale of rum to Wetmores, before the seizure of the schooner, indicate that his agreement with the owners allowed him to bring home cargo on his own account, and it could have been his own rum that he hid up the river before entering Newfield Harbor. Conversely, his account book shows no lapse of several years, making McEwen's prison story apocryphal.

Selby died on May 1, 1825. His daughter Eliza married Curtiss Chatfield, and their house at Waterside remained a center of nautical activities. But as trade from Stratford to the West Indies died, his sloops *Castle* and *Eliza C.* sailed as coasters.

Nathan Wells (1818–1894) called himself a farmer but his business was at sea. It's true that he tended livestock and crops, threshed his own rye, spent time cutting salt hay, and went up to the Pumpkinground to chop his winter wood. He was also the town tax collector and a state legislator. But, although he never sailed a vessel of his own, his major business interest was in coasting schooners out of Stratford.

Watching the schooner *Joseph Baxter* sliding down the ways at Peter White's yard on September 13, 1866, Wells commented that it was "the most beautiful and successful launch I ever saw." He was one of several owners aboard on October 6 when Captain Obed Baxter took it on its maiden voyage to New York. With wind ahead, they beat down past Huntington light, and the next morning took a pilot above Throg's Neck "who took us safe through the gate" to the foot of Wall

Street. Next day a tug towed the *Baxter* over to Jersey City for final fitting out, and Wells came home on the steamer *Schuyler*. *Baxter* sailed the New England coast until it foundered on Narragansett Rocks on the night of September 29, 1873.

On December 6, 1866 Wells finished signing up owners for a new schooner to be built at White's. That day he went over to East Bridgeport to see Captain Marcus Hale, to sign him up as captain and 1/16 owner of a 108.1-ton schooner to be named *Clarissa Allen*. Wells would be managing owner. Wells spent most of the following week in the woods with shipbuilder Peter White, locating timber for the vessel. On the 13th, the 16 stockholders held a meeting at Captain Park's house, where Wells was appointed treasurer and collector.

August 1867 was a good month for Nathan Wells. On the 5th he received his first dividend from the schooner *Joseph Baxter*—$50.10—and on the 24th he watched as the masts were hoisted into place aboard *Clarissa Allen*. On September 2 on the afternoon tide *Clarissa Allen* slid cleanly down the launching ways at White's yard. On the 12th, Nathan took the night boat *Bridgeport* into New York (11:00 p.m. to 4:00 a.m.) and spent the day settling some of the schooner's bills, then took the dayboat *J.B. Schuyler* back to Bridgeport (2:00 p.m. to 7:00 p.m.) and hopped a train to Stratford.

Clarissa Allen sailed for New York on the 18th, where Captain Hale completed fitting her out and found a cargo for Corpus Christi, Texas. He left New York on December 21, and Nathan Wells went back to farming. On February 21 he received a letter announcing that the *Allen* had arrived at Corpus. Confident, he went to New York in April to renew the insurance. Marcus Hale commanded the schooner until 1871.

The coasting business seemed good, so on April 4, 1868 Nathan Wells, Captain Park, and J.H. Stagg went down to the upper wharf to look over the 66.1-ton schooner *Margaret Kennedy* from Philadelphia, and on the 8th they bought her for $1,750.

The *Kennedy* was taken to Milford, where at 5:00 a.m. on November 17 a severe gale sank her in Milford Roads. In December Wells was able to hire the schooner *Eveline Ross* to help raise the *Kennedy* and the tug *Knickerbocker* to tow her over to White's yard in Stratford for repair. In May the vessel was still in the yard, and Wells had to take the train to New York to purchase a new ship's wheel and windlass, which arrived at the steamboat wharf a few days later.

Meanwhile, *Clarissa Allen* had returned to Bridgeport in December 1868, where, checking over all her papers with Captain Hale, Wells concluded that everything looked good, but after paying for her insurance, had "not done anything for her owners." After consultation with Captain Hale in the spring of 1869, Wells had the *Allen* hauled at Ren & Walker's yard in Black Rock. After a couple of successful seasons the owners were able to divide up their profit in January 1871. That April Wells secured the services of Captain Hiram Hodgden for the next four years. In July the managing owner took a steamer to New York and treated the *Allen* to a new suit of sails. The schooner operated that summer out of Fair Haven, and in mid December Wells went up to New Haven to settle up with the captain. In 1872 Hodgden continued to work *Clarissa Allen* in eastern Long Island Sound.

In 1873 Nathan Wells put *Clarissa Allen* to its most important use. In February 1869 he had "got title to the lot below the hoop skirt shop for St. John's Lodge No. 8 and paid [H.A. Sutton] for the same." In February 1870 the citizens at a town meeting discussed the possibility of building a new town hall, but took no action. But now the schooner was to play a vital role in this major step for the town. Wells's diary reads:

> 22 Aug 1873. Arrived in Newburyport [MA] at 7 oclock PM, Went on board th schr *Clarissa Allen* bound for Calais Maine.
>
> 23 Got under weigh at 8 oclock AM. Crew composed of Capt Hodgden, Wm Fields of Boston, mate, John Cogill of Haverhill Mass before the mast, James Martin of Calais Maine steward. Went into the harbor of Kittery, Maine.
>
> 24 sunrise Sunday. AM got under weigh with wind fresh from the Northwest which before noon blew a gale. Shortened sail to jib and double reefed fore and main sails. Before night burst jib and foresails.
>
> 26 Shortly after noon a light breeze sprung up. We proceeded on our voyage. Saw a school of 20 or 30 whales playing and gamboling about all the PM.
>
> 27 About noon entered the Bay of Fundy, passing in close to Passamaquoddy Head, the island of Grand Manan being in sight on the starboard side. Just at night entered the St. Croix River and passed Lubec and Eastport. Anchored about 12 oclock.
>
> 28 Thursday AM got under weigh and proceeded to Calais. Arrived at 5 oclock PM.
>
> 29 Capt Hodgden and myself interviewed the lumber dealers with a view to purchase lumber for the masonic hall. Could not succeed on account of scarcity of water for sawing. Capt. H. took a load of lumber for South Kingston [RI] and hauled into dock for loading.
>
> 4 Sept. Finished [loading] and towed down to the ledge 3 miles below the city.
>
> 6 Saturday AM Passed Eastport and Lubec and about noon passed Passamaquoddy Head with light wind which continued until 12 oclock at night.
>
> 9 Tuesday AM passed Cape Cod and Tuesday night came over Nantucket Shoals and
>
> 10 Wednesday run into South Kingston where we were bound but the wind being east the Capt thought it prudent to run for Dutch Island where we anchored about sundown.

Unsuccessful in obtaining lumber for the new Masonic hall, Wells left the vessel and came home by train. Hodgden brought the schooner home on September 20,

In 1875 the new Masonic building and Stratford town hall was completed, thanks to trips up and down the coast by Charlie Wells's schooner Clarissa Allen *to find materials.*

and in November Wells tied up *Clarissa Allen* for the winter. Meanwhile, work proceeded on the new lodge hall and on May 12, 1874 the cornerstone laying ceremony took place. On the 25th masons began to lay brickwork on the stone foundation. On June 1 Captain Hodgden brought *Clarissa Allen* home again, this time with the needed lumber. On September 26 the selectmen signed a ten-year lease for a town office in the building. (In 1887 the town would buy the building.) On the 28th plastering commenced. *Clarissa Allen* most likely brought the bricks from the Hudson valley and the lime from the Connecticut valley or from the coast of Maine.

On December 23 *Clarissa Allen* and *Margaret Kennedy* went into Ferry Creek to wait out the winter, and on February 9, 1875 the new hall was dedicated in an elaborate ceremony. With the building completed, *Clarissa Allen* was released to regular duty. On March 7, 1878 she was auctioned off for $2,600 at West Stratford to Charlie Wakeley.

After selling the *Allen*, Wells and Ezra Whiting went to Milford to arrange the *Margaret Kennedy's* 1878 season. In 1880 Wells took passage on the *Rosedale* to New York to buy a replacement windlass for the *Kennedy*, and when it arrived at the *Rosedale* office in Bridgeport, he sent it on to Milford to be installed.

Although he continued to be interested in things nautical, Wells's diary does not mention the schooner *Margaret Kennedy* after 1880, although she was registered at the Customs House through 1882. He may have turned over management of the schooner to one of his younger partners and returned to farming.

Captain George Culver brought up his boys as mariners, and from Ferry Creek he owned and sailed his sloops. In January 1870 Alexander St. John became full owner of the 48.8 ton sloop *Whippoorwill*, but on July 25, 1871 Captain Culver registered as owner and master. Culver did whatever brought a living, using *Whippoorwill* for both oystering and transport. On July 20, 1877 Culver first registered as master of Nathan Wells's coasting schooner *Margaret Kennedy*, and he kept that job through 1881. In 1882 customs records list him as master of Charles Wakeley's steam canal boat *L.G. Smith*. From 1893 through 1896 he worked the natural beds with his sloop *Ella May*. From time to time, Culver and his sons worked the shad seines, as well. He gave his name to Culver's Bar.

With so much seaman's work to do, George Culver's sons grew up as experts in the business. In 1896 both were listed as oystermen, still living at home. In 1916, when they had their own growing families, Irving worked as an oysterman and Robert was a mariner. Like his father, "Captain Bob" had a master mariner's license, of unlimited tonnage. He commanded the towboat when the draw span of the present railroad bridge was put into place *c.* 1905. By 1962 he had the greatest number of reissues of any captain in the Third Coast Guard District. Robert's son Reginald served on battleships in World War I, then worked aboard the steamer *Stratford* for his father, but is best remembered as a decoy carver.

The 69.6-ton sloop *Commodore Jones* was built in Derby in 1835 for the Hudson River brick trade and to ply between the Housatonic and the Tappan Zee. She was

The last operating schooners hauled kerosene, coal, and lumber and served the oyster trade. This working boat, its topmasts long removed, shared Bedell's Shipyard with sailing yachts in 1911. (Robert Treat sketch.)

the first centerboarder built in Derby, and was said to be very fast. She was owned by Thomas Aldridge and her captain was John Payne of Fishkill. In August 1838 Charles Edmond of Stratford became her captain, but by 1844 Truman Hotchkiss was master and Isaac Wheeler had bought a quarter share from Hotchkiss. In 1853 *Commodore Jones* hailed from Bridgeport, owned by Sherwood Sterling, but soon returned to Stratford. Among her jobs were delivery of lumber from Catskill-on-the-Hudson to build Selleck Batterson's house on Elm Street in 1842—when her shoal draft enabled her to come in to the end of Mack's Harbor and project her bowsprit over Elm Street—and later to help to build the Stratford breakwater. For several years after 1890 *Commodore Jones* could be seen in tow of the tug *Evona*, loaded with stone from Derby, as contractor Thomas Anderson struggled to construct the breakwater. It was completed in 1914 and the old sloop was retired.

Abel Drew of Stratford began in 1863 by purchasing the aging 54-foot 47.8-ton sloop *Emperor*, built in 1839, hiring Timothy Miller as skipper. From 1866 through 1875 his 96.2-ton *Jacob Lorillard* sailed out of Stratford. In February 1867 Marcus Hale commanded the 69.7-ton schooner *Henry B. Drew*, out of Stratford, registered to Charles T. Leonard. In September Captain Timothy Miller took over the *Drew*, owned by Abel Drew and others. When Miller transferred to the *Jacob Lorillard* in 1871, Drew brought in Captain James K. Kaen to run the *Drew*. In 1875 co-owner William E Wheeler became Drew's managing owner. 1870 saw two more schooners added to the Drew fleet, the *Charles S. Hazzard* and the *Anson Brown*. Captain Philander Clark had the 81.2-ton *Hazzard* for three years, then when he went over to the larger *Jacob Lorillard* in late 1873 he turned the *Hazzard* over to Henry Parker from Brewer, Maine. The *Anson Brown* was registered to Abel Drew from late 1870 through 1874, with Daniel Mills, then

Bridgeport harbor c. 1870 was home to every kind of activity. In the foreground is the Bridgeport Yacht Club. Across the harbor, schooners line the wharves in front of the Housatonic Railroad freight yards and a domed roundhouse. At right a tug noses a schooner into a wharf at Water Street. The grain elevator looms behind.

Nelson Wakelee as masters. On April 19, 1875 the managing owner was William E. Wheeler and master David L. Mills. In 1877 Franklin G. Coley took over as master, and in 1878 George A. Cleveland. The same partnership operated *Anson Brown* from Stratford through 1882. Jacob Lorrillard's last enrollment in the Bridgeport Customs House, on November 1, 1875, lists banker Henry B. Drew of Bridgeport as owner.

From 1730 when Philip Nichols opened his store in the Pequonnock, the number of Newfield merchants grew. Into the nineteenth century, as trade from Stratford wharves declined, ever more vessels departed Newfield harbor (renamed Bridgeport in 1800), with cargos fed by highways from the north, then by the Naugatuck and Housatonic Railroads. The local hub of early nineteenth-century water commerce was Bridgeport harbor. While the War of 1812 was still on, the *Connecticut Courier* of November 29, 1815 displayed this ad by merchants Foote & Brooks:

> Have just received from New York a choice selection of GROCERIES which they offer for sale at their store, near Knapp's Hotel, at a small advance from cost, consisting of the following articles, viz. Old Antigua Spirits, St. Croix Rum, Cogniac Brandy, Holland Gin, Cider Brandy, Madiera and Lisbon Wines, Hyson & Souchong Teas, Lump and Brown Sugars, Rice, Coffee, Chocolate, Pepper, Alspice, Ginger, Nutmegs, Alum, Starch, Hand & Paper Tobacco, Soap & Candles, Indigo, Pipes and Segars, Snuff, &c. ALSO a handsome assortment of CROCKERY and a few hundred bushels of Turk's' Island SALT of the 1st quality. They will pay cash for a few hundred bushels CORN.

Samuel Burr & Son on Water Street offered much the same supplies as Brooks, together with "salt nitre, battle powder, and shot. David Minot & Co. had a like list, with 60 quintals of cod, a few barrels of "mess shad," plus "Swedes iron," German, English blisterd, Crawley, and American steel, and a variety of wrought nails. Minot also sponsored the sloop *General Pike*, James Fayerweather master, to New York and Boston.

Fayerweather and Hubbell at the yellow store on Water Street offered a long list of dry goods from all over the world with their groceries, together with "Swedes and Russia iron, suitable for Cart and Waggon tire." William King sold dry goods, groceries, and crockery, with a note that the packet sloop *Young Fox*, captain Samuel Pennoyer, would sail for New York every Tuesday evening. DeForest, Wade & Co. had a similar list.

Lewis & Hayt's drygoods included broadcloths, cassimeres, black bombazine silk stockings, silk gloves, crepes, shawls, and fancy cravats. Roswell Lewis offered all this plus spotted martin and white fur. Barnum Beach added ladies' and gentlemen's boots and shoes, plus ladies' leather, Morocco, kid, Northampton sole leather, and wax and grained upper leather. At Lambert Lockwood's Hardware & Book Store customers found the latest books from New York. Curtis

& Smith announced white lead, red lead, paint supplies, and whale oil for sale. Hinman Sterling & Hyde went further afield for their wares. They announced "have received by the ship *Minerva Smith*, Captain Allen, from Liverpool, a general assortment of crockery and glassware," then went on to list a large supply of dishware from Britain.

After 1800, transoceanic traffic grew so great that larger vessels—brigs and ships—prevailed. The import trade shifted to deepwater ports—New York, New London, Providence, Boston—and sloops and schooners were relegated to the coasting trade. Depth across the bar at the Housatonic's mouth was only 3 feet at low tide, and the bar at Newfield harbor measured 5 feet, so Stratford, Newfield, Huntington, and Derby were served by coasters.

Although after 1824 steamboats began to take over passengers and freight, some travelers and shippers preferred to sail, for lower cost and fear of boiler explosion. Judge Robert Fairchild's daybook shows how one patron used the coasters:

> July 6, 1825 Capt McColly, sloop *Commodore Hull*, Julia's passage to New York $1.00.
>
> Oct 15, 1826 Capt Chatfield, my passages to & from N York & board in full $2.17.
>
> Oct 31, 1826 Capt Levi Wheeler, flax put on board your sloop *Toleration* for Boston.
>
> Mar 3, 1828 Memo: This day I received from NY by Capt Curtis of the *Parthenia* a bbl Richmond flour sent me by my son Robt. Price $5.32.
>
> Apr 8, 1828 At 5 oclock PM I sailed from Stratford for New York in the sloop *Parthenia*, Capt Curtis. I arrived there next morning at 8 oclock.
>
> Jan 26, 1829 Capt McColly of *Othello*, paid Lyman Osborne for passage &c from NY in Sept. or Oct.
>
> 27 Nov, 1830 On Saturday night at 10 oclock sailed for NY with my son Alfred in the Bridgeport sloop *Champion*, $1.25.
>
> Sept 17, 1831 8 oclock from Bpt in sloop *Sabina*, Capt Layfield, and arrived next morning at 8 oclock 75¢.

When the nineteenth century ended, the coasting trade ended too. Steamships, railroads, and then motor trucks succeeded the old schooners as the twentieth century began. For a while, lumber schooners and coal schooners continued to unload at Waklee's Coal and Lumber wharf at the upper dock, and in 1914 Alfred Waklee built a three story concrete block warehouse, which promptly burned down when watchman Frank Monahan's lighted pipe ignited rubble. The warehouse was rebuilt as a two story building, but the coasting trade vanished and it served as an aircraft factory, a shipyard shop, and a commercial school. It was demolished in 1999.

Old hulls rotted out, old sailing vessels ended up on rocks and shoals, some turned to oystering. By World War II few remained, and the sailing coasters became a memory.

STEAMBOATS ON THE SOUND

On Wednesday September 22, 1824, Stratford residents lined the lower wharf to watch as a trail of black smoke moved up the Sound, and a sidewheel steamboat appeared from behind the headlands at Stratford Point and steamed up the river to the wharf. Next day, Judge Robert Fairchild noted in his daybook, "Last evening the *General LaFayette* arrived from New York being the first steam boat that ever entered this harbor and this morning she was viewed by the people of Stratford at the Lower Wharf. She is a new boat burthen [92 54/95] tons and is designed to ply between New York and Stratford & Derby." *General LaFayette* was named for the Revolutionary War hero who had passed through town on a triumphal tour the previous June, en route to lay a cornerstone at Bunker Hill.

Some Stratfordites were already familiar with steamboats. In 1807 old Captain John Brooks Sr. took young John Sterling to New York to observe the *Clermont* head for Albany. On an August day in 1787 framer of the Constitution William Samuel Johnson took his colleagues, hot from weather and from debate, down to the Schuylkill to observe his friend John Fitch's steamboat.

General LaFayette was built in New York in May of 1824 for Bridgeport operator Henry Eckford, and first registered there on September 21, the day before she came to Stratford. The Bridgeport Steamboat Company had 72 prominent shipowners as stockholders. The boat was commanded by Thomas Vose in 1824, Joseph French in 1825, William Hanford in 1826, and Ira Bliss in 1827. This ad appeared in the *Connecticut Courier* in 1824:

The first steamboat to enter Stratford harbor was the General LaFayette *in September 1824. Captain Thomas Vose took her up to Derby, then back to New York. (*Connecticut Courier, *1824.)*

STEAMBOAT GEN. LAFAYETTE
Captain Thomas Vose
Will continue the regular routes between this place
and New York through the season, to wit:
Leave Bridgeport every Monday, Wednesday and Friday at 8 o'clock AM
for New York
Leave New York every Tuesday, Thursday and Saturday at 8 o'clock AM
for Bridgeport and every Saturday will proceed on to Stratford and Derby
and will return on Monday (touching at Stratford and Bridgeport) to New York.
For passage or freight apply at the store of D. Sterling & Company,
or to the captain on board.

In 1825 Judge Fairchild chose to take the steamboat over a sailing packet to save time en route:

> On Friday evening July 8th I went to New York in steamboat *LaFayette* of Bridgeport with my daughter Jane. Arrived next morning before Breakfast—next day (Sunday) went to Albany in the steamboat *Chancellor Livingston*. Arrived there before breakfast on Monday & at 10 o'clock am started in the stage for the Springs at Saratoga—travelled 9 miles in stage—then on the Western Canal in the canal boat *Lady Adams* drawn by 3 horses 9 miles & then 19 miles in the stage to Saratoga (37 miles from Albany). I arrived there about sundown. Stopped at Ballstown Springs 7 miles this side of Saratoga half an hour. Drank the mineral water there which operated on me as a powerful cathartic.
>
> Started from Saratoga on Tuesday evening July 12th arrived at Schenectady same evening 22 miles & next morning breakfasted at Albany 15 miles from Schenectady. Next morning July 14 at 10 o'clock embarked on board the *Richmond* & arrived in New York Friday morning 7 o'clock July 15th & the next day at 5 o'clock took the steamboat *LaFayette* with Jane and Alfred. I arrived at Bridgeport that night at 12 o'clock & at home the next morning at 6 o'clock.

The judge paid Captain French $3.50 for his and Alfred's fares down, and $6 for the three return tickets. Julia's passage down on a sailing packet had cost only a dollar. Whether it was the difference in ticket cost or fear of boiler explosions (common in the early days) that drove him, thenceforward he took the packets to New York.

Competition soon arrived. Wording put into the Constitution in 1787 by Stratford's William Samuel Johnson had given the Supreme Court jurisdiction over "laws passed by the legislature of the United States" and in 1824 the Court used that power to rule that Congress could regulate interstate commerce, thus ending New York steamboat monopolies. That same year, John Brooks Jr. took command of a steamboat named for the Chief Justice, running between Norwalk and New York with a stage connection to Bridgeport. In 1828 Captain Benson complained that the *John Marshall* could not stem the tide at "Hurl Gate." At Hallett Point "she essayed 3 times to go out of the eddy, but each time as she struck the current was nearly upset by its force, and was finally compelled to lay up until the tide had flowed in from the Sound."

By then Captain Brooks was operating the steamer *Baltimore*, in competition on the same route. "The large and splendid steamboat *Sun*" was advertised in April 1828, seven hours from New York to Bridgeport, with a stop at Norwalk. After the *John Marshall*, Brooks commanded the steamer *United States*, then the *Hudson*, running to New Haven, and in 1826 and 1827 the *Franklin* on the New York-Poughkeepsie run and the *Governor Wolcott*, New York to New Brunswick. Living with the Vanderbilt family at the time, Brooks became a lifelong friend of Commodore Cornelius Vanderbilt. The long list of Brooks's commands also includes the steamboat *Emerald*, Norwalk to New York; and *Bellona* and *Thistle* to New Brunswick.

Born in 1795, John Brooks Jr. grew up in a sea captain's home, one of ten houses at New Pasture Point in Newfield Harbor. He went to New York at age 15 to work as a clerk in a counting house at Peck Slip. He returned home in 1813, and at age 18 was put in command of Elisha Wilcox's newly built New York-to-Bridgeport coasting sloop *Arab*. In 1814 he transferred to his father's sloop *Intrepid*; in 1815 he commanded the regular packet *Patriot*, owned by Beach & Peck; and in 1816 worked for his father again, as captain of the sloop *Mary Ann*. Thus prepared by command of sailing vessels, Brooks took over the *Marshall* in 1824.

In 1832 Captain Brooks commanded *Citizen*. In 1833 he registered the steamboat *Westchester* in Bridgeport; and in 1834 he registered for the Bridgeport Steamboat Company the steamboat *Nimrod*, named for the Native American who had killed the customs officer's swine in 1651. At age 38 Brooks had already had 21 years at sea, and had commanded nine or more steamboats. *Nimrod* was more than twice the length of *LaFayette*.

The tonnage listed on her licenses increased constantly, from 232.6 tons in 1834 to 336.7 tons by 1842. By 1844 mail that had come into town by stage arrived aboard the *Nimrod*. The vessel served for many years as the Bridgeport boat, safe, reliable, and famous for her Friday night beefsteak-and-onion suppers. William Pendleton's weather diary reports on March 11, 1836, "Steamboat *Nimrod* came up from NY and broke through the ice in Bridgeport harbor," but says on the 27th, "ice not yet broken up between Washington Bridge and Derby." Brooks served as captain of the *Nimrod* through 1847.

In May 1825 the Ousatonic Steamboat Company was organized to run boats from Derby to New York, and by the following year their 81-ton sidewheeler *Ousatonic*, built under supervision of Captain Vose, was running against the *LaFayette*.

In 1844 the Ansonia Brass and Copper Company had an iron hull twin screw propeller driven steamboat built in New York for service to Derby with stops at

From 1834 to 1847 the most frequent steamboat between New York and Bridgeport, with occasional trips to Stratford and Derby, was John Brooks Jr.'s Nimrod. *(Jurgan Frederick Huge painting.)*

Stratford, and named her, appropriately, *Naugatuck* (also known as "the iron pot"). *Naugatuck* was 105 feet on deck, with 6 feet, 8 inches depth of hold.

She was scheduled to leave Derby at 3:00 p.m., Milford at 6:00 p.m., and Stratford at 6:30 p.m., three times a week, for New York. Returning, she would leave Pier 11 at 6:00 p.m. and reach Stratford at about daylight. Pendleton reports her first arrival in Bridgeport on June 1.

In 1847 the operators of the *Naugatuck* paid Julia Curtis and her girls to maintain a lighted beacon at the riverbend below the wharf. The beacon was lighted only on nights when the steamboat was due, at 50¢ per night.

Ansonia was built in 1848 for service on the Derby Line, under Captain Deming, from New York to Bridgeport, Stratford, Devon, and Derby. At 412 tons, she was the largest vessel to travel up the river, and was described as "beautiful as a duck and can give entire satisfaction to all who may have occasion to embark on board of her for the great metropolis." She took six hours to reach New York from Derby.

Norwalk, commanded by Captain Peck, was built in 1849 and fitted with a propeller and a crosshead engine, and ran to Derby in 1854. *Valley City* was another smaller steamer, built in the 1850s by the Atwater Iron and Steel Co. for service on the river.

L.H. Russell sold his shipyard to Peter White in 1854, but continued to receive his grocery supplies by steamboat. Young Lewis Russell's diary in 1859 records:

John Brooks Jr. grew up at New Pasture Point, sailing on his father's coasters. At age 18 he skippered the new packet sloop Arab. *In 1824 he captained his first steamboat,* John Marshall, *and spent the rest of his career in steam.*

June 21. Went down to the dock to see the Propeller tonight and we went all over her. She came from Derby for New York.

June 25. We got up [to harbor] about 4 o'clock PM. The Propeller got up here about the same time that we did.

June 30. The Propeller came up this noon & landed some oil of petriol for AH Stagg & 1 case oil for LHR & Son.

July 1. The str *John Brooks* is going to make an excursion to New York & the str *Valley City* to New Haven Monday [July 4]

July 11. The Propeller came down from Derby tonight & left some wagon springs for Chas. Curtiss [carriagemaker.]

July 21. We went down to the shore in the morn & got what the Propeller brought up yesterday. *Valley City* went down tonight.

July 25. Went down to the Propeller in the evening & she stopped & took on some paper.

July 27. Went down to the dock to the Propeller to catch the lines. She had some stuff for the [Cong.] church [being built.]

July 30. The Propeller got aground outside today & she cannot get in till 10 oclock tonight. We have got freight on her.

Aug. 6. The Propeller came up about 5 o'clock. She left some things for the church & 3 chests of tea for us.

Aug. 8. Went down to the Propeller in eve & she left some springs for G. Nichols & Bro., Old Farm.

Aug. 10. Went down to see the Propeller & she left something for TB Fairchild & something for the church. I heard the *Tom Thumb* was up here getting a boat fixed.

Aug. 11. The Propeller did not get up till 6 o'clock yesterday & she is due at 10 because there is a fog on the sound. She is going down now (12 o'clock.)

Aug. 13. The Propeller came in at 12 o'clock. She brought 66 brls Flour for us & 1 brl Mackerel for TB Fairchild & some oats for Stagg.

Aug. 24. Rainy unpleasant wind NE. The Propeller came in at 1/2 past 9. She was an hour behind and she had such a lot of freight for Stratford that she could not get away soon enough to get across the bar up to the mill & she staid till 1/2 past 5 in the eve.

Aug. 29. Henry & Uncle Meigs went to New York this morning on the boat. The *Naugatuck* got in this morning about 11 o'clock. They had a first rate time.

Sep.21. [Wed.] The Propeller due here at 4 o'clock has not come at 9 oclock Thurs.

Sep. 23 [Fri.] The Propeller came in a 1/2 past 5. She went into Northport LI Wed.

Sep. 28. The Propeller came in at 1 oclock and she was loaded down just as full as she could slick. She had a lot of things for Perry & Smith & a large lot of things for us. I carted all the afte noon & Capt Parks man & Lewis Hubbell.

Oct. 7. The Propeller came outside this morning but grounded on the bar [depth 3 feet] and we went down at 9 oclock. But the tide was not very high & she could not get off. They carried out some coal to the Propeller today.

Oct. 8. Cloudy & unpleasant. The Propeller came in at 1/2 past 8. Went down & saw her. She was loaded down as deep as she could be and her wheel was under water.

Oct. 24. Very pleasant day. Started from Stratford in the Propeller *Valley City* and reached New York at 7 oclock. Going down we met the steamers *Bridgeport, Elm City, Long Island, Mayflower, Island City, Empire State, Granite State,* the Propeller *Thomas Sparks,* Propeller *Osprey.*

Oct. 27. Went down to the dock & the Propeller came down at 1 oclock & took some things. She got the rope in her wheel when she started & was some time before they got it out.

Oct. 29. Went down to the shore in the afternoon and the Propeller came up about 2 oclock. She did not stop. She had been run into by some boat & had a big hole in her bow.

Oct. 31. Went down to Propeller at 1/2 past 4 and she took on freight.

It was the Derby steamboat *Monitor*, a 309-ton sidewheeler built in 1862, that the Washington Bridge collapsed onto on July 15, 1868, delaying the vessel for a few days but eliminating the bridge for the next four years. In 1871 *Monitor* sprang a leak while crossing the bar at the mouth of the river, and sank in 7 feet of water.

Winter ice was a problem on the river. Pendleton wrote in 1836, "Jan 24. Steamboat stopped running. Bridgeport harbor frozen over." then on March 16 "Schooner *Lexington* sailed today for Boston." On March 28, 1843, "Spring floods. Ice broken up between Washington Bridge and Derby." He notes *Naugatuck's* winter trips up the ice-choked Housatonic on November 19, 1844, March 6, 1847, and February 26, 1848, but says on December 5, 1846, "The propeller *Naugatuck* went up the river but could not reach Derby so returned to Stratford." Nathan Wells reports "Feb 13, 1866. Foggy and warm. Ice came down the river and did some damage to Washington Bridge."

Meanwhile, Bridgeport–New York steamboat competition grew. Fare on *Trojan* became 75¢, *Nimrod* and *Eureka* charged 50¢, and a ticket on *Cataline* cost 12¢. In 1844 the Housatonic Railroad's *Mountaineer* reduced its running time to New York to three hours and eight minutes.

In 1848 Captain Brooks left his 336-ton *Nimrod* for command of the 700-ton *Niagara*, a link in the Housatonic Railroad's ice-free route from New York to the west, via Bridgeport, Pittsfield and Albany. After the opening of the Hudson River Railroad doomed the Housatonic Railroad's "ice free route to the west,"

In 1848 Captain Brooks was given command of the Housatonic Railroad's 700-ton Niagara, *connecting New York with the west in wintertime by way of Bridgeport, the Housatonic Railroad, and the Western Railroad of Massachusetts.*

steamboat service to Bridgeport declined, and *Niagara* was taken off the route in 1853.

In January 1855 Captain Brooks was bringing the smaller *Ansonia* to Bridgeport from New York three times a week, and *Cataline*, Captain Charles Weeks, was advertising a four-hour passage, both for 50¢ a passenger.

In 1858 Captain Weeks first brought in the new 734-ton steamboat *Bridgeport*, and Captain Brooks topped that in 1859 with his 240-foot sidewheeler namesake, *John Brooks*. Lewis Russell reported "Thurs June 6. The new Bridgeport boat *John Brooks* came up from NY today to Bport. in 3 hours & 38 min."

It became common practice to take the New York boats from Bridgeport: They were much larger and faster than the Stratford steamboats. After the Civil War, *Jacob Bell*, *Stamford*, *James B. Schuyler*, *City of Bridgeport*, *Crystal Wave*, *Waterbury*, and *Rosedale*, all ran from there. Nathan Wells wrote, "Sep 12, 1867. Went to Bridgeport and took the steamer *Bridgeport* at 11 oclock PM for New York arrived at N York at half past 4 oclock AM. Spent the time till 2 oclock PM in settling bills for schr. *Clarissa Allen* then took the steamer *J.B. Schuyler* for Bridgeport arrived at 7 oclock and took the cars for home."

In 1890 *Nutmeg State* was built (she burned in 1899), and after the New Haven Railroad bought the Bridgeport Steamboat Company in 1903, it operated *Allan Joy*, *William G. Payne* (later renamed as another *Bridgeport*), and *Rosedale*, which had been running since 1877. The railroad's New England Steamship Company operated several passenger steamers in the twentieth century, the last being the *Richard Peck*, which, as a Meseck Line boat went off to serve in the Second World War, and, renamed *Elisha Lee*, never returned to Bridgeport.

In 1877 Captain Charles Jeffries Wakeley commanded the 82.6-ton schooner *Loon* for Andrew Winton in Bridgeport. In 1878 he was in business for himself, registered as master and owner of the *Clarissa Allen*, bought from Nathan Wells at auction. With his bankroll built up, Wakeley abandoned sail and entered the newer world of steam. In 1880 he registered as owner and master of the 128.87-ton steam canal boat *City of Ithaca* (99.14 tons per an 1882 Act of Congress). Based at the upper wharf, Wakeley operated the *Ithaca* on the Sound, the Hudson River, and the Erie Canal, from Stratford and Bridgeport to Buffalo and beyond. Business was so good that in 1882 he took over Alonzo Beardsley's 112.8-ton canal boat *L.G. Smith*, and then the *Alice Wakeley*.

Gradually, as the railroads built in 1849 became faster and more efficient, steamboat service at Stratford declined to non-scheduled freight boats and steam tugs. With one small steamer, the *Minnie B.*, and four freighters, the Derby Line folded in 1889. In 1904–1905, the Merchants' Line operated the *William V. Wilson* from Bridgeport to New York, with an occasional trip to Derby. Steamer service on the Housatonic shrank to the infrequent tugboat hauling barges up the river to deliver coal or construction goods. Coal went to the Youghiogheny Coal Company yard south of the railroad (now the Dock Shopping Center), the CL&P power station built in Devon in 1920, and to Derby. When use of coal declined, oil took its place. Today, all steamboats have been replaced by diesel boats, and

The last regular steamboat from Bridgeport to New York, in the 1930s, was the speedy propeller-driven day boat Richard Peck.

what oil is still delivered—and it is not much—comes in on the huge barges *Maine* and *Connecticut*, pushed by Moran diesel tugs. In 1991 through 1993 a diesel driven sternwheeler named *Victorian Princess* took passengers on excursion cruises in the river and prop-driven *Mister Lucky* came cruising by from Captain's Cove in Black Rock, but now even those are gone.

KEEPERS OF THE LIGHT

Stratford Point, formed by glacial deposits reshaped by aeons of Housatonic river water flow, juts out more than a mile from the Connecticut shore. The bluffs at Stratford Point extended west along Bennett's Cove, some 40 feet in height. North of the point the shoreline melded into Half Moon Cove, where Short Beach is today. Currents at the river mouth were swift and treacherous, and bars left only 2 feet of water at low tide. In colonial times, in low visibility or when a ship was due, a bonfire on the point served as a beacon to guide mariners past the shoals at the river's mouth. Later, an iron basket was erected on a pole to house the signal fire.

The point itself served as a landmark for ships on both sides during the Revolution. The journal of HMS *Rose* for December 30, 1777 reads ". . . came to with best bower, in 7 fm soft Bottom Veered to a Cable, the entrance of New Haven NE by N 8 Miles, Stratford Point W by S, anchored the Convoy . . ."

This line sketch by Assistant Keeper Fred Lillingston in 1867 shows the high bluffs, the keeper's cottage, the covered walkway, and the wooden light tower and bell at lonely Stratford Point.

The light at Stratford Point was the third one on the Sound. On March 3, 1821 Congress authorized expending $4,000. In May the United States purchased 2 acres at the point from widow Betsy Walker, and on June 20 an ad appeared in the *Connecticut Courier*:

> Proposals for furnishing all the materials and building a Lighthouse, and a small house for the Keeper, on Stratford Point, will be received at the collector's office in New London until the 1st day of July next. The Light House must be of wood, about 28 feet high to the foot of the Lanthern, and similar in the foundations, and in all its dimensions, to that on Five-Mile Point, at the entrance of New Haven harbor. . . . the undertaker will please to state the lowest sum for which he will undertake the job.
>
> T.H. CUSHING, Superintendent
> of Light Houses in Connecticut.

Contractor Judson Curtis built well; a hurricane on September 3 destroyed the lighthouse at Black Rock, but Curtis's half-built wooden frame at Stratford Point survived. It was completed in the winter of 1822.

The tower was a tapered octagon, 28 feet tall (the light was 50 feet above mean high water), painted alternately black and white. Its light was at first a set of eight lamps with fixed reflectors, fueled by whale oil, later by lard oil, stored in a brass reservoir above the lantern, warmed by the flames below it. Even with a coal stove in the middle gallery for added warmth, on cold winter nights the lard would congeal, the light would go out, and the keeper would have to climb the tower, carve out the solid lard, and remelt it.

Samuel Buddington, first of ten lightkeepers, was paid $300 a year, raised to $350 in 1829. He and Amy raised seven children at the lighthouse, sending them two miles to Old South School at Sandy Hollow in season. A barn, a henhouse, and a garden on the reservation allowed the Buddingtons to supply themselves with milk (although the rules forbade a cow), eggs, meat, and vegetables, and to store supplies for their winter of isolation. Samuel Buddington watched the first sidewheeler *General LaFayette* round the point and steam up the river in 1824, and he must have seen the *Lexington* burning across the Sound at Eaton's Neck on that icy January night in 1840.

It isn't clear whether the keeper's job was a patronage reward, but Buddington served under a series of Democratic regimes, then was replaced by William Merwin during Whig John Tyler's presidency. As soon as the tally showed that Democrat James Polk had won in 1844, Buddington was back on the job.

When Samuel died in 1848, his widow Amy stayed in the keeper's cottage and took on the keeper's job. By now her youngest child Amy Jane was grown and married and her son Rufus and his wife Eliza were raising a family of their own. They appear to have moved in with her and taken over some of the duties as she aged, because on February 12, 1861 Rufus Warren Buddington became the fourth keeper of the Stratford Light, at the handsome salary of $600 a year. They had eight children in the little cottage at the light, but in the winter of 1861–1862 disaster struck at Stratford Point when four of the children died of diphtheria. Rufus was the last Buddington to keep the light; he held the job until relieved by Benedict Lillingston in 1869.

During the Buddington years, Stratford Light underwent remarkable improvements. Within a year of its installation, the light was changed. A Captain Winslow Lewis talked the government into installing his patented rotating-lamp-and-parabolic-reflector system, with ten whale oil lamps and ten 16-inch reflectors, driven by Simon Willard's patented clockwork mechanism. In 1842 the light was a revolving white light with a 2.15 minute period, and in 1855 six Argand lamps with 21-inch reflectors were installed. When Eliza's brother Captain Truman Hotchkiss came down to visit in 1860, a fog signal bell known as a Stevens Striking Apparatus was on order—Congress had authorized $1,200 for it on June 20—but it did not arrive until 1864 when the Civil War was nearly ended. The bell was housed in a 30-foot high white wooden framework. A weight suspended on a cable powered a hammer to strike the 1,305 pound bell every 15 seconds. In 1863 a third-order fresnel lens imported from France was installed, flashing white.

"Stratford Light dim for half hour last night" was the message received in late October 1871 by the Lighthouse Department in Washington from the captain of the sound steamer *Elm City*. On August 30, 1869 Keeper Benedict Lillingston lived there with his invalid wife Marilla, his son and assistant Frederick, and his little granddaughter Lottie. The keeper's rule was that never must he and his assistant leave the light at the same time, but on this wild October night, with a nor'east gale howling around the creaking wooden tower, the keeper spotted a signal. He rushed through the covered passage from the tower to the cottage, yelling "There's a vessel in distress off the point, son! 'Twill take both of us, in this gale, to be of any help! Lottie must take care of the light!"

Donning poncho and sou-westers, the men rushed out into the stormy night, leaving the girl alone, her ailing grandmother upstairs in bed. For a half hour she sat there, waiting for the men's return, then remembering that the *Elm City* was due to pass at 11:00 p.m., she decided to go check the light. Lighting a small brass alcohol-fueled safety lantern, she found her way through the passage and into the base of the tower. The light tower was a three-story structure, with tanks and cleaning equipment stored in the base. Lottie climbed the staircase to the middle landing, where a coal stove heated the lard oil to keep it from congealing on cold winter nights. She looked at the steep, narrow ladder that led up to the lantern room, where the lamp's burner sat within the fresnel lens, fed through a tube from the brass tank mounted above it. She had never been up there before but, grasping the rungs, she hauled herself up, and found the light was out! Stopping the clockwork mechanism that rotated the light, Lottie carefully hung her little brass lantern in the center, then set the works rotating again. Fifteen minutes later, the *Elm City* steamed by, and wrote its message, "Stratford Light dim for half hour!"

In September 1874 John L. Brush became acting lighthouse keeper, and on April 1, 1876 he was officially appointed to the job. He earned $560 per year (same as Lillingston), but his wife Abigail, as assistant, brought in another $425. On March 7, 1879 Jerome B. Tuttle succeeded him for a year, and his wife Mary received the $425. Captain Theodore D. Judson took over the keeper's job on March 31, 1880, and his wife Kate likewise became assistant. Her office was abolished by the service in 1882, but "Theed" ran the lighthouse for 41 years, assisted by Kate, son Henry, and daughter Agnes.

Agnes was more than helper, she was a beautiful girl and a prizewinning swimmer. One afternoon, aged 17, she saw from the lantern tower two fishermen in a small boat in choppy seas below the cliff, attempting to raise their anchor. As she watched, the boat lurched and both men went overboard. Agnes didn't hesitate: She rang the alarm, dashed down, and plunged into the roiling water. As the men struggled, she passed a rope to one and, when Henry arrived, towed them both to shore. They saved the lives of Edward Lowe and Herman Chase. Agnes's comment was ". . . same as anyone would have done."

When Judson first took on his duties, a new lighthouse was already planned. The old wooden tower was leaking badly, and was in serious disrepair. The new light tower was the first in the Sound, perhaps first in the district, of the new cast iron construction developed by noted engineer General James C. Duane. Five courses of curved cast iron plates, flanged and bolted together, form the shell. It

146

The night the keeper's granddaughter Lottie relit the light she had to climb three stories to the lantern room, insert a lamp, and restart the fresnel lens's rotating mechanism.

is mounted on a concrete footing 3 feet high, is 21 feet in diameter at the base, 18 at the top, and rises 35 feet to the plane of the light. The interior is an open space, with a cast iron stairway curving along the shell to the lantern gallery. The lantern cage itself, 1,100 pounds of glass and cast iron, is encircled by an outside railed catwalk. The third-order fresnel lens and clockwork from the old light tower (a 45-second period) were retained, as was the bell mechanism.

The fog bell took 20 minutes to wind, and ran for two-and-a-half hours, striking every 30 seconds. Captain Judson told of one stormy February when a blinding snow storm required him to sound the bell for 104 hours, going outside to wind it 42 times. Then, after a four-hour respite, the storm returned for 103 more hours.

In 1911 a pneumatic fog warning system replaced the ancient bell when a new brick building was built, housing two bronze diaphone horns, with their two trumpets projecting through the roof. Inside were air compressors, driven by two diesel engines, later by electric generators. Although Judson hired William Petzolt as assistant in 1913, the job remained a lonely one. On foggy days, imagination could run rampant. "Theed's" uptown relatives called him "Crazy Judson," and this 1915 press interview may explain why:

147

Three days ago, on July 4, I saw a shoal of mermaids off Lighthouse Point. I've seen them again and again, but it's only once I laid hands on one. She scratched me well, but I got her brush away from her and I've got it yet. It's generally in the early morning or late afternoon that they gather around the rocks off the point. Sometimes I've counted as many as 12 or 15 of them, their yellow hair glistening and their scaly tails flashing. They're a grand sight.

It was late afternoon when I happened to be out there alone. The sky was thickening for a storm and a fog was creeping up and I had just set the fog horn going. It seems to have an attraction for mermaids, just as the light has for moths. But all of a sudden I noticed this one sitting there all by herself, combing her long golden hair. I took a long look at her before I crept up to her and it's well I did, else I wouldn't be able to give you much of a description, everything happened so quick, once I touched her. I didn't have time to notice anything after that. Well, her hair was wet, but she was brushing it and trying to get it dry. She had lovely gazelle eyes and a fair skin. She was just like a woman to her waist and below that all silver-spangled scales. I should say her tail was about three feet long. The upper part of her body was a little smaller than the average woman. I should say she weighed about 75 pounds. She was a beauty. She didn't wear seaweed clothes. She was bare to the waist. . . .

The mermaid didn't either scream or speak, but she had a tongue and beautiful white teeth. The only sound she made was a hissing noise and it matched well to her temper.

Judson went on to describe how the mermaid slipped out of his grasp. His wife and his assistant Will backed up his story and produced the mermaid's hairbrush. "Theed" explained that they get their combs and brushes from the staterooms of wrecked steamers.

Old "Theed" lasted at the job for six more years, then in 1921 his assistant Will Petzolt took over. No more mermaids were reported, and during the depression, passenger steamers also vanished from the Sound, commercial traffic turned to tug-towed barges, and fewer oyster sloops went out, but small recreational power boats appeared. In 1932 the illuminating apparatus was changed to a fourth-order fresnel lens with a 290,000 candlepower incandescent oil vapor lamp, flashing white at 30 second intervals. In 1939 the lamp was electrified. When Petzolt retired in 1945 the wartime Sound was a submarine training ground and home to passing destroyers.

The last civilian lightkeeper at Stratford Point was Daniel Francis McCoart. "Cap'n Dan" spent 45 years with the Lighthouse Service and the Coast Guard, the last 18 at Stratford.

At Stratford, McCoart and his assistant William A. Shackley served as mechanic, steamfitter, plumber, carpenter, and painter. Four times a night, at 15 minutes before sunset, midnight, 3:00 a.m. and 6:15 a.m., one of them had to

A pneumatic fog warning system replaced the bell in 1911. A pair of large bronze diaphones were sounded by air from compressors driven by electric motors.

cross to the tower, climb the 33 steps and seven ladder rungs to the light, to wind the mechanical clockwork and raise the 35-pound weight suspended from the works that still rotated the lens. (Actually, the clock could run for 5 hours, 20 minutes unattended.)

McCoart received "Excellent" ratings at annual inspections, and had some 20 commendations from the service, ending with the Albert Gallatin award on the day of his retirement (and the end of civilian keepers at the light), on October 31, 1963.

By now, the Coast Guard's program to automate its lights was in high gear. In 1965 the service replaced the deep-voiced diaphones by a higher pitch fog horn, and made plans to automate the light and control it from the Eaton's Neck station. In 1969 a new automated lens, with 1,000-watt lamp, group flashing 20 seconds, was mounted on the tower. Its size required removal of the lantern cage so, at the request of the Historical Society, the Coast Guard commander of the third district donated the cage to them. It was stored in Boothe Park for 20 years.

Although Stratford Light was now completely automated, the keeper's cottage became the living quarters for personnel of the new New Haven Coast Guard Station. A fortunate set of circumstances then occurred. First, Coast Guard policy recognized the value of preserving old lights and beacons, and second, Senior Chief Paul Vanderkaay and his family were assigned to live at Stratford Light. Chief Vanderkaay soon discovered that the old lantern cage still existed. He knew that the light at Stratford was mismatched. Its luminous range (how far it shined) was twice its geographic range (the distance it could be seen allowing for the curvature of the earth). In other words, even though the lighthouse keeper at Faulkner Island 18 miles away could see it, a powerboat east of Branford and 14 nautical miles off could not. The answer was to replace the 1,000-watt light with an efficient 150-watter, put the cupola back on, and restore the light to its classic appearance, while saving $450 a month.

Things moved rapidly in 1990. In February, First District personnel visited the light to check the feasibility; in March Commander Collins of the Long Island Sound Group formally requested it; and on June 28 Coast Guardsmen reset it. The illuminating apparatus today is an FA-251 lens, flashing twice every 20 seconds.

Stratford's lighthouse is photogenic. A pastel belonging to Howard Hyde shows it in its early days when his ancestors the Buddingtons were the keepers. Another, by George Wolfe, adds the bell tower. A Lillingston painting captures a quiet nineteenth-century Stratford. In about 1940, artist Stevan Dohanos painted his "Lordship Light." Photographer Al Mathewson did one of his famous camera sketches in 1957, and a Robert Treat pen-and-ink sketch shows the same scene. The history of Stratford Point light has been well illustrated.

Light Keeper "Theed" Judson stands with his assistant Will Petzolt, hired in 1913. Will took over as keeper in 1921.

5. At Sea around the World

Departing New York in October 1799, Ezekiel Hubbell's ship *Enterprise* was among the first visitors to the Orient. Several Hubbells subsequently made annual voyages to Canton and Manila, as late as 1828. Meanwhile Curtiss Blakeman took *Triton*, *Trident*, and *Macedonian* to Canton, returning with tea, silk, and chinaware. Through the first half of the nineteenth century Stratford men continued to command oceangoing ships for New York merchants to Liverpool, Canton, and Manila. There were Edward Nicoll, his brother-in-law George Dowdall, his brother Samuel Nicoll, his brother-in-law Pulaski Benjamin, John Sterling and his brother-in-law Robert Waterman from Fairfield. Their ships included *Adonis*, *Ajax*, *Blooming Rose*, *China*, *Citizen*, *Columbia*, *Eunice*, *Europa*, *Garonne*, *Helena*, *John G. Coster*, *Memnon*, *Nimrod*, *Panama*, *Sabina*, *South America*, *Splendid*, *Superior*, and *York*, a cross section of the New York fleet.

The Canton Captains

In 1782 14-year-old Ezekiel Hubbell became a clerk aboard Richard and Amos Hubbell's vessels between Newfield and the West Indies. He soon commanded them, and married his employer's daughter Catherine Hubbell. In 1791 he sailed as master of Matthias Nicoll's and the Wetmores' 40-ton sloop *Lord John* out of Stratford. When the Wetmores forfeited their schooner *St. Joseph* for skipping duty payments, Hubbell won it at a Customs Office auction in New York and in 1797 owned it, the brig *Caroline*, and the ship *Sally & Betsy*. He made several voyages to Havana in command of the armed ship *Citizen*, 16 guns and 50 men. The *New York Commercial Advertiser* of July 15, 1798 reports, "Ship *Citizen*, Hubbell master, off Newfield Thursday last, via Halifax, where she had been taken by an English cruiser, and, after a close examination of the crew and papers, was released." On December 6 the paper says "This day came up the armed ship *Citizen*, Capt. E. Hubbell, sixteen guns, nineteen days from Havana. Came out with eighteen vessels under convoy, and parted with them on the coast. Left a French privateer lying off Havana, but she did not seem inclined to come out." Early in 1799 *Citizen* put in at Vera Cruz in Mexico but, not being allowed to land his goods, Hubbell took her to Honduras, then to Havana and New York.

To avoid harassment from the British and the French in the West Indies, and to tap the wealth of Spanish Pacific coast colonies, Hubbell and his associates Isaac Moses & Son, and Hoyt & Tom purchased the ship *Enterprise*, 250 tons. He left New York in October 1799, with a crew of 30 men and boys, a cargo of valuables to trade with the Spaniards in Chile and Peru, and trinkets for the Indians of northwest North America.

After a slow trip southward, they found a harbor on the coast of Patagonia where they careened the ship to clear the hull of barnacles and seaweed. Rounding Cape Horn in early February, after battling storms and mountainous seas, they had fine southerly breezes to carry them up the west coast, and in early March 1800 dropped anchor in Valparaiso harbor. There they found that only Spanish flag vessels were allowed to trade but, since the crew were suffering from scurvy, the governor allowed them to remain and recover. Captain Hubbell took advantage of the time to obtain a passport and travel inland to Santiago, the capital, to seek permission from the viceroy, General O'Higgins, to sell his cargo. The viceroy turned him down, but after some haggling the governor of Valparaiso agreed to purchase most of the goods for 150,000 Spanish dollars, to be delivered at Concepcion, some 300 miles to the south. Taking an agent aboard, they sailed to Concepcion Bay.

The morning was fair, the scenery magnificent, a beautiful bay and harbor could be seen, overtopped by the snow-capped cordilleras in the distance, as the ship glided to her haven. The agent landed and proceeded towards a thicket a short distance away, but instead of finding friends to answer his countersign, he was surprised by a squad of cavalry in ambush. Seeing at once the treachery of the officers and his own defeat, he sprang for his life towards the boat, into which the crew took refuge also. He barely escaped the coils of a lasso as they pushed off for the ship, which they reached in safety except for a wound received by one of the officers. Some years afterwards Hubbell learned that the silver coin sent to Concepcion Bay [by the governor] was seized by the viceroy and confiscated.

Enterprise then sailed to the northwest coast of North America, to trade for furs with Indians at Nootka Sound, then on to Russian-colonized Kamchatka, the Sandwich [Hawaiian] Islands, and Canton, in China [modern-day Guangzhou]. This became a favored approach—get furs, then trade for tea. With a cargo of Bohea tea and other goods, Hubbell left Canton in January, and arrived off Newfield June 27, 1802, 140 days from Canton, the first New York–area captain to circumnavigate the globe.

In the spring of 1803 Ezekiel Hubbell purchased shares in the 200-ton *Catharine Ray* and sailed her to Canton for silk, returning to New York a year later. In 1804–1805 he repeated the voyage, and in May 1805 he visited Canton in his old ship *Citizen*, with $150,000 in Spanish coin to purchase silk, arriving home in May 1806.

In October 1807 he took his and his associates' ship *Augustus* to Canton. He delivered cotton and loaded up with tea. For the tea, he left a $103,000 note with the Hong merchant Houqua. The tea was landed in Amsterdam in the warehouses of Louis Bonaparte, King of Holland. *Augustus* returned to New York in December 1808. Houqua's receipt said "Received pay in full, with interest, as adjusted, $119,000. Houqua." Captain Hubbell's annotation read "Paid, thank God!"

Hubbell remained home until 1817 when he took the *Citizen* to Manila for sugar. *Citizen* made two more trips to Manila. In 1821 Hubbell commanded the newly built ship *Ajax* to Manila, leaving his sons there to establish a trading house. Captain Hubbell made four voyages to Manila in *Ajax* before selling her. Within four months of her sale, in 1825, *Ajax* foundered. In June 1825 Hubbell made a Manila voyage commanding the ship *Sabina*. Again, on December 26, 1826 he took *Sabina* out, this time to Rio De Janiero, Valparaiso, Lima, Patu, Guayaquil in Equador, the Sandwich Islands, and Manila, returning to New York on April 14, 1828. This was his last voyage. Ezekiel Hubbell had sailed more than 245,000 miles, and helped open the Orient to American trade.

Born inland at Daniel's Farm in Stratford on October 24, 1777, Curtiss Blakeman found shipboard work at an early age. By 1799 he and his wife Lavinia were living in New York and he was master of the 53.9-ton sloop *Hiram*, owned by Tom Hoyt and John Gould, coasting between New York and New London. In 1803 the Blakemans moved to the borough of Bridgeport.

On May 2, 1804 Blakeman departed New York toward Canton, for merchants Oliver Wolcott & Co. as master of their ship *Triton*, a new 320-ton ship built in New York. Wolcott leased *Triton* from its owners Isaac Bell and Thomas Carberry. (Some documents list Carbury as captain and Bell as supercargo.) Instructions

Captain Ezekiel Hubbell commanded ships contemporary to this nineteenth-century bark— Enterprise, Catherine Ray, Augustus, Citizen, Ajax, Sabina—*to* Canton *and* Manila.

were to bring home 3,000 chests of tea—Hyson, Hyson Skin, Young Hyson, best Souchong, 2nd Souchong, Gunpowder, and Imperial.)

That November, *Triton* was one of five New York ships among the 28 American vessels in the port of Canton, arriving with 70,372 Spanish dollars and 9,533 beaver pelts purchased in Montreal the previous year. Following Chinese regulations (in force before the treaty ports were opened in 1842) the cargo was unloaded at Whampoa Reach and lightered 12 miles up to the hongs (factories) at Canton. Each ship was assigned a "fiador," a principal merchant, and a "comprador" to furnish provisions, lighters (sampans), and linguists. The "hoppo man" was the customs agent, who measured the ship for duty, and expected a gratuity, a "cumshaw." *Triton's* fiador was named Cheonqua.

Home in Bridgeport in 1805, Blakeman wrote to Wolcott asking to be named master of Wolcott's new ship *Trident*. In September 27-year-old Captain Curtiss Blakeman was busy supervising *Trident's* outfitting for her maiden voyage, at a salary of $45 per month. *Trident* was built for Wolcott by Adam and Noah Brown in their yard at Corlear's Hook in the East River. Her construction process was typical of the time, wherein the owner served as prime contractor. *Trident* grossed 461 tons "custom house measure," or 501 tons "carpenter's measure," as calculated and built (at $49 per ton) by the Browns. She scaled 111 feet in length. She was built of live oak, locust, and cedar, copper fastened and copper sheathed. Rigging—outfitting and cordage, sails, blocks, pumps, ironwork, anchors and such—was separately contracted by the owners: Isaac Bell bought timber for $1,178, Wolcott paid a blockmaker $400 for "all articles in the blockmaker's line," Bell purchased an anchor for $209, Flemish sail cloth from Amsterdam cost $2,003, and Richard Sawyer was paid for three coats of paint. Even launching brought a separate bill. The Browns reminded Wolcott "Sir, we have always understood that the owners of the vessels did pay for injoining to watter."

On April 14, 1806 *Trident* left New York for Canton, "drawing seventeen feet nine inches water." The crew totalled forty men—Captain Blakeman, three mates (his brother Elijah was second mate), a captain's mate, doctor, sailmaker, carpenter, cook, and 31 seamen.

Trident kept a careful watch for sails: This was the period when the British Navy was impressing seamen from American ships. But she had no trouble, and the passage was swift. On July 27 Blakeman wrote to Wolcott from Anjier in Java that he was pleased with the ship's performance, but brother Elijah had crippled himself by a fall from the mizzen topsail yard to the deck in a squall.

In Canton, the captain stayed at the factory while the return cargo was being loaded. Blakeman himself shipped 690 pounds of long white nankeens of handloomed cotton, which on return he sold to Stratford storekeeper Elijah Ufford.

After two months in Canton, Blakeman departed for New York in November with 760 tons of cargo. The homeward voyage was fraught with problems, beginning with ten hours aground on a mud bank in Banca Strait. Next, *Trident* was stopped and held for 40 hours by a British warship. In Sunda Strait the ship lay for four days in a dead calm. Seven crewmen were sick, and the captain worried that he might not have enough men to work the ship through the straits. Finally he cleared the straits, crossed the Indian Ocean into the Atlantic, and after a round trip total of about 245 days at sea, reached New York on the evening of March 20, 1807.

Blakeman was home less than three months before his next voyage began on May 12. Heavy gales made this passage a rough one, with damaged rigging and flooding in the hold. Blakeman wrote to Wolcott that the roundhouse (deckhouse) was filled with water and, "had not the *Trident* proved excellent the consequence must have proved fatal to us."

A letter from Wolcott to Blakeman on July 11 described a June 22 incident when the 50-gun British frigate HMS *Leopard* attacked the 38-gun *Chesapeake*, caused 21 casualties, and impressed four seamen. Wolcott cautioned that there might be war, that Blakeman should avoid other ships on his homeward voyage, and that if war did occur, he and his men would receive "a liberal donation."

Trident reached Whampoa Reach 113 days from New York. The outbound cargo, 173,000 Spanish silver dollars, some brandy, Madeira wine, and a small amount of ginseng, was traded for 1,379 chests of tea, 106,250 pieces of nankeen cloth, 8,500 pounds of cassia (cinnamon), and some chinaware. Blakeman himself bought 59 boxes of chinaware to sell.

On December 21, 1807, while *Trident* was still at sea, Congress passed the Embargo Act, shutting off all American trade. When Blakeman landed at New York on March 20, 1808, he learned that the ship had earned a profit of $74,000 on its second trip, but *Trident's* next voyage to the Orient was cancelled.

Jefferson signed the repeal of the Embargo Act on March 1, 1809 and on May 15 Blakeman put to sea, pledging to defend his ship if attacked. Aside from the captain, four officers, Dr. Thomas Griswold, a carpenter, and a sailmaker, the crew numbered 35. Blakeman received $50 a month plus 12 tons "priviledge," first mate Abraham Jennings $35 a month and three tons, second mate Thomas Watterman $30 and two tons, third mate John Thompson $25, and Dr. Griswold $30 and two tons.

Incidents en route included the loss of Avory the sailmaker, who jumped overboard and, when a boat attempted to rescue him, swam away from it. In the China Sea, a severe typhoon struck the ship, causing damage but no injuries. One Mr. Roberts "conducted unfavorably bad," by speaking in favor of the British navy, and was dismissed at Canton. The return cargo was mainly tea and nankeen, plus some chinaware.

The homeward trip was another trial. The ship leaked continuously after Sunda Strait, so badly that both pump and men were "worn down." Finally, the captain decided to put into a port in the Atlantic. Not sure whether the United States was at war with Britain, he decided to avoid St. Helena, and reached Ascension Island on March 6, 1810, where the men captured turtles for food. Then northward to the equator and the doldrums. For two days the ship lay motionless, while water seeped into her lower hold. Finally on March 20 they picked up the northeast trades but were forced to go to Barbados eight days later to repair the leak. On April 2 they began their final leg, and reached New York on May 3, 1810, after 132 days at sea.

Trident's first three passages proved profitable, but now she was to be sold. *Trident's* new registration, issued on June 23, 1810, listed Isaac Bell, Richard Black, and John Graham as her owners.

The new owners immediately put the ship into Transatlantic service, and engaged Blakeman to take her on the initial run, to Greenock in Scotland. On July 27, 1810 *Trident* departed New York on the North Atlantic run to Greenock and arrived back in New York on November 26, after a 43 day westward passage.

After Congress declared war on Britain on June 18, 1812, Blakeman found employment in the West Indies trade. He made at least two trips to Puerto Rico as master of the schooner *Venus*: one from Florida on January 13, 1813 with a "Fairfield cargo outbound foreign," and another on June 13. In spite of the war, Blakeman went to work in Transatlantic service as master of John Jacob Astor's ship *Hannibal*. On July 22, 1813 he left New York for Gottenburg. One of his passengers was French General Jean Marie Victor Moreau, en route to help the allies overthrow Napoleon. Arriving in Bremen, Blakeman was forced to sell the ship to a neutral to avoid its capture by the British. He returned to New York as a passenger on *Hannibal*, now in neutral hands, on November 8, 1814.

Blakeman continued in the employ of Astor, as master of his brig *Macedonian*. On January 14, 1815, unaware that the war had ended on December 24, Blakeman left the East River with a load of furs and ginseng, headed for the Far East in company with several Navy vessels bound to attack British shipping in the Pacific. After losing her foremast and escaping a British frigate, *Macedonian* reached Canton on July 2, 163 days en route. Astor had feared that the brig was lost, but a year after its departure, on January 18, 1816, *Macedonian* reentered New York harbor.

Two months later Blakeman took *Macedonian* to Canton on another yearlong trip, returning on January 26, 1817. Then in April he took Astor's *William and Mary* to Gibraltar, where he loaded a cargo of quicksilver and lead for Canton. On April 27, 1818 Captain Curtiss Blakeman returned Astor's ship to New York, and never went to sea again. At age 42 he came ashore, moved to Illinois, and became a farmer.

New York Custom House records of July 11, 1820 list the arrival of the 300-ton ship *Columbia*, Captain George Robert Dowdall, from Ireland. On November 13 Dowdall arrived again on the ship *Adonis*, from Antwerp via Newport. Born in 1783, Dowdall, like many shipmasters, spent years in the Transatlantic trade before heading toward the Orient. But his next assignment was to China. On April 5, 1822 he arrived in New York from Canton in the ship *China*.

Like John Sterling from Stratford, he commanded ships for Charles Hall & Co., and was the first captain of Hall's new ship *Superior*, 575 tons, built by Isaac Webb. He brought *Superior* home from Canton on May 21, 1823, and again on April 20, 1824.

This Cantonware came from China in New York ships with Stratford skippers. Except for tea, chinaware like this was the primary return cargo.

Through his friendship with the Nicoll brothers, Samuel of privateering fame and Edward, he met their sister Eliza, married her in 1821, and moved to Stratford. There he bought a lot on Elm Street and built a mansion for Eliza. While the house was being built, Hall assigned Captain Phillips to *Superior's* Canton runs, but in 1826 Dowdall took command again and brought her home to New York on April 16, 1827.

At this time a new *Ajax* was being built, taking the name of the ship that had foundered in 1825 shortly after Ezekiel Hubbell sold it. This *Ajax*, 627 tons, was built in Kensington, Pennsylvania, and sailed out of New York for owners Robert Kermit & Stephen Whitney. In 1827, after Dowdall brought *Superior* in, his turnaround was swift: The records show him bringing *Ajax* into New York on April 23, 1828.

Meanwhile Edward Nicoll was busy on North Atlantic runs. Working for Peterson & Mensch, he had command of *Europa* when she left Hamburg for New York on February 15, 1827.

In the spring of 1829 Dowdall took *Ajax* to Canton once again, with his brother-in-law Edward Nicoll as mate. In the fall of 1829, plague raged through Canton, and *Ajax* was not spared. An epitaph in the Episcopal cemetery in Stratford commemorates the captain's death on November 1 and the mate's demise on October 27.

April 9, 1836. A cloudy morning, followed by a warm, pleasant spring day. The full-rigged 642-ton ship *Panama* passed the narrows and eased into her berth in New York Harbor, 99 days from Canton. Captain D. Pulaski Benjamin took

George Dowdall from England commanded transatlantic runs for Charles Hall & Co., married a fellow captain's sister, built a mansion in Stratford, and entered the China trade. (Courtesy Yale University Art Gallery.)

the steamboat for Stratford. On his arrival home, Reverend Shepard solemnly informed him that his dear wife Susan had left this earth in November, "but she died loving the Lord." "The Hell she did!" replied the crusty captain, "She never loved anyone but me!"

Deliverance (or Delucina) Pulaski Benjamin made some of the fastest runs to Canton in his day. Born May 22, 1796, his life at sea began at age 16 during the War of 1812. His story, written in 1879, begins:

> I was but a boy on board of the ship *Pallas*, bound for Cadiz, and we were in sight of that town when our ship was overhauled and captured on December 24, 1812, by the British ship-of-war *Scheff*, and sent into Gibraltar, kept there for some time and then sent with other prisoners to England in a British 74-gun ship, arriving there in April 1813. We were then confined on one of a number of old prison hulks moored in the River Medway near Chatham. On board this old ship called the *Glory*, there were 1,200 French prisoners and 200 of us Americans.

In the fall of 1814 young Benjamin was sent with many others to the notorious Dartmoor Prison, where fierce Atlantic storms swept across the desolate moor. It covered 30 acres and housed 10,000 French and American prisoners. The jailer, bloodthirsty Captain Shortland, made it a living hell. Long after the Treaty of Ghent was signed in December, Yankee prisoners were retained. In fact, the situation worsened. In March Captain Shortland ordered the food ration cut from one-and-a-half pounds of bread to a pound of moldy biscuit:

> To every prisoner in his charge a pound, not one ounce more,
> Though a pound and a half each man received the very day before
> As that was due by right and rule to prisoner young and old
> Confined there, his just due share, 'twas cheating to behold,
> One half a pound! remorseless and unfeeling man this jailer sure must be
> From every prisoner to exact so large, so great a fee!
> Nor he nor cre nor feeling had, but feeling for himself,
> And thus he meant his purse to fill by such illgotten pelf.

Benjamin's story continued:

> We refused to accept the musty sea biscuit. Our allowance each day was one and one-half pounds of bread, one-half pound of meat, three ounces of Scotch barley, half an ounce of salt, quarter of an ounce of onions to each man. All this was put into huge boilers and made into soup, thus the bread was an important item. On account of our refusal they called

On July 11, 1820 Captain George Dowdall brought the 300-ton ship Columbia *into New York from Ireland. He spent several years in the transatlantic trade. (Peabody Essex Museum.)*

out the troops and threatened to fire on us. . . . finally at midnight we got our bread fresh from the ovens as they had to bake it for us. Shortland was very angry that he could not make us eat his mouldy biscuits and said he would fix the damn Yankees first chance he had.

That chance came on April 6. The prison was divided by a wall, with prisoners on one side and barracks and hospital on the other:

The prisoners were in the habit of playing ball and sometimes the ball would go over the wall on the soldiers side and they would throw it back, but this time they did not return the ball and one of the American prisoners made a hole in the division wall and crawled through and got the ball. As soon as this was discovered by the guard the alarm bell rang and we all rushed to see what was the matter. The troops were drawn up in the square and at the order of Captain Shortland, the commanding officer, fired at us, as we were all huddled together. Ten were killed, more died later from their wounds. There were 6,000 or 7,000 of us in the inclosure. I think many more of us would have met the same fate but the soldiers, knowing the injustice of the order to fire, aimed high. It was nothing less than a massacre, for it was wholly unprovoked.

> Fire! Fire! my lads, the murdrer cried, the trigger then he drew
> And swift as lightning on the wing their deadly bullets flew
> Sixty brave tars by Shortland's means lay weltering in their gore
> High heaven itself had ne'er beheld such cowardly acts before.

On May 19, 1815, freed with 2,400 other American prisoners, Benjamin finally sailed for Boston. He arrived home a grown man, hardly recognized by his family.

At every opportunity he went to sea. In 1820 his sister Elvira Nicoll wrote "Pulaski has gone on a long voyage to Valparaiso in the *Warrior*, Captain Nixon; expects to be gone at least a year. It was called a fine berth for him." His ship had sailed in early February on his first trip around the Horn.

By 1827 Pulaski Benjamin was captain of the 388-ton ship *Courier*, crossing the Atlantic every 106 days from New York to Liverpool, Glasgow, or Hamburg. By 1835 he was sailing for N.L. & G. Griswold in the China trade. The Griswolds owned a series of ships named *Panama*, and the words printed on every wooden box of tea aboard, "*Panama*, N L & G Griswold," were so familiar that it became known as Panama Tea. Five times, from 1836 to 1841, Benjamin brought the 509-ton *Panama* home from Canton.

A marked-up chart of the Canton (Pearl, or Chu Kiang) River shows that Benjamin went into both Macao to the west and Hong Kong to the east. It also shows bearings taken all the way up to Whampoa Reach: One is from Lung-Est or Dragon's Cave, another lines up a Chop House with Saddle Hill.

Another chart shows part of the East Indies south of Singapore. East of Sumatra is Banca Strait and the island of Banca (Bangka), and between that and Billiton

Deliverance Pulaski Benjamin spent his life on the water, in European traffic and in the China trade. He saw the destination port move from Canton to Hong Kong and ships grow from packets to clippers. He retired at age 52 and spent the next 35 years sailing around the harbor.

Island are the Gaspar Straits. Billiton Strait is the widest and most easterly of three entries to the South China Sea. This part of the chart is erased clean, indicating many passages by its owner. While sailing *Panama* in 1836 Benjamin added Vegas Shoal to the chart, and moved Magdalen's Shoal about 4 miles south of it. Navy Captain John Vest recalled that many charts he used in World War II were those of China trade captains of the 1800s.

Benjamin's chart of Sunda Strait is similarly marked up. One fix in Batavia Road shows that Benjamin anchored at this Dutch colony on Java. His plots show his usual route to be southward through the China Sea, through the Gaspar Straits into the Java Sea, thence southwest through Sunda Strait between Java and Sumatra, and into the Indian Ocean. This is a busy route today.

His chart of the northern half of the South China Sea shows travel from Canton along the east shore of Cochin China (Vietnam), past Camraigne (Kamchon) Point, then south past Sincapour (Singapore) toward Gaspar Straits. Benjamin marked a new rock at 5° 23' north latitude, 107° 34' east longitude and added shoals in the vicinity of 9° north latitude, 112° east longitude. His route from Manila passed west of Panay, down past Mindanao into the Celebes Sea, and southwestward through Macassar Strait between Borneo and Celebes Islands. On Celebes is his note "All this coast and the adjacent islands are placed about 10 miles too far west on this chart. D.P. Benjamin."

In 1836, when Benjamin brought *Panama* home in 99 days, it was good time. Captain Griswold had taken 94, but John Sterling in the old packet *York* had done well at 104 days.

As Benjamin's reputation for fast passages grew, The Griswolds gave him larger ships. When he arrived home from Canton in *Panama* on April 17, 1841, *Helena* was already on the ways at William Webb's. *Helena* grossed 598 tons, and her moderately sharp hull and heavy rig made her able to make as fast passage as the earlier Baltimore clippers while stowing a much greater tonnage. Called a "clipper," she was not a true clipper of the type built in the 1850s, but was clipper rigged.

Benjamin took *Helena* out on her first voyage to Canton, around the Horn and via Valparaiso, on October 30, 1841. On December 4, south of the line, she came up with the ship-of-the-line USS *Delaware*, and within 24 hours *Delaware* was out of sight astern. Captain Benjamin's temper flared a few days later. He writes "Fresh breezes with much rain. House all afloat. Not a dry spot in it. I wish the Devil had all such houses."

Although weather was not especially favorable, she made Valparaiso from New York in 83 days. On rounding the Horn, Benjamin wrote on May 19:

> Fine breeze SE and cloudy weather. Studding sails set below and aloft. This is the most remarkably good fortune I have ever heard of in doubling the Cape in the winter. We have had continued Easterly winds now for four days and the breeze is still fresh from the SE and the weather pleasant. The Lord be praised!

One reason for continual record breaking passages was cooperation between ships' captains and the Navy's Depot of Charts and Instruments. Under the leadership of Lieutenant Matthew Fontaine Maury from 1842 to 1861, the depot compiled reports on weather, winds, currents, and tides from all over the world. Benjamin exchanged his logs for free charts. Information from these logs was entered onto new charts, and showed the clipper masters what routes to sail for the fastest passages. The average time from New York to California was cut by 47 days, and American ship owners saved—thanks to Maury and to their own cooperation—some $2 million a year. In 1845 Benjamin broke a Transpacific record by taking *Helena* from Callao to Hong Kong in 51 days. *Helena* was a fast ship.

The following year he was awarded an even larger ship, the 714-ton *John G. Coster*, built in New York in 1841 and owned by Joshua Atkins, then by Howland & Aspinwall. New York Custom House records show *Coster's* arrival in New York from Canton on October 2, 1846.

Pulaski Benjamin's last ship was the clipper *Memnon*. *Helena* was fast, *Memnon* was faster. Designed by Griffiths to be an improvement on *Sea Witch*, and built in 1847 by Smith & Dimon in New York "of clipper mould" for F.A. Delano of the Swallowtail Line, she grossed 1,068 tons. Benjamin took the clipper on her first

In 1827 Pulaski Benjamin was master of the 381-ton ship Courier, *which had been one of the first four Black Ballers in 1818, crossing the Atlantic every 106 days, forerunner to this 1,400-ton ship.*

two runs to Liverpool. Customs records show him bringing her in to New York on March 13 and June 29 in 1848, before handing her over to Oliver Eldridge, then to Joseph Gordon. Gordon made a record 14-day Liverpool run, then took *Memnon* to San Francisco and Canton several times, competing against John Sterling's brother-in-law Robert Waterman's *Sea Witch*, until he lost her in the Gaspar Straits in 1851.

For Pulaski Benjamin, now 52, it was time to retire from the sea. From the sea, but not from the water. In *Lippincott's Magazine* in 1879, Ellen Olney Kirk reported on his sailing activities in Stratford in his little cutter *Adele*. "He carried all sorts of precious cargoes, but no matter what rich merchandise freighted his ships in the old days, his present sailboat, which cuts the blue waters of Stratford Harbor on a summer's day, contained treasures yet more priceless. The *Adele* is noted for its pretty crews, and, surrounded by bright eyes, rosy cheeks, and girlish figures, the last Dartmoor prisoner enjoys a different sort of captivity."

None of his children went to sea. John and Pulaski helped form the Housatonic Boat Club, and John became a member of the New York Stock Exchange. The old sailor died in October 1883, and there is a story that in his memory *Adele* was scuttled in Selby's Pond, where her mast projected above the surface for many years.

Benjamin took the pre-clipper China packet Helena *on her first voyage to Canton for N. & L.G. Griswold in 1841. She had sharp underwater lines and plenty of canvas, but did not sport double topsails or topgallants. (Courtesy Mystic Seaport, Mystic, CT.)*

Retired from the sea, Captain Benjamin kept his hand in by skippering ladies up and down the river in his little catboat Adele, *seen in this image from the July 1879* Lippincott's Magazine *at the warehouse at the lower wharf.*

JOHN STERLING, MASTER MARINER

John William Sterling spent 10 years and 19 voyages rehearsing for his Oriental trips. Born in 1796 when America was getting its sea legs, Sterling was early attracted to the sea. To discourage the boy and steer him toward a Yale College education, his father in November 1810 put him aboard Levi Coit's ship *Aristomenes*, with his uncle Daniel Sterling master, bound from New York toward Liverpool and Archangel. His papers, drawn up to protect him from British navy impressment, read "an American seaman, aged 14 years, of the height of 4 ft. 8 inches and a half, dark complexion, dark hair, black eyes."

Far from dissuading John, the voyage decided his career. In Liverpool on a three-month winter layover, John studied navigation. His notebook, labeled "Problems in Navigation" in his own neat hand, gives insight into navigation processes and cargo handling methods of the day. Procedures we consider modern, with logarithms and trig tables, were in common use. Plane sailing—solving for dL and dLo knowing course and distance—was routine. But longitude was difficult to determine, so parallel sailing (wherein the ship sailed to the latitude of its destination, then sailed east or west until it arrived) was substituted. Lunar observation, (wherein the observer measured the distance between the moon and a star and found from tables just when such a distance would occur) was also still in use.

By springtime, saturated with nautical knowledge, John was ready to continue on *Aristomenes's* voyage to Russia. At Archangel he was "filled with wonder at the

Old sea captains conspired to steer John Sterling away from Yale and toward the sea. In August 1808 Captain John Brooks Sr. took him to New York to see Fulton's Clermont *on its first trip up the Hudson. (Samuel Ward Stanton painting.)*

bursting Arctic summer." Back to Liverpool, then home to New York, *Aristomenes* arrived in October 1811.

On June 18, 1812 Congress declared war on Britain. John shipped again on *Aristomenes*, this time under Captain Brewster, New York to Charleston, Lisbon, and Boston.

With the War of 1812 underway, John signed aboard a schooner under Swedish colors, sailing from New London to Halifax and back to New Haven in late 1813. In 1814 he served as second mate aboard the cartel ship (ship commissioned to sail under safe-conduct to exchange prisoners) *Fingal*, carrying General Proctor home to England after his defeat at Tippecanoe. It was a stormy passage, and the old general feared that the ship would founder, trusted to a boy of 18. *Fingal* was at Havre de Grace when Napoleon returned from Elba in 1815, and Sterling observed the riotous celebration of the French and the rapid departure of English ships.

When *Fingal* returned to New York in April 1815, the war was over. John signed on in June as second mate of the brig *Wrangler*, Captain Aldrich, to Charleston for cotton. Promoted to first mate, he made another trip to Charleston, then to Martinico, returning to New York in December. From January to April 1816 John sailed as second mate of the ship *Minerva Smyth*, Captain J.W. Allen, owner Archibald Gracie of New York, to Liverpool.

John Sterling's ninth voyage was as mate of the new 482-ton ship *Nestor*, uncle Daniel Sterling master, to Liverpool and back. John's journal says:

> Monday May 20th 1816. At 4pm cast off from the wharf & drop'd off into the North River and came too. May 22 at 1pm beat down as far as Statin Island & came too. Mon May 27 At 11am a fine breeze from NW. Hove up our anchor & stood out. This day contains but 12 hours. [i.e. noon of the 27th, civil time, begins the 28th, nautical time.]

On June 10 the journal reports pleasant breezes from the south and all sails set. At half past eleven they saw the moon in total eclipse, and after midnight took in steering sails (Sterling always referred to studdingsails or stu'ns'ls as steering sails) and royals, then the fore topgallant.

On June 15 they spoke an Irish fishing hooker, bought some mackerel, and got directions to Holyhead. On the 17th they saw St. David's Head, and at 2:00 a.m. on the 18th they passed Holyhead and took a pilot. They beat up the Mersey, and at meridian on the 19th moored with their kedge in the Sloyne, across the river from the docks, until the tide should be right for opening the gates.

After discharging cargo, the new ship was hove downriver to graving dock no. 2 to be coppered. This done, and cargo stowed, on August 5, "Hove up our anchor and stood out." By August 28 they were off the Grand Banks, and on September 11, "At 6pm got a pilot about 8 miles from the Hook. At 10pm came to anchor at the quarantine ground. At 9am the doctor came on board, permitted us to pass Got underway & beat up the North River & haul'd into the dock about 2pm."

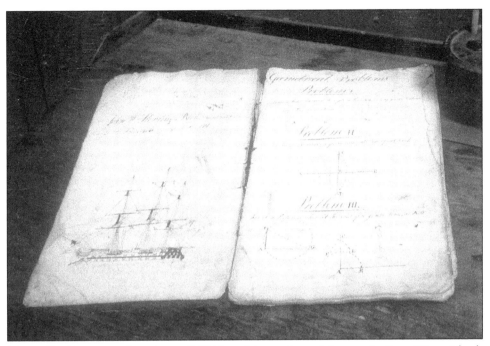

Young Sterling spent the winter of 1811 at Liverpool, studying navigation. His notebook shows geometry problems, alongside what may be the a diagram of the Aristomenes.

On December 6 *Nestor* departed for Liverpool again. On January 3, 1817 she hauled into George's Dock, 28 days en route. The return trip began on Friday, March 14 and she reached New York in May.

With first mate's experience behind him, Sterling accepted command of a brig, engaged a crew, and supervised its loading, but when the underwriters found out that he was only 20 years old, they refused to insure the brig. The owners then offered him the job of mate, but he answered that where he had been master he could not be man. Again, he shipped as mate on *Nestor*, now one of three ships of the newly formed Black Ball Line. *Nestor* sailed for Liverpool in June, with captain A. Scott and 18 other crewmen.

On *Nestor*'s fifth voyage, Daniel Sterling was in command again, on a stormy eastbound passage. Ship's pumps were constantly at work. On November 9, "Made Holy Head Light bearing east. 10am got a pilot." Next day *Nestor* was in Queen's Dock, 22 days from New York. The westbound trip began on Christmas day and *Nestor* reached New York on February 24, 1818. She continued to cross to Liverpool for the Black Ball Line until lost in 1824.

After five trips to Liverpool on *Nestor*, Sterling signed on as first mate of the 296-ton ship *Garonne* (built in 1815 in Milford), captain Edward Whiting, bound for Trieste, departing March 29. On April 20 the mate reported "Observations of the moon and Regulus were taken," and on the 21st, the mean of several observations of the moon and Antares was used, although "taken with a quadrant

& supposed not to be correct." On the 22nd they sighted Gibraltar, and "at 6pm made the apes hill." On May 11th, "pass'd St. Salvaro & anchor'd at Trieste. At Meridian ready for discharging. Were quarantin'd 5 days."

After completing loading and caulking the hatches, on June 6 *Garonne* set sail, passed Gibraltar at midnight on the 27th, and Cape Trafalgar at 4:00 a.m. She spent all of July crossing the Atlantic and on the 31st arrived in New York, 56 days from Trieste.

At age 21 John Sterling received his first command, as master of *Garonne*, New York to Havana, from August 12 to November 8, 1818. Spain had just opened its Cuban colony to foreign trade, and *Garonne* was among the first ships to carry its sugar, coffee, and cocoa to New York.

As soon as *Garonne* reached New York, Sterling set out again, this time as master of the brig *Eunice*, for St. Thomas in the Danish Virgins. By Monday December 7, "At 10am made Virgin Gorda bearing South dist 30 miles." Sterling, who had not sailed these waters before, was surprised to find the island of Anegada, which rises only 15 feet out of the sea, between him and Virgin Gorda's thousand-foot peaks. From St. Thomas harbor *Eunice* reached the south coast of Cuba on February 8. "At 1am was up with Cumberlan Harbour [Guantanamo] . . . At 1pm took a pilot [at Santiago]. At 2, came too off the moro went up to town in the boat."

In port for 107 days, sickness overtook the crew: "Lost 3 of the crew who died of West Indies fever." Finally on April 25 the brig dropped down to the morro and, with a cargo of sugar and molasses and a single passenger, set off for New York. By 7:00 p.m. on May 20th *Eunice* lay fast alongside the wharf in the East River. Sterling headed for home, and stayed six days.

On June 2, 1819 he sailed for Charleston, Havre de Grace in France, Gibraltar, and Malaga. Ghosting down the coast, he wrote:

> June 6th. This past day ends with a light breeze scarcely sufficient to stem the current, which creates a great deal of impatience on my part, and a prospect of a long passage. Thurs June 10 It is an old saying that "a bad beginning makes a good ending" of course must be content with hoping it may prove true. The wind has been directly ahead since we have been out.

Europe was hungry for American cotton and tobacco, and in Charleston Sterling loaded 325 bales of one and 50 hogsheads of the other. *Eunice* spent a month crossing the Atlantic. On Friday June 25, in dense fog but knowing that he was close to port, Sterling took in sail and stood off until morning, when the weather cleared, revealing Cape la Hague. At noon, when the sea day of the 26th began, he reached le Havre and commenced discharging.

On to Gibraltar and Malaga for wine and fruit, then to New York on Friday November 12, "Very thick and foggy. At 2pm made the black buoy on the east bank, got a pilot. At 6pm came too alongside the wharf."

After a month's layover, Sterling again took *Eunice* out, to Charleston, Havre, Gibraltar, Malaga, Gibraltar, and New York. As *Eunice* headed up the English Channel beyond Ushant Light an English pilot boat informed them that "the mad monarch who had lost America had died," and George IV was king.

They took in 50 hogsheads of tobacco and on March 9 made sail from Le Havre's dock gates. On the 26th they dropped the bower in 9 fathoms of water in Gibraltar harbor. Here they discharged the tobacco and took aboard 104 pipes (1 pipe = 4 barrels = 126 gallons) of wine. At Malaga, *Eunice* loaded 500 more casks of wine for New York. Finally on June 23, "At 4pm took a pilot. At 10 came to anchor at the Quarantine to lay 2 days." *Eunice* was home.

John Sterling's eighteenth voyage, as master of the ship *Blooming Rose*, from New York to Rio de Janeiro, Montevideo, and Buenos Aires, commenced on August 1, 1820. At Buenos Aires, the dictator General Puyerredon had just been deposed, and there was rioting in the streets. A mob was burning and pillaging the business district of the city. With loaded pistols, Sterling went to the banking house, withdrew his ship's money and papers, and carried them through the mob to his ship and the safety of the U.S. flag. On April 1, 1821 he was home in New York.

On May 10, commanding the ship *Nimrod*, he departed New York again for Montevideo and Buenos Aires, returning on January 17, 1822.

Nimrod, John Sterling's first command to Canton, *must have looked much like the* Hazard, *built for the East India trade.*

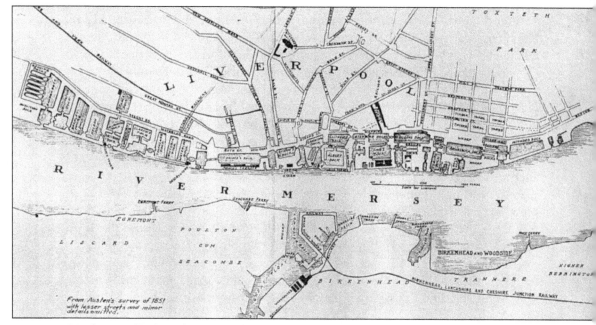

Uncle Daniel's ship's layover in 1811 acquainted John Sterling with the docks at Liverpool, where he would later berth at George's Dock Basin. Austen's 1851 survey shows gated docks to deal with the Mersey's extreme tides. Ships waiting for the gates to open anchored across the river at the Sloyne, at Birkenhead.

On March 20 Sterling and *Nimrod* left New York again. It was his twentieth voyage, and his first to Canton, thence to South America. With light breezes and fair weather, at 3° 18" north latitude he lost the northeast trades, but the next day at 2° 36' south latitude he picked up southeast trades. On May 19, approaching the Indian Ocean, he "caught a booby, meas'd tip to tip of the wings 6 ft 6 in and an albatross meas'd 9 ft 3 in."

On June 20 Sterling reported, "fresh breezes and pleasant weather. Took in the steering [studding] sails Got guns on deck. At 9am took in the royal yard. Log 14138 miles." They had crossed the Indian Ocean, and were heading into the pirate-troubled Sunda Strait, between Java and Sumatra.

As they felt their way into the Gaspar Straits, they "kept the little island to west'd of Middle Isl. just open on the starboard bow."

Sterling recorded their arrival the next day:

> July 21; At 1:30pm saw the land & a ship to leeward standing to the North. At 8pm was up with Little Ladrone. At 10 pass'd Potok or Passage Island At 10:30 took a pilot. Gave him $8 to take us to Macao Roads & $7 for the use of his boat to bring off a river pilot to us. At 11:30 came too in Macao Roads in 5 $\frac{1}{2}$ fths water. The supercargo went ashore for a River Pilot. 2 English ships came in with us in the night.

At 10am another English ship came in & the American ship *Phoenix* 114 days from Philadelphia.

Nimrod took a pilot up the Pearl (or Chu Kiang) River to Whampoa Reach, where 22 other American ships lay at anchor. Sterling remained at Whampoa for four months, and in November witnessed the great fire of Canton. Ship's stores purchased for the homeward trip included a sow, 12 pigs, 24 geese, 36 capons, and 72 fowls, plus yams, potatoes, onions, oranges, pickles, plantain, eggs, paddy (unmilled rice), flour, bran, pumpkins, ground nuts, fine rice, common rice, molasses, curry powder, salt, pepper, and garlic.

On Monday November 25 at 4:00 a.m. they warped down a short distance, then, catching a breeze, sailed down past the other ships. On Tuesday the pilot went ashore to register the ship's papers, then at 7:00 a.m. they passed Tiger Island.

Helped by a southerly current and in company with other ships, *Nimrod* beat down the China Sea past Sumatra and into Lampoon Bay (now Telak Lampung). On December 14, "At meridian, the peak on Crockatoa bore SE by S" and on December 17, 21 days out, they were in the Indian Ocean.

On January 20, 1823 the ship passed about 100 miles south of Cape Agulhas, the southern tip of Africa, and on the 27th Captain Sterling encountered trouble: "Turn'd the second mate out of the cabin for trafficking with the men & selling the cook his pistols. Took the pistols from the cook." That seemed to end the matter.

On March 4 *Nimrod* passed Lobos Island into Montevideo. A chronometer check at Lobos showed longitude was off by 5 miles—the clock was nearly 20 seconds slow. Proceeding with a pilot up the Plate River to Buenos Aires, they commenced loading hides.

Hides were a major South American export. In the undeveloped Argentine, wild cattle roamed the pampas, available for the taking, yielding hides, tallow, horns, bone ash, and smoked beef. Sterling wrote on Tuesday June 3:

> With 15,274 hides, 400 bags of sugar, and 133 lbs. card. in the hold, got clear of the shore and ready for sea.
>
> July 25th. 50 days out. At daylight made the Highlands. At 10 took a pilot. At 3pm came to anchor at Quarantine and lay til our cargo was discharged, with 15,000 evil smelling hides, they unloaded in the stream. Then got permission to take the ship to town. The *Nimrod* has been from the N York docks 17 mos and 12 days.

On December 22, 1823, 27-year-old John Sterling began his 21st voyage, as master of the 642-ton ship *Splendid*, which was just completed and was one of the largest merchant ships afloat. Built by Isaac Webb & Co. in New York and owned by Charles Hall, she was chartered by Smith & Nicoll—Francis Holland Nicoll, from Stratford. *Splendid* measured 136.6 feet on deck. Sterling's journal continues:

> Ship *Splendid*, from N York towards New Orleans.
> Mon Dec 22 1823 at 30'pm got underway. At 3.45 discharged pilot.
> When about half way from the Hook to the floating light took an obs.
> for the chr. Made the long. 74.4 West. Set the fore top, M and lower
> steering sails.

The following day the wind increased to strong gales. The crew spent much time aloft, tending sails in the cold and stormy seas:

> At 8 close reefed the topsails . . . took in the gib & mainsails . . . Double
> reefed the foresail & took in the miz topsail . . . set the mainsail single
> reefed . . . set the gib . . . at M split the gib took it in.
> Wed Dec 24 . . . At 10am took in the main topsail all hands with the
> mates on the yard now furling it. Hous'd the miz top gal mast. A sea
> struck our larboard quarter boat and stove a hole in her.

In haste to get to sea, *Splendid's* rigging had been set up too slack. Now gales, squalls, and choppy seas brought pitching and rolling motions that further stretched the wet hempen shrouds and threatened to snap the spars. On Christmas day Sterling recorded:

> Kept the ship up to the west'd to head the sea, our rigging being very
> slack. At daylight called all hands & commenced setting up the lower
> rigging & back stays. Carried away the strop of the lower deadeye, main
> swifter. Ends calm with a heavy swell.

By New Years Day of 1824 *Splendid* had rounded Grand Caycos (Caicos) Island, and headed west past the north coast of Cuba. On January 8 the ship was at a mouth of the Mississippi, back on civil time, and facing new problems with the elements:

> Midnight haul'd by the wind & tack'd every 2 hours till daylight. At 11:30
> being nearly over the bar the wind died away & the ship grounded. Got
> out the kedge & stream anchor to heave off. Could not start her, the tide
> falling. Furl'd all our sails & lay waiting for the tide. Several sail passed us
> bound up. Got out our longboat in order to carry off our best bower.

Next morning the ship hove off on a rising tide and sailed upriver to the Balize, but had to pay a pilot $15 to retrieve the stream anchor. There they swapped the bar pilot for a river pilot (another $35) and on the 10th reached Poverty Point under sail, then when the wind died, warped up to Morgan Plantation. When the steam tug *Port Boy* came down the river, Sterling grudgingly paid Captain Badger $90 for a tow up to town, and $10 more to bring him the recovered stream anchor and cable.

John Sterling went to sea as an eager boy in 1810 and came ashore as a tired 39-year-old in 1835. Unlike his fiery brother-in-law Robert Waterman, Sterling was a slight man of even temperament. A cautious, safety conscious captain, he satisfied the owners of his ships for more than 25 years.

At sunset on Sunday the 11th, *Splendid* came to anchor abreast of downtown New Orleans in 20 fathoms, 21 days from New York, and on Monday hauled into a berth alongside the *Herald* from New York. They discharged their freight, and on the 28th hired a steamboat to tow them up to the Point, where they waited two months for a cargo. The price of cotton had bottomed out in Europe, and it would be difficult to make a profit.

Finally on April 18 *Port Boy* towed *Splendid* down to the loading docks, and on May 21 the hold was full, with 1,500 pressed bales and 552 unpressed. Crewmen to replace two deserters were nowhere to be found, but by giving the landlords $3 per head and offering wages of $12 per month, men were rounded up. The next problem was to cross the bar at the Mississippi's mouth and get to sea.

The ship drew 14 feet forward, 15 aft. On June 2, by hanging the anchor between two boats and carrying it out to the channel, *Splendid* was slowly worked out to the stream, where she lay aground across the current. When the tide rose 2 feet in two hours, the ship swung around. Next day, with a tidal rise of only 6 inches, she would not budge. Other ships trapped at the bar were the *Bengal*, drawing 15 feet, 3 inches; *Comet*, 15 feet, 2 inches; *Marathon* and *William Nelson* bound for Liverpool; and *Honan* and *Hamilton* for New York.

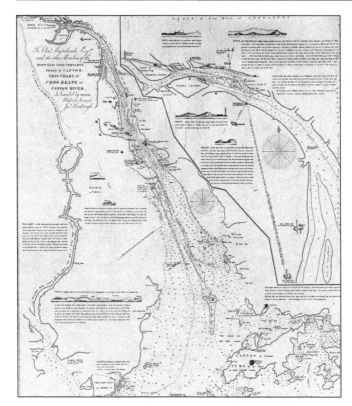

Sterling's chart of the Pearl or Chu Kiang River shows landmarks along the 50-mile stretch to Canton. Chinese pilots were brought aboard for the trip upriver to Whampoa Reach.

Over the next few days, with the water the lowest it had been for six months, the ship moved a couple of ship lengths, and on the 9th cleared the bar. With water casks filled and boats stowed, *Splendid* set out toward Havre de Grace on June 10.

Splendid was in mid Atlantic when Sterling wrote, "Fresh breezes and cold. Think there must be ice to the north of us. Wind very flawy and unsteady, weather quite cold, some flakes of snow."

On the 19th *Splendid* reached the outer roads of Le Havre, and at the spring tides on the 25th the dockmaster sent three boats to warp the ship into the dock. Sterling wrote: "Tuesday, discharged 500 bales. Wednesday, not permitted to work, the Duchess of Berry being in town. Thursday, discharged 500 bales, Friday . . . 304, Saturday . . . 204, Monday . . . 350, Tuesday the remainder."

After taking on ballast, *Splendid* headed for Cowes on the Isle of Wight, and on August 13 anchored in St. Helen's Roads. On Sunday, "Received on board our arms and canvas." Underway for Canton on August 19, they passed Palma on September 3, and on September 10, "it fell calm. We are extremely unfortunate in losing the trade winds so far north."

On September 24, 1824, the day the little sidewheeler *General LaFayette* was paying Stratford its first-ever steamboat visit, Sterling was struggling to cross the equator, complaining, "One of the miseries of human life is to be becalmed when there is a high sea up." On October 11 he knew he was rounding Africa when he ". . . saw many small grey gulls some albatrosses & Cape pigeons."

Ninety days out of Cowes, across the Indian Ocean in strong squalls and baffling winds, Sandalwood Island appeared, and soon they were struggling through Sunda Strait. "Dec. 2. At daylight saw Pantas Island," and, "Dec. 5. At 2am came up with and spoke the *Benjamin Rush* of & from Philadelphia 116 days out."

Past the Puelo Capes east of Singapore, past Kekit Island, Lawn Islands, Pulo Pisang, and near St. David's Islands on December 23, "At 11am had several canoes alongside who brot off coconuts, the only thing that grows on the island. Knives was al they valu'd in exchange for them," and, "Fri. 24. Light air. The canoes kept alongside till nearly night. Two of the natives decided to stay with us. We had to drive them into their boats."

On New Years Day of 1825, slatting in the South China Sea, "134th day out. Faint baffling breezes with a heavy swell from the north'd. O misery!" On the 11th:

> Many fishing boats in sight. At 2pm took a fish pilot. Gave him $30 to take us to Lintin and bring on board the Macao pilot. At 3pm was boarded by the compradore [provision supplier] boats. At 2am left the ship to go for a river pilot. The ship went under Lintin and anchor'd. Wednesday waiting for the pilot: agreeable to custom it is always necessary to wait 24 hours for them before being able to get the necessary chop [papers] for passing up the river.

With pilot aboard, *Splendid* finally reached Whampoa Reach on Sunday, and on Monday morning commenced discharging ballast: "Tuesday January 25th commenced taking in our cargo not being able to get through the necessary forms at the Hoppoo [customs officer] or Custom House any earlier. Saturday Feb. 5. Took in our chow chow chop [supplies] and got ready for sea."

On February 6 *Splendid* departed for New York, anchoring in the Pearl on every flood tide and drifting down on the ebb. On the 10th they discharged the pilot off Macao and headed down the China Sea, driven by a north-northeast wind in thick weather. Twelve days out, the ship passed Discovery Rock in the Gaspar Straits, and spoke the English brig *Corsair*. Next day they saw Sumatra, spoke the *Rita* from Manila, sighted the Brothers, and reached the entrance to Sunda Strait. "There being no prospect of being able to get through the straits, came too with small bower. The boats went on shore and fill'd 3 casks of water." Sterling's 1819 chart says, "Mew Bay, the watering place on Java, is convenient in the Easterly Monsoon. The water is excellent, falling from the Rock in a Cascade, and may be filled with a hose into the Boats." The following day more casks were filled, and turtles purchased for food from friendly natives. Then, "We drifted close under the Peak on Crockatoa within one quarter mile of the shore."

Through the Indian Ocean again, *Splendid* crossed the prime meridian south of Africa, and on Sunday May 29 reached New York. Sterling's final comments on his 21st voyage were:

Thanks God—here ends a long tedious voyage of 7 months. Many & various are the vexations difficulties and troubles attendant on so long a voyage. One experiences every difficulty in navigation. He has all the troubles that a variety of ____ scoundrels that generally compose a ships crew can give him and is continually vexed with calms, squalls, & contrary winds. It is not very strange a shipmaster should be petulant in his temper. . .

Here the tirade became indecipherable. John Sterling was the opposite of his brother-in-law Robert Waterman of Fairfield: Waterman, tall and slender with a cold, hard face, was a driver. Although he had served under Sterling on the *Nimrod* and the *Splendid*, none of Sterling's temperament had rubbed off. He was known as "Killer" after he bashed in the skulls of two mutinous crewmen, but he made record-smashing voyages on his Canton trips. Sterling, on the other hand, was a small, mild mannered man, averse to risk and content with the normal hazards of the sea, who made good but not sensational passages, with profit to his owners.

Tired and discouraged, Sterling spent the summer of 1825 ashore, then in October set to sea again, commanding *Splendid* on her second journey to Canton. The 151-day voyage began on October 17 with a fine breeze. At 1:30 p.m. they discharged the pilot, and at 5:30 p.m. set the steering sails. Sterling complained that the ship was trimmed too much down by the stern and did not sail well. Next day they entered the Gulf Stream at about 4:00 p.m., and rode to a confused sea all night, taking water on deck and leaking badly due to movement of slack rigging and working of the waterway seam:

> Fri Oct 21 The ship has made more water than she did all the last voyage. She works very much in her waterway seam. . . . Some of our cargo will be damaged. I feel determined never to come to sea again so unprepared to meet bad weather. Our rigging should have been set up in port & the ship properly trimmed.
>
> Oct 22 A high swell. All hands employ'd in trimming ship & setting up the rigging.
>
> Oct 28 The ship does not sail as well as she has done, by 1 knot/hour.

The captain complained that with trade winds from the southeast, "we are extremely unfortunate & shall never be able to cross the line." All hands continued to tighten the rigging. On November 19, *Splendid* crossed the equator. On the 21st they opened the main hatches and threw overboard about 11 tons of ballast. The entry on the 22nd says, "The ship works and leaks considerable through the waterway seams & through the bind on the larboard side. Found some of the tin damaged, moved it to a dry place."

Just before Christmas *Splendid* passed into the Indian Ocean about 250 nautical miles south of Capetown. *Splendid* found no calms here. The January 12, 1826 entry reads:

In 1810 blank journals were issued by the New York Nautical Institution and Ship Masters' society to be filled out by members. In this copy of Sterling's from his 20th voyage, the title page portrays a typical ship of the period, probably similar to Aristomenes.

R. Tyrell, Printer.

The wind blowing a gale. The sea very high and bothered, but very little abaft the beam. The ship rolling very deep. At times was obliged to keep off on account of the heavy seas. At 8am the ship made several extreme heavy rolls. The load & every thing between decks fetched away & before we could get things secur'd several boxes of olives was stove & one keg of specie although all were well pin'd. Ends the wind blowing in heavy squalls the sea very high.

Friday Jan 13 The wind blowing in heavy squalls The sea very high & in gales the ship leaking very much through her waterway seams & rolling extremely hard. At 6am set two Mtop steering sails At 9am split the starboard one. At 10 in attempting to set, when through the carelessness of the 2d mate tore it all to pieces Ends a strong breeze Set the lower S sails.

On February 3, 110 days from New York, "At 11pm smel't the land but could not see it. At daylight saw Sandlewood [Island]." They had reached Sunda Strait. The next several days were spent shifting sails constantly against winds from every point of the compass. Sterling vowed that he would never make another voyage to Canton.

On February 17 they saw a ship nearby, and received her boat aboard. She was a whaler, *Coquette* of London, 28 months at sea:

Had 2700 bbls oil She was commanded by Capt Spiers Spencer who was mate til her commander was murdered by the Spaniards on the Island of Guam. 14 months since he reports having spoke the ship *Fanny* of Philadelphia. On the 30 June 140 days out from Gibraltar bound to Canton.

A week later, on the 24th, his journal reports:

At 11 by the reflection of the moon saw a white streak on the water ahead of us. Immediately put the helm a lee. The wind falling nearly calm & a strong eddy current taking us on the bow, she would not come around but struck on a shoal of coral rocks. Hove all aback & trim'd the lead & tin between decks & in the hold aft. When she back'd off she hung 30 degrees. There was not the least swell nor any appearance of breakers. While on we had 20 fths water in the M chains and 12 feet where her forefoot was, about 5 feet of which touched the rocks. We could very plainly see the extent of the shoal. We struck on its middle. It appear'd a 1/2 mile long N & S and about 200 feet wide under our bowsprit There were some rocks about 4 feet above water when the ship swung off. I steer'd West, SSW & SE 3/4 of an hour & run about 4 miles. When I haul'd up E & stood on, we saw the shoal in sufficient time to have tack'd, but unfortunately she was prevented from coming around by the strong eddy current which set South past the Shoal 2 knots. She however lost her way before striking, grounded very lightly making scarcely a jar & she went off so easy it could only be perceiv'd by the head. It is a very dangerous shoal and if it is a part of the Helens it must be a detach'd body of rocks . . . I am confident that the shoal we struck on has never before been discover'd or its latitude not correctly given.

On March 16, 151 days out, *Splendid* took a pilot from the compradore boat at Lintin anchorage and went up to Boca Tigris. Next day, river pilot aboard, they continued up the Pearl to Whampoa.

It took a month to unload, take on a return cargo, and head downriver to Macao Roads. On Sunday, April 23, 1826, they entered the China Sea. A week later, "Calm. At 2pm had a light breeze from the North'd which continued throughout the day, with a high swell from SW the sails slapping & thrashing very much & the ship going ahead very little. 5 men sick. 'As hot as the devil.' " By mid May, they were slatting through the Gaspar Straits in company with several other ships:

16 May Light baffling breezes At 10am was boarded by Capt. Giles of ship *Augusta* 30 days out fm Manila bound to Batavia. Also saw the ship *Citizen* to leeward. The *Ben Rush* & *T. Scattergood* just in sight bearing WSW. At M Gap Rock bore SW by S.

17 May At 10am let go the kedge. Boarded the ships *Citizen* & *Augusta* Capt. Keene.

18 May Augusta,, *B. Rush*, & *T. Scattergood* & *Citizen* near us, also 4 proas in sight.

On the night of the 26th, they were still beating through the Gaspar Straits with *Citizen* ahead and *Augusta* astern. On the 29th, *Splendid* drifted along in water too deep to use the bower anchor, to within a mile of the "storm rock," then towed off with the ship's boats. She had drifted very near to a reef which some of the company's ships had previously struck.

Splendid stood over towards Java, then dropped anchor in 12 fathoms in Anjier Roads, in company with *Citizen*. Underway next day, "The wind very light. Crockatoa NE by E. Java Head in sight over Prince [now Pana-itan] Island. The *Citizen* ahead of us." They were leaving the Great Channel, with Java to the south and Sumatra to the north.

After a month in the Indian Ocean, on June 30 the ship was 20 miles off the coast of Africa, "rolling and tumbling so much we were in great danger of losing her masts." A strong gale with heavy squalls came on, and "got into a most outrageous sea, the ship rolling her plank shears under and plunging her bowsprit & gib boom in." Then Cape Delgado came into sight. Sterling was learning to use less southing when rounding Africa.

On July 12, still not past Good Hope but in clear weather, "the wind came on to blow in a most violent squall. We split the fore & main top sails & fore sails. Obliged to keep off before the wind to furl them. At 10 a heavy sea struck our head & started the figure some inches. Carried away the head rail & boards, the starboard side. Later part a heavier gale than we have yet had, the ship lying too under bare poles." On the 13th, "The sea flying over, the ship gulled abundantly . . . the water rolling across our decks filling the roundhouse & forecastle two most uncomfortable places . . . had our deck binnacle & some of our waist boards washed away."

When the storm subsided and *Splendid* was in the Atlantic with light trade winds the crew opened the forehatch and moved 300 boxes of tea aft to the 'tween decks, to trim the ship by the stern. They found several boxes of tea soaked, from leaks caused by the working of the foremast.

In the near calm of the north Atlantic, "painting ship" and "light winds" appear in the journal each day. Finally on September 1, "finished painting ship outside." On September 8 at 10:00 a.m., "it came to blow a hurricane in squalls which took away our miz. top mast & blow'd away the fore topsail. Kept off before the wind." On the 9th:

> The wind blowing a hurricane all hands employed getting in the wreck of the miz. top mast. Obliged to keep the ship before the wind to save the spars. The sea very high & singular, boarding her waist boards on each side. It swept away our starboard quarter boat & waist boards

on each side, a great deal of water came through the cabin windows though the dead lights were well hove in. Also much water came in through the rudder port. At 4am a little more moderate, bro't the ship too under bare poles. About 5am two heavy seas struck us on the larboard quarter, took off many of our waist boards & filled the cabin on deck nearly full of water At 10am set the foresail reef'd & at M set the close reef'd M topsail.

On September 12, 142 days out and in a thick fog, sounding revealed 45 fathoms and oozy mud. On the 13th, "Light air of wind and very foggy. We are most cursedly unfortunate." On September 14, 1826 *Splendid* arrived in New York, 144 days en route, completing Sterling's 22nd voyage.

Tired of the hard work and tension of a life at sea, John Sterling decided to try his hand at life ashore. He was now 30 years old and unmarried. He knew the value the Chinese placed on ginseng, and knew that a variety grew wild in the northern United States. After staying home all winter, he set out in May for New York state and Vermont to locate the medicinal root, but returned empty handed in November.

After another winter at home, Sterling took the ship *Sabina* out to Manila in 1828. On April 23 that year, Stratford Captain George Dowdall arrived in New York from Canton aboard *Ajax*, and they must have compared notes. When Sterling left port aboard *Sabina* on May 23, his first entry read:

> Let them go to sea who like it better than I do. A berth in the back woods of Vermont is preferable. May fortune so smile on the writer of this journal as to enable him to remain at home when he gets there. [Sterling's wish was not granted, as he was to make another voyage.]

An accomplished linguist, Sterling occasionally lapsed into Spanish. On "Viernes, 6 de Junio," his journal read:

> Todavia dura el viento al sud. El dios de los vientos ha determina no que la *Sabina* no haia una pasage corte y todos los diablos estace opanidas a nosetros, que pedemos iacer? [The wind continues from the south. The gods of the winds have determined that *Sabina* will not have an easy passage. All the devils are against us. What can we do?]

Later, sailing southward through mostly calm seas, he fussed:

> One half of this day calm. I had a bit of fever & ague have not been well since I left Nyork.
> Tues 15 July. Morning a ship in sight in the east. By her signal knew her to be the *Beaver*. This is the second time the *Beaver* has come up with us while we were becalmed.

Before the opium wars, the only open anchorage in China was Whampoa Reach, 40 miles up the Pearl River, and 10 miles below Canton. From here sampans took cargo to the Hongs at Canton.

Sterling continued to fret each time the *Beaver* ghosted past *Sabina*. Nearly across the calms of the Indian Ocean on August 26, the 96th day out, he wrote, "A very light breeze from the north'd all this day all sail set. That fickle bitch Dame Fortune has smil'd & frown'd on us alternately since we left but now seems determined that we shall have a long passage. She may go to the devil!"

On September 3 the lookout sighted Christmas Island 23 miles off, and on the 4th Java Head bore north-northwest. On the 5th *Sabina* hauled in for Anjier, but chose to sail past. "At daylight was boarded by the Anger boats, got a supply of chickens, plantains, pine apples, coconuts, monkeys, and Java sparrows. At Meridian enter'd the Java Sea."

Arriving at the Gaspar Straits on September 8, the captain worried that he would run into shoals: "At 5 pm came to anchor with the stream in 17 fths thinking it not prudent to run through the strait in the night. . . . At 9am . . . had soundings from 9 to 11 fths . . . in Horseburgh's Chart no such soundings are given, neither have I ever had such shoal soundings in passing the straits three times before this." By the 20th, heading across the South China Sea on his first trip to Manila, Sterling grew anxious:

> Improve your time: time is money &c. There is at least half a dozen old maxims as it regards improving time, but I cannot conceive how they

These Stratford citizens in 1859 were all connected with the sea. Standing are Captain Pulaski Benjamin, General Loomis, Captain Thomas Austin, geographer Jesse Olney, merchants Henry Plant and T.B. Fairchild. Seated are Admiral Joshua Sands, William Benjamin, Captain John Sterling and his son John, mill owner Edwards Johnson, and James Olney, plus three children.

can at all times be followed in the China Sea with a headwind and the current. Time is certainly lost or . . . a ship will make lee way and lee way is a bad way of improving time.

Sun 21 Sept . . . but a headwind is not the only disagreeable thing I have to contend with. My Spanish passenger continually muttering at his face. This morning he got sulky & would eat no breakfast. I despise him but endeavor not to notice his discontents for the sake of quietness on board; my mates at times too lazy to do anything but eat. They hang about the deck like a wet swab taking every opportunity to sleep in their watch when I am below.

Monday 22nd of September. I have almost resolved never to attempt making another voyage to the eastern world. The vexations and difficulties of so long a navigation are not balanced by the small compensation one receives; with a little exertion I could certainly get a hiring on shore and am quite sure of never being able to make a fortune in the China Sea.

All melancholy disappeared when the Phillipines appeared, and at 10:00 p.m. on the 26th *Sabina* dropped anchor at Corregidor. Next day the ship went in to Manila bar, where government officials came aboard, after which the ship put into port 128 days from New York.

Sabina left again for New York on Thursday December 4, 1828: "A light air of wind from south'd. At 4 pm got underway and stood out for the Corregidor. At 11 pass'd the Haycock & steer'd our course for Sapata. Latter part a heavy swell from the north'd & increasing."

With the China Sea, Gaspar Straits, Java Sea, and Sunda Strait behind her, *Sabina* enjoyed a fresh breeze and fine weather in the Indian Ocean on Christmas day. "This being Christmas, had a roast goose, pumpkin pize & a very good salad of the mustard plant rais'd on board, with a bottle of champaigne for dinner." Next day the captain planted more mustard seed and lettuce in boxes of earth. By now the ship was passing the Cocos Islands. On the 30th the journal reported, "My musk cat jump'd overboard. Lower'd the boat but could not save her."

Then in the western Indian Ocean on January 17:

> A moderate breeze. An hermaphrodite brig in sight standing to the S & E At 1 pm she fired 2 guns hoisted the French flag & kept away for us. hove too & speak him, when he got within about 3 miles of us he haul'd again on a wind & stood to the south'd & east'd. He had many men on board. His main rigging & foretop were full while he was standing for us. I at first suppos'd he was in distress but his conduct made me think he might be a pirate. Ends a light breeze.

Sixty-five days out from Manila, Sterling passed Good Hope. He saw the Cape as he passed the English ship *Easter*, and bore northwest into the Atlantic. On Wednesday, March 4, Sterling wrote, "Who is President this day? Jackson or Adams? Quien sabe?" At that very moment, some 3,200 miles from *Sabina's* position near the Brazil Rocks in mid–South Atlantic, Andrew Jackson was being sworn in. A month later, on April 6:

> At 4pm saw the land above Jersey shore. At sunset haul'd to west'd. Wore & stood to north. At 8am took a pilot & at 6pm civil time came to anchor at the Quarantine ground. Tuesday mornng haul'd into the wharf foot of Rector St. and breakfasted on shore.

On May 17, 1829 Captain Sterling took *Sabina* on a 323-day round trip to Manila and Canton. The ship reached Manila on September 4, 110 days en route. She sailed from there to Canton on October 9, arriving at Whampoa on the 23rd, to find Canton overwhelmed by a ravaging plague. On the 27th, Sterling's Stratford neighbor Edward Nicoll, mate of the ship *Ajax*, died of the plague, and on November 1 *Ajax* Captain George Dowdall succumbed. Both were interred at Canton. Sterling sailed for New York with the sad news, leaving Whampoa on Christmas day in 1829 and reaching Rector Street on April 5, 1830.

With a one-month turnaround, *Sabina* sailed again on May 12, for Liverpool, Manila, and New York. It was Sterling's 25th trip. Sailing down the Atlantic from Liverpool, in the southeast trades with all sail set *Sabina* clocked daily runs of 182, 186, 179, and 180 miles, and crossed the equator on July 23. Then daily runs decreased to 113, 70, 116, and 67 miles. On August 4 Sterling reported "Anson Hubbell, who left Liverpool sick, died this day at 9:31 am. His disease was without doubt consumption. Five days before his death he was delerious & continu'd so while he lived." On the next day, "at 8pm committed the body of Anson E. Hubbell to the deep."

Miserably wet from bad weather in the Indian Ocean, Sterling wrote:

> My mate decidedly hypocondriac, his complaints of pains in the breast mostly imaginary, he declares he has the consumption, that he is losing flesh; today he does not spit enough, the other day he spit too much, in the morning he says he ought to feel better, in the evening worse, because Doct. Thomas says so. Last night he had a sweat, which is also a bad sign with him, he has a good appetite but does not eat much, to me he does not appear to suffer in the least from pain, though without doubt he may feel some slight pains in his breast & side which his fears magnify into something serious; he feels confident he has the consumption. I feel confident he will have what is worse unless he will exert himself to shake the disease out of his head.

On September 10, "at M the fog clearing off saw Amsterdam [Island]." Daily runs now measured 212, 158, and 216 nautical miles. Sterling was pleased at the contrast between this and previous trips. On September 26 he wrote, "*Sabina's* passage through the Straits of Sunda is quite remarkable, having enter'd them in the evening & passing quite through before daylight." On September 29, "At 2 pm clear of Gaspar Straits. Never came through more pleasantly."

At sunset on October 13 *Sabina* passed the Haycock, was boarded by the Spanish officials, then lay to the kedge next day with Manila and Cavite in sight. At 4:00 p.m. they beat up to the anchorage.

On December 29, 1830 *Sabina* left Manila for New York. In a fresh monsoon, Sterling discovered the ship leaking badly through the stem, and had to keep one pump constantly at work to outpace the leak. Inspection in smooth seas showed the leak above the waterline and after several days they plugged and copper sheathed the bobstay hole, where the stem had rotted.

On January 8 they entered Gaspar Straits again, and on the 13th were past Crockatoa (Krakatoa) and Prince's Island (Pana-itan) and entering open ocean. Fine trade winds enabled *Sabina* to clock close to 200 nautical miles a day. Approaching the southern tip of Africa, Sterling wrote, "13 Feb. 47th day out. The ship plunging deep, leaking very much. A long spell at the pumps every half hour."

Rounding the Cape, *Sabina* recorded gradually decreasing distances, of 182, 161, 152, 177, 168, 147, 125, and 84 miles per day—"a bad day's work" wrote Sterling—as she approached the equator. But once in the North Atlantic, the distances increased again as springtime northeast trades persisted. On March 25, "A fine trade wind from ENE all this day. At 9am saw Sargasso weed for the first time."

Again the winds lightened, and rain squalls erupted. On April 6 they spoke the brig *Duke of Clarence*, bound from Santiago, Cuba, toward Liverpool, and "learnt that France & England had renewed kings since we left Liverpool." Then, "very high sea . . . ship plunging deep and leaking, two spells every half hour." On April 11, "Pas'd the inner edge of the Gulph. At 4 had a very heavy squall with sharp lightning & much rain."

On April 14, 1831 *Sabina* reached New York and went to the yard to have her stem repaired. John Sterling spent nearly a year at home. On January 18, 1832 he married 24-year-old Mary Judson. In March he took passage on the ship *Napoleon* (first class, $140) to Liverpool, to take command of the ship *Superior*, bound for Canton, and in May he was once more at sea. *Superior* was a 576-ton ship, measuring 126 feet, built by Isaac Webb in 1822. Aboard *Superior*, in the Mersey at Liverpool, he wrote:

> Thursday May 10th [1832] civil time—at 7am hove up our anchor with two small steamboats alongside to tow us out. At M discharg'd the pilot and steamboats, made sail.
>
> Friday May 11th sea account. Tack'd ship often beating down towards Holy Head, at 6am close in with Point Linas tack'd off Wind N. At Meridian pass'd the Head. Kept off for the Tuskar [light].

It took 58 days to reach Good Hope. A few days later, with a wind that "blew very flawy" and the ship rolling and plunging, the entry reads, "A great many birds around us most of them small Peterals & Cape Pigeons very few albatross & boobies." On August 2, Christmas Island bore east about 20 miles away. Next day at noon they were 3 miles from Friar's Rock at Java Head. Heading up Sunda Strait, on August 4, "At 8pm pas'd Fourth Point At 9 saw two ships at anchor off Anger [Anjier]. At 9 came too with the stream. Calm all night. Morning went on shore. At 10am the company ship *Canning* anchored."

On Sunday the 5th *Superior* was underway at 5:00 a.m. On Tuesday Bangka Island lay ahead, and two company ships followed *Superior* into Gaspar Straits. On August 16, the 98th day out, they paid $10 for an outside pilot ("The compradore boat would not go in with us") and at 9:00 a.m. they sent Henry Wilson Hubbell ashore to obtain a river pilot, while the ship sailed past Lintin to anchor at Macao Roads.

On December 8, Sterling hoisted anchor with the help of a boat crew from the sloop-of-war USS *Peacock*. With moderate breezes, *Superior* headed down the China Sea. On December 22, with Bangka Island in sight, they came to anchor with *London* and another company ship. Christmas day of 1832 was spent beating down toward Sunda Strait. The next day, "our ill luck continues. At 4pm anchor'd off the Sisters in 21 fth. water, the stupid fellow in the chains singing out 'by the deep nine.'"

Approaching Anjier, they bought a turtle and some plantains from a canoe, and then the boat from Anjier sold Sterling 200 delicious mangusteens, and handed him a pack of mail for home from Forestier & Co. Tacking back and forth between Stroom Rock and Zuctphen Islands, *Superior* finally cleared the channel, and on the 30th Java Head came in sight over Prince's Island [Panaitan]. On December 31, "after 21 days of light winds and calms we are clear of the China Sea."

Sterling's competitiveness showed up when he had completed his run across the Indian Ocean and passed Good Hope.

> 13 Feb. The ship about 5 miles ahead the *Martha* which we pass'd 30 days since. We outsail her very much, she must have been more favour'd with winds than we have been.
>
> 14 Feb. Spoke the *Martha*. She reports having spoken the *Walter* on the 6th which left Lintin on the 14th Dec., 7 days after us. She is now probably ahead having pas'd the Cape in company with the *Martha* the day before we did. How very unfortunate I am this passage, in being so beaten. We outsail *Martha* but by ill luck we cannot get ahead of her.

As the end of the voyage approached they sent the royal yards down, and in heavy squalls single reefed the main topsail and double reefed the fore and mizzen. On Saturday April 6, 1833 they passed Highland Light and took a pilot. The newsboat boarded them at 4:00 a.m. and at 6:00 p.m. *Superior* was alongside the wharf, 120 days from Lintin. *Superior* went on to a long career, but Sterling spent a year at home with his bride Mary.

John Sterling's last command was the elegant little ship *York*. At 433 tons, she was half the size of *Splendid*, built in New York by William Crockett and operated by Fish & Grinnell as a luxurious two-deck, three-mast Transatlantic packet. York was 118 feet in length, copper fastened and sheathed. On her stern were carved gilt symbols of the City of New York, two female figures, and a sheaf of wheat. The roundhouse was carpeted, with scenes of America painted on the walls. Descending a handsome stairway with mahogany handrails, the passenger saw a 16- by 40-foot paneled cabin, with redwood pillars and paneled doors to 20 staterooms. It had a mahogany table, mahogany sideboard, and a small library of leather-bound books. The mirrored ladies' cabin beyond contained a large crimson sofa on one side and a piano on the other. The 41 steerage passengers subsisted with little more than 6 feet of headroom and a caulked overhead to keep them dry. Six times a year, on the eighth of alternate months, *York* sailed for England, to London, Cowes, or Liverpool, as a Swallowtail Line packet.

In 1834 Fish & Grinnell replaced *York* with larger ships and put her in the China trade under Captain Sterling. His first journal entry reads:

> Ship *York*, from New York towards Liverpool bound from thence to Canton.
> Feb. 16, 1834. At 10am left the wharf, tow'd by the steamboat *Rufus King*—took the letter bags, as the packet of the 18th, the Old Line ship to sail this day, not having arrived."

Next day they set off in company with the ship *Charles Carroll*. On March 24 Tuskar Light was sighted, and soon afterward *York* was at Prince's Dock in Liverpool. By April 15 a new cargo was aboard and *York* stood down the Mersey with a fresh breeze.

Sterling's journal confirms that disease was ever present on shipboard. Eight days out, reaching down St. George's Channel:

> My 2nd mate has been sick since Wednesday his face & body is full of pustules & we don't know whether he has the small pock or measles.
> 22 April. The 2nd mate no better. His disease has now the appearance of being the small pock.
> 23 April. 2d mate no better, two other men taken sick besides one man been sick with the venereal ever since leaving port.
> 24 April. Two of the men turn'd to this morning.

It wasn't until May 22 that *York* finally crossed the line into the southern hemisphere. Sterling's entries read, "Another man sick with the small pox. This is the fourth case of it since leaving Lpool. All except the 2d mate had it very lightly. One was only off duty two days the other is not yet well his ancle being yet swell'd. We are very fortunate in having it so mild."

On June 4, as *York* passed the Cape of Good Hope Sterling wrote, "Cape pigeons seen for the first time." On July 29 Java Head appeared, and in calm seas the ship rode the current into the straits. Next day Sterling reported passing the ship *Splendid* of Philadelphia, but it is unknown if this was his old ship or another. Tacking back and forth, *York* came within three shiplengths of the beach, so Sterling decided to put in to Anjier for the night. Then, battling the current in company with a Dutch man-o-war, Sterling reported that he "never had a more tedious time in the Straits of Sunda." In contrast, on August 3 he wrote, "Have had a very pleasant time through the Straits of Gaspar." On August 14, the 122nd day out from Liverpool, *York* sighted Great Ladrone, picked up an outside pilot, and came to with the small bower in the Cap Sing passage at Macao.

On the 27th, having taken aboard 2,258 pigs of lead from the ship *Logan*, and with pilot aboard, *York* started up the Pearl to Whampoa against a strong current. At sunset they came to anchor off Chuen Pee, and put the pilot ashore for the

Foreign merchants were restricted by the Chinese to a single district at Canton, where they built their hongs, or warehouses and offices. Here all business was conducted.

required pass. Getting underway at sunrise, they were moored at Whampoa off the Junk River by sunset.

By September 4 the hold was empty except for woolens. On the 5th Sterling went in to Canton to confer, all communications between there and Whampoa having been cut due to disputes between the Chinese and the British (which culminated in the opium wars and the founding of the British colony of Hong Kong). It was November 18 before the last of the cargo was unloaded, after which they built three charcoal fires in the hold to kill the rats, about 20 altogether. A Chinese painter was then hired to paint the ship inside and out, Sterling to provide the gold leaf.

By January 7, 1835 *York* was underway once again: "At M discharg'd the pilot a few miles south of Lintin. . . . a strong breeze the sea getting up. At 5am carried away fore top steering sail boom. The ship leaking badly, pump her every hour."

Next day a hard gale with squalls sprang up, and pumping continued at the same pace. Squalls and rain continued all down the South China Sea and through the straits, until the lookout reported, "Java Head in sight over Prince's Island." As *York* entered the Indian Ocean once again, she exchanged signals with Sterling's old ship *Sabina*, now skippered by McEwen, who was undoubtedly trying to beat his own 1834 record of 90 days from Canton to New York.

York fought light westerlies together with *Adelaide* and *Sabina*. On the 23rd Sterling recorded "*Sabina* in sight," and on Sunday the 24th, "The *Sabina* about 6 miles NE of us." On Monday, "The Sabina coming up with us." Then, "Morning. a ship in sight ahead. Suppose it the *Sabina*." Sterling must have hoped that his small ship might outsail his old command.

When leakage appeared at the stem, men were put to work caulking at the starboard bow. *Sabina* had by now disappeared ahead. As *York* approached the African coast, the winds became more easterly, and on February 16, the anniversary of his departure from New York, the captain praised the fine weather, fine trade wind, and current setting to the west. Nearing Cape Agulhas, soundings on February 27 showed 70 fathoms. With strong breezes and topgallant sails set, the distance made on March 1 was 225 miles. The leaks continued however, and as the ship crossed the equator on March 24 in a fresh wind and with steering sails set, the pumps were manned every hour.

York arrived at Rector Street on April 20, 1835, 104 days en route. The ship went on to a long career: from 1841 to 1847 she made two voyages as a whaler (plush quarters for a whaling crew), and in 1849 she spent 170 days carrying 38 "Forty-Niners" from Boston to San Francisco.

But John Sterling never went to sea again. For a quarter century he had served the prominent merchants of the day: Howlands, Minturns, Aspinwalls, Grinnells—and continued to receive offers of commands.

Mary died in 1838, and in 1839 John married her cousin Catharine Plant and settled down as a local businessman, bank director, and community leader until his death in 1866. The boy so eager to go to sea had become a disillusioned man, exhausted by the sea. But he had greatly influenced the development of American world trade.

Captain Sterling sent his son to Yale, not to sea, and young John became wealthy as a corporate attorney and advisor to business barons Daniel Drew, Jim Fiske, and Jay Gould. But the seagoing genes were not inherited: when he had to cross the Hudson to New Jersey where his clients had fled from New York law, young John Sterling got seasick on the ferry.

BEFORE THE MAST ON *LEBANON*

Shipboard accounts kept by working sailors are far less common than officers' logs or diaries. This is the journal of 22-year-old Stratford seaman Lewis Barnum aboard the 697-ton ship *Lebanon*, on a voyage from New York to Manila in 1847–1848. Barnum's journal reveals rare details of shipboard life as seen through the eyes of an Able Seaman of the mid-nineteenth century:

> Went on board of the ship *Lebanon* on Friday morning Oct 1 1847 at 8 oclock and at 1/2 past 8 the Tow Boat came a long side and towed us out in the stream whare we anchored and lay their all day getting the Crew on board and putting things to rights. On Saturday morning about 10 ocl the Tow Boat came off and towed us down below Governors Island when a light breeze springing up astearn we cast off from her and made

As Lebanon *departed New York harbor in 1847, seaman Barnum would have viewed this active scene. Steam ferries and excursion boats plied the river, but ocean sailing ships still crowded busy wharves.*

sail. The wind continued fair till 3pm their being barely sufficient to stem the tides which was setting us in when as we was passing the old Fort Dimond the wind hauled ahead so as to obblidge us to go about. We continued beating down till 1/2 past 4 when we came to anchor a little below Fort Hamilton and lay their all night. At 4 ocl the nex we had a fair wind and a good breeze. at 1/2 past 4 hove up anchor and made sail again. at 1/2 past 7 passed the US sloop-of-war *Albany* with a steamboat alongside towing her in. At 8 ocl we was outside of Sandy Hook Light and at 9 a pilot boat came along side and the pilot and Mr Gordon one of the owners left us after bidding us good bye and wishing us a prosporous Voyage and we stood on our course with a fine breeze and all our sail set. At 11 ocl the land was out of sight and with a long lingering look I bid adue to my native land and went to work withe the rest to stow the anchor a get the cables below which we finished about 2 pm and I spent the rest of the day in getting aquainted with my ship mates and triing to comfor those who had never been to sea before most of them being dreadfully Sea sick their being concidarble of a sea runing and this endid my first day at Sea on board of the ship *Lebanon*.

Saturday Oct 7 This week commenced with a strong breeze from the NW which lasted until Thursday when it hauled ahead and continued so till Saturday when it increased to a gale so as to oblidge us to double reef our top sailes and furl the main sail. We lay to untill Sunday afternoon when we mad sail again.

Saturday Oct 23 Lat 18.20N Long 42.20W This week for the most part light winds and some squalls of rain. On Tuesday saw a large ship bound to the Easward. Exchanged Coullars with her when she proved to be English. Also saw a Barque on the other tack but did not come near her.

Saturday Oct 30 This week light rains with constant showers of rain which enabled us to catch enough water to fill all our casks and have plenty to wash up with. Latter part of the week it was calm most of the time.

Saturday Nov 6 This week a head wind with constant squalls of wind and rain. On Thursday saw several sharks around the Ship. Tryed to catch one of them with a hook baited with a piece of pork but they would not bite so we left t hook overboard and about 9 oclock in the evening the man at the helm hearing a splash in the water we went their and found one hooked. Hoisted him in. When he proved to be about 10 feet long cut him open and took out his liver and threw the rest of him over board.

Saturday Nov 20 The first part of this Week fine weather but a head wind. Later part a fair wind but squally weather—on Friday morning found ourselves surrunded by 4 Brigs and a Ship all standing the same way. At 2 pm tacked Ship and spoke the Brig *Eirabeth* of Boston bound

Was Triumphant *hypothetical or real? This silhouette of a typical mid-nineteenth-century ship was found on a wall panel of an ancient house not far from Lewis Barnum's home.*

to Valparaiso 51 days out. Also spoke the Ship *Cygnet* from New York bound to Canton 48 days out.

Saturday Dec 5 Lat 24.45S Long 19.17W This week for the most part a good breeze and pleasant weather. On Monday morning made the Island of Trinidad or Martin Vas. bearing S by E distant about 3 miles. Cept the ship off so as to pass to the Westward of it. At 3 pm we was abreast of it and about 8 miles distant when it had the appearance of being nothing but a heap of barren rocks and is uninhabited except sometimes the Brazilians put Convicts there. The next morning it was out of sight On Saturday saw a Brig ahead under short sail and by her appearance we supposed her to be a Man-of-War cruising for Slavers. Passed her about 8 pm and by her lights she was about half a mile.

Saturday Dec 19 Lat 36.50S Long 20.10E This week for the most part a good breeze and pleasant weather. On Sunday saw a Brig ahead standing the same way as ourselves.

Saturday Jan 1, 1848 Lat 41.10S Long 74.20E This week commenced with a good breeze and a fair wind. At sun down the wind increased so as to obblige us to furl topgallant sails and on Tuesday doubble reefed the topsailes and furled the jibb and main sail. On Wednesday saw a Barque ahead under close reefed topsailes. Passed about 1/4 a mile to leeward of her and by her appearance she was a spouter having 5 boats on deck. On Thursday morning saw a large ship on our lee bow and under snug sail. Passed her and at 10 oclock she was about 4 miles to leeward of us when she shook a reef out of her topsailes and set her jibb. When she overhauled us very fast at 12 oclock she was about 2 miles astern of us when we perceived her to be a Friggate. At 2 pm she was about 1/2 a mile astern of us and to windward when she showed English Coullars with a blue penant. She bore down fast and tried to speak us but their was so much sea that she darst not come near enough to be heard. Her decks was crowded with men and by the appearance she had transports [convicts sentenced to be exiled to New Zealand or Australia] on board. She passed us and by sundown she was hull down to windward when she tacked and stood to the Northward by which we supposed her to be bound to Calcutty or Bombay. On Friday saw a Barque to windward standing the same way as ourselves. At sundown she was out of sight to windward.

In January, seaman Barnum finally looked up from his work and noticed land, as *Lebanon* entered Sunda Strait and ran down the coast of Java:

Saturday Jan 15 Lat 24.30S Long 111.20E This week a good breeze and fair wind with some rain. Saturday morning the NW coast of New Holland [Java] was in sight to leeward but the weather was so thick that we could not see it plain.

Saturday Jan 29 On Monday morning saw several sharks around the Ship. Tryed to catch one of them with a hook but they would not bite so the captain got the harpoon and succeeded in hitting one but it would not enter him. When finding all our efforts vain the Captain tried to shoot them but a ball had no more effect on them than the harpoon till finely one of them bit but before we could haul him in he broke the line carrying away with him the hook and about 7 fathoms of line. At 8 pm made Sandle Wood Island [on the weather bow about 20 miles distant]. Kept the Ship off so as to pass to the Southward of it On Friday made the Islands of Timore and Ombay [now Alor]. The next morning found ourselves at the entrance of the Strait of Timore. At 9 am saw 2 sail ahead one of wch having only 1 mast an 2 stumps. At 12 ocl it fell calm, the dismasted Ship being about a mile ahead of us when we lowerd the boat and 4 of us pulled the Captain on board when she proved to be the ship *Hoquagh*, of New York, Capt Low [William H. Low of A.A. Low & Bros. had *Houqua*, 600 tons and 143 feet LOA, built by Brown & Bell in 1844] bound to Canton 88 days out. On the 15 she experanced a heavy gale of wind which increased to a hurricane so that the topgallant went by the bord before they could cut them adrift. She was knocked down on her beams end and the mizen mast carried away when she shiped a sea which swept her decks carring away the house amidships and all her boats. Stove the bulwarks washing away all the poarts and filled the cabbin half full of water so that they was obbliged to cut away the main mast to right her. She also had 4 feet of water in her hole when she was righted but there was no one lost from her. We learned news from home until the 3 of November. She also spoke a Brig the day before from Manila bound to Sydney who reported the *Sea Witch* arrival after 90 days passage from New York. She had as many spars as she had rigging for and so finding we could render her no assistance we left her and pulled aboard of our own ship again. At sundown we ware abreast of the north point of Ombay [Alor] and a mile distant from it. Is very high as are all the others we have seen and covered with verdure.

Saturday Feb 5 Lat 25 miles N Long 133.40E This week commenced with a good breeze and rainy weather. On Sunday morning we were most out of sight of Timore into the Bandy [Banda] sea. On tuesday made the Island of Bora [Buru] the *Cygnet* being in company with us. On Saturday morning made Boo [Buru] Island and at 6 pm we was about 4 miles from the entrance of Dampier Straits when we tacked Ship and stood off again under short sail. At 10 pm hove her to with the main topsail to the mast and remained so until daylight.

Saturday Feb 12 Lat 3.50N Long 135.20E The next morning found ourselves about 2 miles from the land and right at the entrance of the Straits. About 7 ocl saw a great many canoes coming off to us and not as they would be peacible. We got one of the guns on the forecastle and

When Lebanon *met* Houqua *in the South China Sea, a typhoon had claimed two masts and a topmast, but Captain Low insisted that he could manage without help. The* Lebanon *later learned that Captain Low had, on March 13, brought* Houqua *into Hong Kong under jury rig. (Courtesy Peabody Essex Museum, Salem, MA.)*

loaded it with slugs. As soon as they saw us loading it they begun to hold up things and make signs that they wanted to trade. They are of the New Ginnea race and have woolly hair but are good featured and well formed. They had shells and mats to sell besides a few coaconuts and lemons for which we gave them old cloths and some small trinkets and tobacco but the thing they wanted most was knifes on which they set a great value. They ware armed with bows and arrows an spears pointed with bone which they offered to exchange for knifes and tobacco. On tuesday we ware out of sight of the land. On thursday we hooked a large shark but as we ware hoisting him in the hook broke and we lost him. The latter part of the week a head wind with a good breeze and some rain.

Saturday Feb 26 This week commenced with a good breeze and fair wind. On Thursday and Friday we had the regular land breeze at night and the sea breeze in the day. Morning we found ourselves about 3 miles from the entrance of Manila bay withe the wind ahead. We continued to beat up and at 11 am we had passed a small island their is in the middle of the entrance and got inside of the bay. They hoisted a flag to us on

194

shore and we showed them our ensign, Manila is situated at the head of the Bay which is 8 miles long. We continued beating up till 2 pm when a gun boat boarded us and after overhawling our papers they left us to proceed. At 7 pm the wind hauled so as to enable us to lay right up the bay and at 9 pm we came to anchor about 3 miles from the Citty.

The voyage had taken 156 days, not good time for 1848. The crew set to work unloading the ship and filled the hold with bales of plantain bark, sappon [probably saffron] wood, and 100 boxes of indigo. By March 20 *Lebanon* was ready to sail. The voyage home was four weeks shorter than the trip outbound. In company with other Yankee ships, they learned from the *Antiss* of Boston that captain Low had brought the *Houqua* into Hong Kong under jury rig on March 13. On May 20 *Lebanon* passed Good Hope and reached New York in mid July. The final entry in Lewis Barnum's journal reads, "Thursday July 20. We got a steamboat along side at 10am and she towed us up to the foot of Fulton Street where we came to anchor about 5 oclock in the stream waiting for a permit from the Mayor to haul along side of the wharf which we did on Friday afternoon and made fast to the ship *Liverpool*."

CRUISE OF THE *COAST PILOT*

It was the winter of 1861, and Truman Hotchkiss was between voyages. The nation was coming apart: in January five southern states joined South Carolina in secession. In New York, Captain Hotchkiss was preparing for his next sailing.

The schooner *Coast Pilot* was the culmination of his career. Born April 10, 1816, Hotchkiss grew up in Stratford and began a life at sea in 1836 on local coasting sloops. In 1844 he skippered Isaac Wheeler's *Commodore Jones*, a fixture on the river. In 1847–1848 he commanded the 66.5-ton *Orin Sherwood*, owned by John Brooks, and in 1849 he skippered Brooks's 48-ton sloop *Guide*. Hotchkiss finally graduated to ocean-going vessels, sailing from New York.

The 298-ton *Coast Pilot* was built in Brookhaven by William Bacon. She had been copper sheathed in 1860. She carried mainsail, foresail, main and fore topsails, inner, outer, and flying jibs, studdingsail, and main and fore trysails. Her owners were Stratford men William Ely, Philip Jones, Edward Plumb, and the captain, who owned a 12/96 share.

While *Coast Pilot* loaded cargo in New York, carpenters and riggers were busy replacing a rotten bowsprit and a jib boom, and sending down the topmasts to be shortened four feet. Hotchkiss negotiated "a charter to Monte Video and Buenos Ayres for a sum of four thousand one hundred dollars."

As his ship was being readied, Hotchkiss spent what time he could in Stratford. On February 22 he attended "a great display of Bunting, Military parade, [on] the anniversary of the birthday of the Father of Our Country, the immortal Washington." Hotchkiss visited his sister Eliza Buddington at Stratford lighthouse and spent an hour skating with his children at Fresh Pond.

On March 11 the steam tug *Corning* towed *Coast Pilot* out into the North River and on March 12, the ship "stood out to sea with everything staunch and strong and properly victualled and manned for the voyage before us."

As the northeast trades set in, the ship moved to a fine breeze. On April 20 *Coast Pilot* crossed the equator, and next day spoke the bark *Warren White*. On April 24 the chronometer stopped, so Hotchkiss reset it using the longitude obtained from *Warren White*, later updating it with a new longitude from the brig *Esther* of Jersey.

Squally weather followed. On May 23 at 3:00 p.m.:

> A terrific squall burst staysail, fore and main trysail into ribband in five minutes time. Wore off before the gale. 4pm a sea pooped her. Filled cockpit, bursting in skylight, letting a large quantity of water into the cabin and bruising your humble servant severely across the wheel. Midnight, gale still in full force. 10am shipped a sea which filled main deck, galley, and center house."

Through most of May the storm continued, and the journal reads, "burst fore topsail," "burst clue of foresail," and "burst bonnet of jib." Finally on June 2 Hotchkiss turned to "run our longitude up by careful soundings," and from a measured 32-fathom depth determined his longitude. On June 4, exchanging signals with the Sardinian bark *Ascension*, 120 days out of Genoa bound for Montevideo, he learned she had 440 passengers aboard and needed provisions. Her boat was soon alongside, and a barrel of bread, a barrel of flour, and one of rice were transferred.

On the afternoon of Friday, June 7, Lobos Island appeared, then Flores Light and the entrance to Montevideo Harbor. Next morning a pilot brought *Coast Pilot* to anchor in the inner harbor, 87 days from New York. As soon as the health officer and the Custom House had completed their checks, "Flag Officer Sands came aboard and made a short visit." Captain Joshua Sands, a veteran Navy man and at the time commodore of the Brazil Squadron, was Truman Hotchkiss's Stratford neighbor. Hotchkiss went ashore to hand his crew list to the American consul and visit his consignees.

Until June 20, *Coast Pilot* remained at Montevideo. Hotchkiss discharged cargo—barrels of rice, cases of lard, barrels of whiskey, boxes of starch, and carriage assemblies—into lighters, had his chronometer repaired, and visited his Navy friends. On Wednesday the 19th, another Hotchkiss neighbor from Stratford, Lieutenant William Barrymore, came aboard for an hour to visit. On Thursday Hotchkiss located the commodore aboard the steamer *Pulaski*, and handed him a letter and $115 in Brazilian gold to give directly to his wife in Stratford. ". . . spent the remainder of my day in looking to my business, and bidding good by and GodSpeed to the Officers of the United States frigate *Congress* which is to sail tomorrow direct for Boston."

On June 20 Hotchkiss had concluded his business and, with pilot John Flynn aboard and a fine southeast breeze, *Coast Pilot* headed up the Plate to Buenos Aires.

The next several days were spent unloading some 900 packages of merchandise onto lighters and then, on the 4th of July, attending a social at the American consulate.

Beating northward up the coast through thunderstorms and pamperos, on Sunday the 11th *Coast Pilot* came to anchor at Paranagua. After completing customs and visiting his consignee Señor Guimmerain, Hotchkiss proceeded to unload the stone ballast he had carried from Buenos Aires. After removing 20 tons, the schooner was shifted across the bar at Bonita Island, then further lightened until all the ballast was removed and loading could begin. The lumber ports were first opened (*Coast Pilot* sported this feature, which was later used on many downeasters, a rectangular port built into the hull on each side of the stem). The agent sent two canoes with 27 pieces of madiera timber (mahogany), "and then we must go to St. Antonio [Antonina, further inland up the bay] for the balance of cargo of timber." At Antonina, attempting to get close to the timber to be loaded, she went aground in the mud. In spite of this, Hotchkiss continued to load timber. On the 29th he sent out an anchor to kedge off, and the schooner slid across the mud and floated. Finally, *Coast Pilot* returned down the bay to Paranagua, where the crew worked at caulking the bow ports, adjusting the rigging, securing cargo, and readying for sea. "Saw in Rio papers statements of heavy battles between North and South, and that our coasts are swarming with privateers."

On Sunday September 22, pilot on board, *Coast Pilot* came to anchor inside the bar, with three other vessels waiting to go out. On Friday, September 27, Hotchkiss wrote:

> 4pm got underway (high water) with a fine breeze from East. Tacked and laid out. After passing white buoy at the Ilha des Palmas touched on rocky bottom but not hard enough to do damage. 6pm discharged our pilot.
>
> Friday 4 October. 8am took pilot. 9am came to anchor in the inner harbor of Monte Video.

Unloading took so many days that Hotchkiss claimed—and collected—demurrage. USS *Pulaski*, which remained on the Brazil station when *Congress* and Commodore Sands were ordered home, had come over from Rio and on the 22nd Hotchkiss went on a picnic up the mountain with a group of Americans. On the 24th he completed his charter, and on the 26th he was again searching for business. Unfortunately he could learn of nothing except a freight of bones and ashes from Patagonia to England at 30¢ per ton, which would not do.

Meanwhile ships continued to arrive from New York. One arrival related, "Fri. Nov. 1st. Arrived schr. *Warring*, Capt. Smith, 67 days from NYork. This vessel has been taken by the Privateer *Jeff Davis*. A prize crew was put on board her—her officers taken out—The cook a coloured man killed the prize crew and took her into New York."

Not all oceangoing ships were square rigged: the schooner rig was handy for beating up estuaries and rivers in interior South America. Coast Pilot's *name hints that she was patterned after contemporary pilot boats.*

Finally on December 2 Captain Hotchkiss again chartered *Coast Pilot* to bring more lumber from the Bay of Paranagua, for $2,100. After taking on 50 tons of sand ballast and sending money to managing owner Mr. Maxwell and a letter to his wife via the New York-bound schooner *J.F. Farland*, Hotchkiss dropped down the river and on December 8 stood out of the harbor. Beating up the coast, *Coast Pilot* on December 18 made Ilha des Palmas, and anchored near the fort.

Next morning, with pilot and boarding officer aboard, *Coast Pilot* sailed into Paranagua and the captain went ashore to give Señor Guimmerain $1,000 in doubloons from Freyer Hermanas the charterer. Removing some of the sand ballast, *Coast Pilot* moved to Bonita Island. Although ballast was completely removed on the 23rd, Señor Lisander refused to begin loading until after the Christmas holiday. On Christmas eve, Truman Hotchkiss, Captain Huntley, and a Señor Isadore took a boat across the bay to Guallaguadava (Guaraquecaba) to attend midnight mass, then to Isadore's brother's home for food and coffee.

As lumber loading began, Hotchkiss had to enlarge the bow port to take the logs. Shifting from spot to spot, loading continued for another month. On

February 6, 1862, *Coast Pilot* returned to Montevideo. There Hotchkiss finally agreed to transport a shipload of bones and ash to England, as no better cargos were available to Yankee ships. On March 1, with a new second mate and a pilot aboard, the schooner headed up the Parana River to load. With strong opposing currents, a pilot reluctant to come aboard, who would not run at night, and used too little sail, "myriads of musketoes and a great many of them weigh a pound," Hotchkiss finally reached Parana 28 days from Montevideo. While the crew maintained the ship, loading of bone and bone ash began.

Serious troubles plagued the *Coast Pilot*. While still loading bone ash, on April 30 a pampero struck, and both anchor chains parted. The captain set the jib and fore staysail and ran four miles up the river to a spot where the boat could be brought close to an island and tied to some trees. But *Coast Pilot* ran aground, and the water level dropped. Hotchkiss had to transfer his cargo into a hired schooner at a cost of 5 oz. gold, to refloat *Coast Pilot*. He wrote to agent Meyers, asking him to purchase a 1,500-pound anchor to use until he could recover his own, which were both on the river bottom. On May 5 he reported "swung off afloat," and ready to resume loading. He searched for his anchors with a grapnel to no effect. He concluded, "This is a hard section of country. Nothing to be had but beef and pumpkins. It is a long time since I have seen a potato."

Finally on May 21 a 1,000-pound anchor arrived from Montevideo, a loan from the steamer USS *Pulaski*. Hotchkiss immediately got underway down river, but reported, "pilot does not know how to work a fore-and-aft schooner and not allowing anyone else to know anything fooled away an hour and came to anchor again at 9am." And later, "sent boat on shore for some fresh meat and William Kitt deserted." On June 1, back in Montevideo, he bought two anchors and 27 fathoms of chain, returned *Pulaski's* anchor to her commander, and took departure on June 22, 1862.

For three weeks *Coast Pilot* headed northeast across the Atlantic, in haze and light breezes. Slatting in a rolling sea caused constant splitting of the mainsail. Sighting Trinidad on July 15, Hotchkiss took the opportunity to fix his position. He made a good profile sketch of Trinidad and Martin Vas Rocks, passed between them, took observations at meridian on the 16th, and corrected his chronometer by bearings.

With a "monstrous high rolling sea" continuing, Hotchkiss reported, "mainsail being burst in a number of places," "carried away fore throat halliards," "burst flying jib and main," and "set main trysail in place of main sail on account of main sail being tender." On the 25th, *Coast Pilot* celebrated crossing the line by bursting the main again. Hotchkiss's journal also describes typical treatment—or lack of treatment—for sickness on board ship:

> Soon after leaving Monte Video [I] took a heavy cold from exposure which brought on chronic rheumatism which continued to grow worse day by day. July 25th, no longer able to get on deck, continued to grow worse. Swelling increasing and becoming more painful until Aug 10th

when it broke, discharging about a teacup full of fester. Commenced getting better at once and this morning Aug 14th went on deck for the first time in twenty days. I am very weak, can just get about by holding on to things.

The trip across the Atlantic continued through light winds and rolling seas, with constant sail repair. Finally on Monday September 8, off the coast of Ireland, Hotchkiss reported, "Fastnet Rock Light bearing NE distance 33 miles." On the 10th the ship passed Kinsale Head and came to anchor in Queenstown, Ireland.

After writing a letter to Maxwell "asking him to make and send us a new main sail and jib," *Coast Pilot* sailed for London. They took a steam tug (*Rover*, for £11) up the Thames, and on September 15 entered Victoria Docks basin to unload the bone and ash.

There Hotchkiss signed up to carry a load of coal from Cardiff or Swansea to Cadiz, then salt to Rio la Plata, and return to Cadiz. Shortly afterwards he received a letter from owner Maxwell saying, "Get your sail made there, then come home, with a cargo or in ballast," but it was too late. On October 15 he was towed down to Gravesend to await a tide and wind. After sailing as far as the Downs at Deal, *Coast Pilot* came to anchor, with westerly winds and a heavy storm preventing movement down the English Channel. When fine weather returned on the 19th, Hotchkiss checked his newly repaired chronometer against the time ball at Deal Castle, and found it three minutes fast.

Finally on October 29, 1862 the weather moderated enough to permit a fleet of some 200 sail to get underway. At the coal drop in Swansea, loading was completed on November 21. Catching a tide on the 23rd, *Coast Pilot* released the line from steam tug *Eagle* and set off down the channel, shifting to nautical time.

Beyond the Scilly Isles, a squall carried away the flying jib sheet and staysail sheet and burst the foresail, then they found the schooner leaking. And in wearing the ship about, the swinging main boom stove the steering wheel. The storms continued, finally clearing off the coast of Portugal. On December 13 they made Cadiz Light and came to anchor opposite the town. Next day a steam tug towed the schooner up to Trocadero to unload her coal.

On his second Christmas away from home, Captain Hotchkiss noted only that work halted. On the 24th, after unloading about 60 tons of coal, he discovered a large leak, apparently at the rudder post. Back at Cadiz, Hotchkiss bought some mats and a half dozen wooden salt shovels, and on January 7 salt loading began. There was no way the captain's impatience could speed up the process. He was completely discouraged.

Finally, bound for the River Plate with salt, *Coast Pilot* recrossed the equator on February 16. It was a decent passage, 58 days to Montevideo. There Hotchkiss found that neutral vessels were earning nearly $9 per ton, twice that of American ships. His orders were to go up the River Uruguay to discharge his salt at San Roman, and there receive a full cargo of tallow for Cadiz. He beat up the river with a fair tide, but after several groundings, it was April 5 before he reached his destination. Then unloading at the "saladero" proceeded at a snail's pace: Lighters did not arrive when promised, and soldiers came and took away workers and horses. As unloading slowly progressed, Hotchkiss and the crew busied themselves with ship maintenance, making a main topsail and a gaff topsail and scraping down the masts.

By July 1, 1863 *Coast Pilot* had loaded 479 pipes of tallow (one pipe = 2 hogsheads or 4 barrels or a half tun) and a load of bones and horn piths. From agent Brown at the saladero Captain Hotchkiss received orders for *Coast Pilot* to "proceed directly to Monte Video for further orders."

So ends this journal. Captain Hotchkiss retired from the sea in the 1860s, and lived in Stratford near the wharves until his death on September 10, 1880.

The last journey of the *Coast Pilot* is a classic example of the difficulties confronting American ocean commerce in the Civil War. As U.S. naval units were ordered home from foreign ports to blockade the extensive Confederate coast, our merchant ships became prey to ocean raiders, privateers, pirates, and revolutionaries around the world. Commodore Sands's old Navy superior Raphael Semmes was the most prominent of these Confederate raiders, and it was the *Coast Pilot's* owners who suffered most from lack of business, high insurance costs, and danger of attack. The decline of American merchant sail had begun.

6. THE BOUNTY OF THE WATERS

The first arriving Englishmen found heaps of oyster shells along the river bank; shellfish were abundant. And in the spring, shad, salmon, and sturgeon surged into the river to spawn. Other fish abounded in the river and the Sound. The colonists soon set up weirs and seines to harvest the anadromous finfish, first for their own use, then to salt them down in barrels and ship them out. They tonged for oysters all winter long and sent them out in trade. The shellfish business grew, and in the nineteenth century oystermen built oyster stores at the lower wharf where they packed barrels for shipment to New York, then to the west coast, and Europe.

They learned to spread the oyster shells, called cultch, on the seabed of the Sound for young oyster spawn to grow. Larger companies took over, tending leased beds. Sailing sloops dragged for oysters while steamboats spread the cultch, killed marauding starfish, and took the harvest. Oystering reached its peak at the start of the twentieth century; then several threats—starfish, hurricanes, parasites, and pollution—brought a long decline. Meanwhile, by 1900 dams and industrial pollutants destroyed fishing in the river. Today dams are being removed, the government is attempting to restock shad and salmon, and the shellfish industry is reviving.

SALMON, STURGEON, SHAD

In 1641, when Governor Winthrop of Massachusetts Bay reported "300,000 dried fish were sent to market," Stratford, still called Cupheag, was in its third year. Unlike the Massachusetts settlers, who went to sea for cod, Stratford planters caught fish in the estuary of the Stratford River.

Fish of all varieties thrived in the clear waters of the river and the Sound. Immense schools of pelagic fish—mackerel, blues, and alewives—arrived in season. Bottom fish—tautog, flounder, fluke—abounded. Menhaden, skate, and sandshark were considered trashfish, as was lobster—fit for fertilizer or feeding servants. Schools of porpoise roamed the Sound. Striped bass 3 feet long abounded in the river. Little mummichogs and killifish inhabited the marsh, food for many of these species.

Before the Ousatonic Water Power Company built its dam at Shelton in 1869, and before factories in the Naugatuck valley polluted the water, the river—as seen in this image from the July 1879 issue of Lippincott's Magazine—*teemed with anadromous fish: shad, salmon, sturgeon, and herring.*

Anadromous fish—Atlantic salmon, Atlantic and shortnose sturgeon, and American shad—are born in freshwater New England rivers, spend their lives in the Atlantic Ocean, and return to rivers to spawn. Of these, the most important were the shad, those aristocrats of the herrings, that came in tens of thousands each spring. Shad averaged under 2 feet long and about 4 pounds in weight, although they could reach 12 pounds.

Each spring in late March the shad returned: as an old resident once said, "when the shad bush starts to bloom." First the buck shad appeared; later the roe shad, which were more numerous. The run upriver was about 50 miles to the great falls at New Milford, and about as far up the Naugatuck. At the mouths of creeks or other shallow spots in the freshwater river, the females cast their eggs, 25,000 to 30,000 each. For their first summer, the young foraged in the river, then headed out to sea, to return to spawn in three to seven years.

For two-and-a-half centuries the people of Stratford harvested shad, for themselves and for market. An article in the *Bridgeport Farmer* in 1912 recalled "the good old days when the king of all tablefish swam up the Housatonic by the thousand and when every resident, rich or poor, was able to fill himself with the seasonable dish. It's even said of the old timers that they ate so many shad in the spring that the bones stuck out all over them and they were unable to remove their shirts until hayin' time when they sweat them out."

The earliest technique for catching shad was the Indian method, standing in the shallows and forking passing fish out onto the bank. A better way, used by both aborigines and settlers, was to build weirs of brush and branches, set into the shallow waters in the shape of a huge pen or pound, with a funneled entryway converging into a narrow opening. Fish entering the weir with inflowing currents could not find an exit, and at ebbtide the fishermen walked in and filled baskets with fish flopping on the sands.

The ultimate device for catching shad was the woven gill net, or seine. Weaving nets was a wintertime occupation. The fisherman would cast a loop over a hook on the wall, then his netting needle—a thin wooden shuttle—would fly, as he knotted loops row by row into a mesh, then carted the completed net off to be stored until the shad arrived in the spring.

Stretched across the current and attached to heavy posts driven into the bottom, the seine caught the fish by the gills as they swam headlong into it. At low tide some seiners came by boat or boot to pick the fish from the mesh. Others had a reel or capstan at one shore, and drew the loaded net onto the capstan to remove the fish. It took about a hundred salted shad to fill a barrel.

In their eagerness or greed, men learned to stretch the net across the whole channel and cut off access to upstream fishers. As early as 1764 the General Assembly ruled:

> that if any person or persons whatsoever shall by weirs, seines, hedges, or by any other means, obstruct the passage or course of the fish in said Housatonick River or any of the streams that empty themselves thereinto, such person or persons shall be subjected to the same penalties as in and by said act is provided.

In 1766 Israel Curtiss and 15 partners received from the General Assembly exclusive rights to fish in the hole and deep water lying in said river between the two channels, the one near Milford side, and the other near Stratford shore, bounded on the south upon a line drawn directly west from a point on Milford shore 20 rods north of a piece of meadow called Ford's Hole, and running and extending the whole breadth between said channels northward 100 rods.

Up the river in Ripton Parish, now the city of Shelton, in 1779 the Assembly granted exclusive rights for 10 years to Moses Wheeler, Philo Shelton, and eight others, "peaceably to use and improve . . . a certain place on the west side of Stratford River, about 100 rods above Hawkings Ferry, for catching fish with a sein without the disturbance or hindrance of any other person or persons."

After the Revolution, the State of Connecticut amended its colonial regulations. The 1784 Act for Encouraging and Regulating Fisheries forbade obstructing the passage of fish in the spring in the "Ousatannick" River, and restricted seining to the months of April, May, and June, between sunset on Monday and sunrise on Saturday. No bush seines were permitted, and the rights of established seiners between the mouth of the Ousatunnick and Leavenworth's Ferry were retained.

In 1798 the law was modified to prohibit drawing seines north of Samuel Wheeler's grist mill in Stratford (Peck's Mill) or north of Ford's Hole in Milford except between sunrise on Monday and sunrise on Saturday during April, May, and June.

In 1816 Ferry Rocks fishing place was assigned to Isaac Pendleton, and in 1832 Beach Wilcox signed over to Samuel Wheeler a twentieth of the rights to the spot between the upper and lower wharves, called the Poverty or Toleration fishing place, "with all my right, title, and interest in the seine, ropes, or whatever else belongs to the fishing place."

Seining for shad became one of the most lucrative occupations in town. Every cellar in Stratford had its half barrel of salted shad, and much was sold and shipped out. Local farmers went to work in the fields weighed down by a breakfast of salt shad and boiled potatoes.

The Wellses built a shad house at the end of Johnson's Lane in Putney to store their barrels of salt fish. In 1838 to 1840 the springtime count from the Housatonic was 12,000 shad a day.

The seines and fishing rights were generally held by partnerships of ten or more owners, and each had to tend the net in turn. The fishing was done on shares, with owners taking half and hired crew the rest.

Many a young man earned his annual income from his springtime work on the seines. It was hard work, and when it was time to take a break, lunch was usually—planked shad. Long before fancy restaurants served this dish, it was standard fare for the fishermen. Each crew kept a fire on the shore, and there they would nail a big buck shad to a board and place it next to the hot fire. The smoky smell of roasting fish filled the air and fanned the appetites of the straining crew, but there was enough for all.

Other places had their shad, but Stratford shad had a reputation as the best. The salted barrels were sent to market by sloop, steamer, and train, and shad made a fine gift for friends and family. Mrs. Thomas Clinton related this memory from her childhood:

> My grandmother lived in New York, and we always took her a fresh shad if we could. One time my father was ill, so I was selected to go down and do the honors for grandmother. One morning in May, Cappy Wicks caught a fresh shad at 4 o'clock that morning in the river. Mother wrapped it in a paper and gave it to me. I was loaded down with flowers and asparagus and shad. Half way to New York [on the train] I noticed a man moving away from me, and I looked down, and the shad was bleeding. There was a great big spot of blood on the floor. If I'd been a little older, I'd have had presence of mind to say "Sorry, don't move away, it's nothing but a shad." But I was embarrassed to tears, so I bought a newspaper, the *New York Herald*, and wrapped it around the shad. When I got home I said, "I"ll take anything to grandmother, but I will not take another shad."

There seemed no end to shad, and all fishing spots were staked out. The fish had to run a gauntlet from the river's mouth all the way up to New Milford. Fishing rights extended beyond the river itself, even into the Great Meadow marsh. In 1868 Nathan Wells reported:

April 17 Helped string the Ferry seine today.
May 8 Went fishing on Ferry seine for Josiah Booth, caught 32.
    13 Caught 50 shad.
    27 Went fishing at the Ferry caught 96 shad.
June 5 Went fishing at the Ferry for Josiah Booth caught 60 shad.
    10 Went fishing at the Ferry caught 43 shad.
    15 Went fishing at the Ferry caught 2 shad.

In 1870 Wells helped Wilson Beardsley string seine, and in May 1871 he observed, "This PM went fishing on the Ferry seine caught about 30 fish not more than half of them saleable shad and the other half very small. Shad is evidently going to run out."

Wells's words were prophetic: Overfishing and pollution in the Naugatuck valley did their work. After the Ousatonic Water Power company completed its dam across the river at Derby in 1869, the shad could no longer reach their spawning ground, and soon the annual shad run was no more. In 1877 a few

Using the same techniques as the Native Americans, colonists built weirs of brush and branches on the flats, shaped to funnel fish into a pool from which they could not exit, then at ebbtide picked them up and filled their baskets. The fish were dried or salted.

Along the river seining rights were doled out by the General Assembly. At the "Poverty" hole this group set their seine from a reel, and periodically wound in the shad.

men were still setting seines—Charles and Nelson Wakeley maintained one at Oronoke Creek—but the haul was negligible. In 1899 the state leased Peck's Mill Pond for 99 years to create a shad hatchery, but the project failed. By the end of the century, the shad were gone from the Housatonic.

Atlantic salmon (*salmo salar*) once shared the Housatonic with the shad. Much larger than the shad, salmon reached 10 to 20 pounds. They spawned in the fall in most New England rivers, depositing eggs in November, to hatch in five or six months. The parr (young salmon) remained in the estuary for a few years, then headed out to sea, to return in a few more. Never as abundant as shad, they were sold individually or in small numbers by storekeepers in the early 1800s. On July 4, 1798 John Selby charged Eleazer Lacey 7s 6d for four of them, probably to prepare an all-American Fourth of July dinner of fresh-picked peas, new potatoes, and salmon at his father's inn at the ferry. By 1850 the salmon were gone from local waters.

John Selby's account book records many more sales of sturgeon than of salmon from 1802 to 1819. Judging from his records, these large ugly acipensers returned from the sea to spawn between June and October. They were bottom feeders, with a conical snout, and a head covered with bony plates. They averaged 6 feet, but could grow to 10 feet and 500 pounds. Selby charged about 2¢ a pound, a little less than for cod. Like salmon, sturgeon disappeared before 1850, victims of polluted streams.

Curtis Chatfield must also have used his coasting sloop for fishing. In 1820 he was selling codfish in his store at the lower wharf. He sold the cod by the quintal, an old weight measure of 100 to 130 pounds, for about 3¢ a pound. Codfishing had another payoff; in 1784 Connecticut, to encourage cod and whale fishing, freed any vessels used in these pursuits for four months per year from being taxed.

The earliest colonists eagerly searched for whales in the Sound. In 1647 the General Court agreed that, "Yf Mr. Whiting wth any others shall make tryall and prsecute a designe for the takeing of Whale, wthin these libertyes, and if uppon tryall wthin the terme of two yeares, they shall like to goe on, noe others shalbe suffered to interrupt them, for the tearme of seaven yeares."

In 1791 Captain Joseph Hull of the town of Huntington took out a license at the Fairfield County Custom House in Newfield "for district, bank, and whale fishery." Whaling was still being done in the Sound and along New England shores, in open boats manned by four or six oarsmen, a steersman, and a harpooner. As the whaling industry grew, Stratford men went whaling in larger vessels, but the town did not share in the profits after Bridgeport became a separate town. The Bridgeport Whaling Company was formed in May 1833, 12 years after the split. On April 12, 1839 the whaling ship *Atlantic* returned to Bridgeport from 567 days at sea, in the Atlantic and Indian Oceans. She reported 907 whales seen, 75 struck, and 34 taken.

Captain Willett Hanford, born in Bridgeport when it was part of Stratford, took the brig *Hamilton* whaling in the Pacific. In 1845 Hanford died at sea from injuries received in battle with a sperm whale. He was buried in Hawaii.

Until 30 years ago, schools of porpoise were common in the Sound. These 5- to 9-foot mammals roamed the waters in search of menhaden and similar fare. Returning from New York aboard the steamer *Schuyler* in October 1866, Nathan Wells reported, "opposite Norwalk Islands passed through a large school of herring hogs . . ."

Bony, silvery-blue menhaden—herring whose processed oil and meal yield one of the highest sources of pure protein—traveled in huge schools in the summertime, pursued by porpoise, stripers, bluefish, and men. Fishermen netted them for oil and fertilizer, but smelly processing plants had to be remote from town. At a town meeting in February 1867 Stratford voters approved leasing part of Long Beach to the Stratford Oil Company. In 1868 the George W. Miles Company leased part of Charles Island to process menhaden, and in 1882 there was a fish works at Welch's Point in Milford.

Menhaden trawling in the Sound remained a viable business into modern times. As other commercial fishing declined, menhaden or bunker trawling increased nationwide to a quarter of the total haul of U.S. fishing boats—more than 1 million tons in 1997. A vessel with a purse seine net could take up to 25 tons in 40 minutes. But bunker fishing was a non-selective process, causing recreational fishermen to complain about loss of other finfish and shellfish species, and pollution of the waters. So in 1997 New York placed a permanent ban on commercial bunker fishing in its half of the Sound, and Connecticut set a two-year ban on boats longer than 50 feet and nets longer than 300 feet.

Sport fishing has always held appeal. In 1859 young Lewis Russell was fascinated by fishing. On April 21 he reported that his brother Ben had gone down to the harbor and got a lot of fish, and again on the 25th had caught a half bushel of flatfish, while up the river the seiners caught 100 shad. On the afternoon of June 25, he and Professor Sedgewick wandered down to the harbor to watch the men hauling seine for sturgeon. They hauled in about 500 whitefish and gave 200 to them, which Sedgewick took home to feed his boarding students. On a sunny Wednesday in July, Lewis and the two Wells boys got 12 flatfish and a half bushel of clams. It was a lazy, sunny summer, a time to fish and visit and to help the steamboat tie up to the wharf.

Albert Laing did most of his duck hunting from his sneakbox—"four black duck, from my box on the flats"—but for serious travel on the water, he owned a little sailboat. His account book shows that he bought and ate a lot of seafood: "2 qts. clams 10¢," "1 peck oysters 56¢," "2 1/2 lbs. flatfish 15¢," "1 lb. blackfish 5¢," "1 shad 5 lbs. 50¢," "terrapin 25¢," and in New York, "oysters & ale 65¢."

But when the hunting season ended in the spring, Laing found time for bass fishing between his horticultural endeavors. In the summer of 1864 he bottom fished for stripers from the lower wharf, using shiners (which he called sturgeon bait), or sand eels (sandworms) as bait. On June 25 he landed a 10-pounder, and on the 26th his catch weighed 13 pounds. In June 1865 he reported, "caught 5 bass, sailing in the bend [the turn in the river at Oldfield Rock, now the Birdseye Street launching ramp]," "a 3 lb. bluefish in bend. Strawberries in their prime," and, "Good fishing in the bend with shiners on bottom first stake below the rocks." In July he was back at the dock, where he landed some 5-pounders, but he was out in the boat as well, as he noted that bluefish had begun to bite outside.
-Laing continued to fish near the rocks from his sailboat. In May 1866, one haul of 15 fish weighed 31 pounds, and in another, Captain Lord Wakely pulled a 12-pounder into the boat. Through 1871 Laing continued to fish for stripers from the boat, or downriver at Skate Bar, or in the Sound for blues. His last fishing entry is on April 11, 1878, "First shad caught on the 'kid glove lure,' 10 pounds."

The following year he was busy trying to stock Selby's Pond: "May 5. Put 12 fine brook trout in pond, politeness of Mr. P H Hodges." (Preston Hodges stocked his own pond at Raven Stream [now Motil's] for guest fishing.) Laing also recorded that on May 19 he "put 8 horned dace & 8 roach in pond from Wheeler's Mills."

Nathan Wells was not a striper fisherman, but did enjoy bringing in an occasional catch once the shad season was over. In July 1872, he took advantage of a bluefish run; on the 2nd he caught 27, then 7 on the 4th, 8 on the 5th, then 3, then 1, until the fish moved on. All summer long he joined other men and boys who spent their days fishing for summer flounder at the railroad bridge. Wells reported an eel chowder cooked up one August evening in 1867 by George Fryer at Benjamin's store, enjoyed with 12 other store-sitters.

Some Stratford seamen went whaling on Bridgeport whaling ships. The Bridgeport Whaling Company was formed in 1833. In 1837–1839 the Atlantic *spent 567 days at sea. Captain Willett Hanford of the brig* Hamilton *died at sea after a battle with a sperm whale.*

Today, when fish farming is the fastest-growing segment of American agriculture, commercial fishing in the Sound is rare, but sport fishing is ever increasing. More and more residents own powerboats. In 1993 the owners of the Dock Shopping Center built a new fishing pier at Washington Bridge. In 1996 the boat launching ramp at Birdseye Street was refurbished for the trailer crowd, and in 1997 Bond's Dock was repaired for use by fishermen. In summer the piers are lined with anglers and the river is crowded with trolling boats. Summer and winter flounder are caught, each in their season, bunker (menhaden) are taken at the town's fishing piers, striped bass are on the increase, mackerel abound in season, and bluefish—snapper, taylor and bunker—are ever popular gamefish, so popular that there is a bluefish contest every year, and the new Bridgeport baseball team calls itself the Bluefish. The blues are savage fighters, and a school of them feeding on smaller fish turns the water foamy white, then crimson as they rip and tear into the bait fish, leaving torn and bloody bits for the gathering gulls.

As we enter the twenty-first century the state Department of Environmental Protection (DEP) is removing dams from the Naugatuck and building improved fish ladders to make the river accessible all the way to the Thomaston Dam. The DEP has transplanted American shad, herring, and alewives from the Connecticut River to the Housatonic/Naugatuck waters where they once grew. Young shad will have no trouble finding their way to the sea, and with better fish passageways and newly implanted "memories" of their home, can be expected to return here to spawn. The DEP has preliminary plans to restore American shad, alewives, blueback herring, sea lamprey, and American eel to the upper Housatonic as well. Osprey and other raptors are increasing, fishermen are enjoying greater catches, and the pristine environment of Stratford's estuary will return.

OYSTERMEN AND SHELLERMEN

Through the ages, the creature with the most profound impact on Stratford waters has been a lowly mollusc with a prestigious name, *crassostrea virginica*, the eastern oyster. These bivalve molluscs covered the bottom of the estuary wherever warm (above 68°F) salt and fresh water mixed (15 to 20 parts per thousand), attached to old shell, rock, or brush, Their shells reached 4 inches in five years, and could become 1 foot long. Between the flat upper shell and the cupped lower shell the creatures worked constantly, filtering phytoplankton nutrients through their gills, pumping 20 to 30 quarts of water an hour. The creature was a succulent mass of meat, reached by severing the adductor muscle and opening the shell.

Looking north from the lower wharf in the late nineteenth century, typical oystermen's and shellermen's working boats line up along the shore. In the foreground are a sharpie, a rowing boat, and a scow. Beyond the shipyard is the H.J. Lewis oyster factory.

The oyster's plebian cousin is the clam. Soft shell clams (Stratfordites call them steamers) grew in intertidal sands along the river and at Lewis' Gut. Round hard-shell clams lay along the bottom, available for the picking. The Native Americans called the hard shell clam "poquau", and added the suffix "haug" to form the plural. The early settlers corrupted this to quahog, the name locals use today. For more than 8,000 years of unrecorded history, oysters and clams formed a major part of the food of the Indian Americans.

Mounds of oyster shells, once Indian kitchen middens, lay along the river from the ferry crossing to the mouth. Across the mouth in Milford, one shellheap covered 24 acres—the largest midden in New England. Borings taken when the breakwater was built showed depths of 80 feet. Immense shell heaps extended a mile northward from Milford Point. Mounds along the Stratford shore from Oldfield Rock to Quenby's Neck and back around Fresh Pond marked the site of a village. These Pequonnock (open field) Indians, part of the Paugussett tribe of the Algonquian nation, enjoyed abundant harvests from the sea—shad and salmon, stripers and sturgeon, eels and herring, crabs and lobster, but mainly clams and oysters—together with duck, goose, and rail, and corn, beans, and pumpkin from plantings in the open field.

When the settlers arrived in the spring of 1639, only small Indian families remained along the Stratford shores, decimated already by the white man's diseases. By 1680 there were only 2,500 in all of Connecticut. But their mounds of discarded oyster shells were valuable to the settlers, ground to powder in our grist mills, calcined to quicklime in our kilns, used in mortar and plaster walls, or ground and spread on croplands to fertilize the soil.

Stratford's early settlers, like the Indians, depended on the plentiful oysters as a major food supply. Gathering meant merely picking them up from intertidal water at ebb tide, or using oyster rakes from boats. Some were a foot long, and all were of rare quality.

From the present Washington Bridge site to the Sound, in water 12 to 20 feet deep, rakes with 22-foot handles were used to gather the harvest into their boats. The boats were commonly dugout canoes, hollowed out from a single pine log 3 feet in diameter and 15 to 30 feet long.

As time went on, harvests increased. Each gatherer took up to 50 bushels per day. The colonial government realized that the supply was not infinite, so in October 1766 the General Assembly passed an act that read:

> Be it enacted . . . that the towns of Newhaven, Fairfield, and all and every town in this Colony bordering on the sea, sound or river, having oysters or clams growing and lying in any river, harbour, cove, creek, or flats, within the bounds of such towns respectively, or adjoining or appertaining thereto, shall have power . . . to make rules and ordinances respecting the preserving such oysters and clams and catching and taking the same, and to lay restrictions and prohibitions against taking such oysters and clams in improper seasons.

Stratford had anticipated the act: In 1764 the town decreed that, "if any parties should take oysters between April 20th and the 10th day of September [the reproductive season] they should pay a fine of ten shillings." From 1790 to 1810 new ordinances restricted not only the time for taking, but the tools for oystering.

When the rest of the country discovered the quality of these luscious Long Island Sound bivalves, demand exploded and more Stratford men took up oystering. From dugout canoes, gundalows, and scows, they tonged with devices that looked like long rakes hinged together. Offshore, an increasing fleet of small sloops began to drag the bottom.

Regulations kept pace. In 1842 the legislature prohibited taking oysters—or oyster shells—from any waters of the state "from the first day of March until the first day of November, in each year," but excluded stopping "any person from retaking any oysters belonging to him, and by him laid down or planted, and not so laid down or planted in or upon any natural oyster beds," indicating that both leased beds and shelling were already in existence.

The expansion of oystering brought need for little sheds and buildings at the shore to prepare the catch for sale and shipment. By 1824, when a warehouse was built on the wharf for the steamboat trade, a line of little shacks began to form along the riverbank. This row of stores between the highway and the river changed hands many times. In 1883 there were 15 oyster stores near the dock; on the wharf itself stood the warehouse/saloon and a large shed, on the corner of the owner's houselot stood the old store once Wheeler's, and in a row along the shore below the bank highway were ten buildings plus three on pilings.

In season, the little shops were very busy. Shells unloaded from sloops at the wharf, or from dugouts or sharpies drawn up on the shore, were carried by cart or wheelbarrow into the oyster stores. By common agreement a path along the shoreline was kept clear for carts and handtrucks to pass from boat to shop—labeled in old deeds the "cartpath."

In the sheds, the oysters were culled—separated from each other and from whatever rocks, shells, or debris the dredger or tonger had brought up, with a blunt metal culling iron, then cleaned up, sized and graded, and packed for shipment. From the cooperage next to the slaughterhouse, or from cooper Asa Curtis's shop, came barrels of about three bushels capacity. Filled with oysters, they were closed with burlap or wooden barrelheads, and shipped down the coast in sailing coasters or in steamboats, or even across the Atlantic to European ports. With moderately cool storage and moisture, oysters would last for weeks.

With the arrival of the railroad in 1849, and of commercially available ice, oyster processing changed. In the little stores below the bank at the lower wharf, shuckers now cracked the shells, cut out the meat, and packed it in one-gallon—or larger—wooden kegs, added ice, and sealed the kegs. Horse-drawn wagons carried them to the depot, where the morning accommodation train took them to New York, for delivery to Delmonico's or to the Fulton Street Fish Market. The first refrigerated boxcars were built to transport barrels of oysters packed in ice to San Francisco.

Ashabel Bond's oyster sloop Samuel C. Bond, *built at Bedell's in Stratford, races home from the oyster beds in a disturbed sea, her crew clustered in the cockpit.*

The owners of the stores were the owners of the fleet, a single vessel or at most two or three family owned sloops. Generations of owners carried on the business. The Lewises were typical. Captain William Augustus Lewis was in Bridgeport in the 1850s with the 18.4-ton sloop *Bellport*, then with the 21.7-ton *Palestine*. When Stratford began to lease oyster grounds in 1861, Lewis was the first man to take an acre. His first Stratford vessel was the *Peri*, 22.4 tons, in 1864–1866; then in 1867 he bought the 38-ton *J.C.R. Brown* and operated it until 1879, when at age 62 he was listed as "managing owner" and John Savage of Westchester was its master.

His occupation extended to his social life. Nathan Wells's diary notes on June 9, 1868, "After closing [their Masonic lodge meeting] the brethern were invited to Capt. William A Lewis's to partake of oysters. Had a good time." It got better. On May 3, 1869 Wells wrote, "This evening attended lodge after which went to Capt. Wm A Lewis's house and partook of an oyster supper and had a *splendid* time."

A good oystering skipper could handle other jobs as well. For a time, Captain Lewis ran the Lewis Shorehouse on Bridgeport's Seaview Avenue. And when Wells's coasting schooner was left down the coast without a master in 1874, his first thought was Lewis: "24 Nov Went to see Capt Lewis at West Stratford to get him to go to Wilmington Del to bring home schr *Clarissa Allen* but he could not go."

When Lewis died in 1883, his role was already filled. His son, also William Augustus Lewis, born in 1857, went aboard the *Brown* as a teenager and oystered all his life. "Captain Bill" was known not only as an oysterman, but as one of the finest racing skippers on the Sound. Commodore of the Park City Yacht Club and sailing member of the Pootatuck, he hired out to sail the yachts of local businessmen. Many a sandbagger he sailed to victory, with hired oystermen as crew. He had his oyster sloop *Arrow* designed by yacht designer Crit Smith, and she was fast. With *Arrow*, Captain Bill routinely won the oysterboat races held at Larchmont, and would race at the drop of a signal flag. His son J. Fletcher once related, "When I was a lad of five, my father would take me out with him to the oyster grounds. Many a time a good looking yacht would come by and my father would yell, 'Haul in the dredge!' They would shove me under the counter and race that yacht all the way to the damn Thimbles!"

In the late nineteenth century, burgeoning demand for oysters in the cities brought out every potential harvester on the coast. On September 1, 1868 Nathan Wells wrote, "The oyster law was off today and a fleet of 175 sail was dredging off Long Beach, a splendid sight." All along the Housatonic, oyster sloops were built and launched to compete with sloops from Bridgeport, Milford, New Haven, and across the Sound, dredging in crowded offshore beds. In 1885 Ashabel Bond built his own oyster steamer *Bond Currier* at his brother's wharf. By 1881 leased beds

This fleet of oyster sloops is busy dredging under sail. In the foreground are, from left to right, Saxton, Priscilla, Bernice, *and* Shadow. *(Courtesy Tallmadge Brothers.)*

were common, and boundary disputes arose between the dredgers. In a chaotic situation, the state established the Connecticut Shellfish Commission to control the fishermen. The new Commission, in their second annual report in 1883, mapped the oyster grounds. The Stratford Natural Bed, 3,057 acres, stretched across the Milford and Bridgeport boundaries. South of the natural bed, leased beds belonged to F.J. Beardsley, Judson and Whiting, H.J. Lewis, H.C. Rowe, W.M. Rowland & Co., J. Smith & Sons, Stratford Oyster Co., G.H. Townsend, and P.F. West.

In outlining the natural beds, which were defined as having contained self-propagating oysters within the last ten years, the commissioners held noisy hearings, with one side arguing for larger natural beds and another claiming that they were played out and should be leased to "oyster growers," as the ones who prepared their own beds and had exclusive rights were called.

Stratford vessels licensed to work the natural beds in 1893 included *Amateur*, William Lewis; *Harry*, Housatonic Oyster Co., Captain Samuel Wakelee; *Ella May*, owned and operated by George Culver; *Jennie & Alice*, owned and captained by Henry Fordham; *Jesse*, owner Wilbur Hine and Captain Nelson Wakelee; George Richardson's *Stormy Petrel*, Captain George Merrill; *Laura V.*, Fillmore Baker and Captain Charles D. Wicks; *Alida*, owner/operator G.W. Mattson; *Ino*, owner/operator Edward Thompson; and Henry Lewis's *Alice C.*, skipper John Holberg.

In 1896, the *Harry*; Culver's *Ella May*; Fordham's *Jennie & Alice*; Richardson's *Stormy Petrel*; George Jack's *Elmie*; and *Marguerite*, registered to Mary Garry and run by Marcus Garry, listed Stratford as their "hailing place." New registrants were Charles Jack, with *Mary Underhill*; Captain John Loundes and C.W. Blakeslee, owner/captain of *Waghenicut*; and Daniel Talmadge, owner/operator of *Little Jane*. Although Bill Lewis lived in West Stratford, *Amateur* was registered in Bridgeport. Over 80 Stratford oystermen are listed in the 1896 city directory. In 1897 the Stratford-Bridgeport oyster industry boasted 19 steamers and 200 schooners and sloops, and 60,000 bushels of oysters were shipped to Europe alone.

As 1900 approached, Stratford's largest oyster companies, Bluepoint, Housatonic, Stratford, and H.J. Lewis, dominated the scene. In 1898 Henry Porter's Bluepoint Oyster Company issued 284 shares of stock priced at $3,550 and held by many of the local oystermen themselves, and by others in the business—Andrew Radel, D.M. Tallmadge, and F.M. Rowley. The Housatonic Oyster Company, H.H. Judson president and Frank Sammis treasurer, reported 140 shares worth $9,142 in 1897, held mostly by local people. The same year, Stratford Oyster Company had eight stockholders, 400 shares, and $10,000 capitalization, per president Ezra Whiting and treasurer Albert Wilcoxson, with H.J. Lewis the major holder.

Henry Lewis was president of his own large H.J. Lewis Oyster Co., which had $100,000 of stock paid in. He owned 3,988 shares, Mary Lewis held one, Albert Lewis held one, and treasurer James Herring had one.

Working the leased oyster beds was a year-round chore. In 1894 the Stratford Oyster Co. spread 10,500 bushels of shells and 141,780 bushels of gravel and sand to prepare for the set. The statewide total was 2,119,800 bushels of shells and 1,291,780 bushels of gravel. In 1895, Stratford Oyster spread 10,622 bushels of shells out of 1,711,069 statewide. H.J. Lewis was ten times as large.

The oyster harvests peaked about 1900, after which Stratford's role in the industry changed significantly. In 1903 H.J. Lewis moved to Bridgeport from its Housatonic River site and leased its large waterfront building near Broad Street to the Pootatuck Yacht Club. When Henry J. Lewis died in 1909 his son H. LeRoy Lewis, who continued to live in Stratford, took over the company and, at his death in the hurricane of 1938, also owned the Narragansett Bay Oyster Company and the Modern Oyster Company in Greenport. The small Housatonic Oyster Company continued to operate in Stratford: in 1915 its address was that of its treasurer Frank Sammis on Academy Hill.

Starr Beardsley's Stratford Oyster Company was absorbed into the Sealshipt Oyster System, which in 1911 took over Merwin & Sons and its facilities in Milford harbor. In 1912 the company, now based in Milford, put Charles E. (Shang) Wheeler in charge of its office and docks in Milford, beginning his 34-year career as oyster farm manager, decoy carver, legislator, and naturalist. In 1913 the firm renamed itself the Connecticut Oyster Farms Company, subsidiary of North Atlantic Oyster Farms, Inc. In 1929 Connecticut Oyster Farms was swallowed by the Bluepoints Company,—itself a part of General Foods —with oyster beds spread throughout Connecticut, Rhode Island, and Long Island waters. By 1910 Rhode Island overtook Connecticut in oysters harvested—15 million pounds versus 10 million—and Stratford had lost its largest oyster companies but retained its leased and natural beds, its sprawling grounds for seed oysters, and its shell mounds.

The brackish waters in and near the Housatonic supplied nearly all the seed for northern oyster waters, and deep shellpiles near its mouth supplied the covering for their beds.

In the nineteenth century these shells were taken from the river and spread on oyster beds in the Sound. This unique local industry began in Stratford. One of the first shellermen was Little Mack, apparently a half-Indian from the Scatacook Mack family. Mack stored his harvest at a place soon called Shellkeep Point, at the south end of present day Stratford Festival property, and the harbor called Cupheag, or Stratford Harbor, became Mack's Harbor. His customers included builders, who calcined the shells into quicklime for wallplaster, and oystermen, who at the start of the nineteenth century were just beginning to recycle their cultch (shells) to line the oyster beds.

Early shellermen worked from scows and skiffs, lifting shells with tongs and rakes from depths as great as 16 feet. A boatload of 60 bushels was a good day's work. Each shellerman had his own pile somewhere on the shore; some were in Ferry Creek—the log of the gas boat *Billo* mentions "finished loading on Goodsell shell, Somers shell, in Broad Creek."

Knell's Island became the main repository for these oyster shells. At the end of their day the shellermen took their dugouts, scows, skiffs, and sharpies up the river to the marsh island, where they shoveled their loads into wheelbarrows and wheeled them ashore on planks to their piles of shells. In the spring their work paid off when oyster planters bought the shells and loaded them onto their own sloops, schooners, and steamers, to spread them on their leased beds as cultch. There were never many shellermen, but some 50 of them were constantly employed. Harbormaster Fletch Lewis wrote, "Many of our well known watermen engaged in this lucrative but man-killing business. Some of the names which come back to me from the early 1900s are: John Goodsell, William Hubbell, Charles Crane, Ren Smith, Wilbur Hine, Robert Plumb, Henry Fordham, Andy McTaggart, and Charles Loper."

The law forbade the use of power to harvest shells, but in 1908 it occurred to someone that it said nothing about using power to make water flow. By rigging a large propeller onto a steeply angled propshaft, it became possible to moor a boat where it could direct a stream of water down onto ancient beds of shells and dislodge enough to scoop them up with ease. Any old shallow draft boat, sharpie, or sandbagger, could be fitted with a five-horsepower make-or-break engine and a large low-speed prop, but later rigs had up to 150 horsepower. Thus "shell kicking" came into being and the "kicker boat" was born. It was a procedure unique to the Housatonic.

Fred Goodsell and his men tong the bottom for shells aboard a scow near the mouth of the river. The shells were piled on the marsh for sale to leased-bed operators.

In the mid-twentieth century, shellermen were still piling shells onto the marsh. Here young men at their summer jobs wheel barrowfuls of shells aboard waiting schooners. Tallyman Shang Wheeler, with umbrella, counts the loads.

The procedure was simple. The boat was positioned with its stern to the underwater bank of shells, with two lines leading from its bow, sternwards to distant anchors on shore or underwater, one on each side and at a large angle to each other. When the flywheel was spun and the engine started, the boat was restrained from moving forward and its thrust drove water onto the shells, dislodging them into a loose heap or driving them up onto the top of the shellbank. By moving the tiller, the "kicker" could be pivoted about its bow through a large arc, and thus direct its thrust along a length of shellbank without repositioning the boat. The shells were tonged into the waiting scows and taken to the shellpiles, for sale in the spring.

In the 1930s the wheelbarrow men who carted shells up the planks onto the buyers' waiting scows or schooners were young college students, tanning bodies and building muscles during their summers off. Allan Poole, a business major, was chosen for the job of "tallyman" or counter, ticking off the count of barrow loads on his clipboard. As each barrowman passed Poole with his load, he shouted "tally one" or "tally two," and Poole made a mark on his sheet. Each mark was worth a penny to the barrowman.

When the oyster business declined after World War I, so did shelling. A few men kept it up: John and Frederick Goodsell were two of them. The total number of shellermen at Stratford tapered to about two dozen, then as oystering declined, the shell heaps disappeared and shelling became a memory.

By 1915 the number of oystermen in the Stratford directory had dropped from 82 counted in 1896 to 37. There were better jobs in factories, and nature and man were working together to destroy the oyster industry. In 1918 the U.S. Bureau of Fisheries set up a laboratory in Milford to work together with the Connecticut Shellfish Commission to improve the crop, but starfish depredations increased. In 1935 they began to apply lime—calcium oxide—at 480 pounds to the acre, to kill starfish on the beds. It was 80 percent effective, but could be used only in seasons when there were no commercial fish larvae in the waters. Old Bill Lewis commented, "We might as well try to bail out Long Island Sound with a teaspoon as try to blot out the starfish with lime!"

In 1932 there was no oyster set in Milford. In 1939 Captain Bill, after 70 years in oystering, commented, "The oyster business is a gamble, pure and simple. Last year the oyster growers spent plenty of money planting shells to attract an oyster set in the water off New Haven, Milford, Bridgeport, Stratford, the entire cultivated vicinity. But did they get a large and early set? They did not!" The little captain went on to remark, "But the Housatonic River [natural beds] had an elegant set! If there weren't any shells planted in the Housatonic, where did the fine set come from?"

But fine sets became rare. Industrial chemicals dumped into the Naugatuck upstream destroyed shellfish. By 1950 even barnacles gave up growing on boat hulls. Raw and undertreated sewage from towns along the coast and up the valley contaminated the crop. Captain Lewis in 1939 said, "But the sewer system of Bridgeport drove us out of business. Today all oysters that are raised in these waters have to be transplanted to Great South Bay and Gardiner's Bay and other maturing grounds so that they will be purified and fit to eat."

Oystermen will not forget the hurricane of September 21, 1938. Henry Leroy Lewis, president of the H.J. Lewis Oyster Company, and Mrs. Lewis were drowned that day, when immense seas swept over their vacation island in the Thimbles. Their oyster beds and many others were ripped up and covered by silt, and laid waste by ravaging floodwaters pouring from the river.

During World War II the industry languished. Young men went to war, and old men tried to work alone. The Ventulette family, Louis and his sons Robert and Murty, natural growthers, had two boats, the little *Beatrice* (they called her the *Dishpan*) and the *J.F. Penny*, a 50-foot sloop brought from New Jersey in 1939. Robert recalled, "Things were a little rough during the war. He [his father] couldn't get no help or anything. Things were getting rough for him, so he sank the *Penny* so she would keep swelled up and everything, and wouldn't open up. Down in Johnson's Creek. So when we come back out of service, you know, we reconditioned her up again. Like I say, we put all new sails on her, new engine, all new railings."

In 1950, the year the Ventulettes quit oystering, a few sails of oyster vessels were still visible on the Sound, but the industry was moribund. No more than a dozen natural growthers were left on the Bridgeport and Housatonic natural beds. By the 1960s most shellfish firms had vanished.

But the oysters are returning. In 1971 the 90-year-old Shellfish Commission was absorbed into the new Department of Environmental Protection (DEP), and in 1972 was renamed the Aquaculture Division, to administer 40,000 acres of leased, franchised, and natural or public beds from its Milford office. That same year the Congress passed the Federal Clean Water Act. From a low of 32,000 bushels in 1972, the statewide crop grew to 133,000 bushels in 1982, and 244,000 in 1984. The Aquaculture Division, aided by local industry, spread some $30,000 worth of shells on the Stratford, Milford, and Bridgeport grounds by 1986. In 1973 the division issued 31 boat and 49 personal licenses. The 1973 leasers of the lots off Stratford were:

Leaser	Acres
Andrew Radel Oyster Co.	206.6
Bloom Brothers	354.2
Long Island Oyster Farms, Inc.	1,451.1
Pine Island Oyster Farms, Inc.	206.6
Shellfish, Inc.	206.0

Blistering heat and sharp shells tormented young workers as they sorted and bagged the catch brought up from the bottom aboard the Catherine M. Wedmore. *(Courtesy Hillard Bloom, Talmadge Brothers.)*

Years of effort by the DEP have reduced industrial pollution and improved sewage treatment in the Housatonic and the Sound. Cleaner waters, better control of predators, better beds, and luck paid off with a larger crop. By 1992 Connecticut produced some 6.9 million pounds of oyster meat, worth $44 million at dockside, and issued 108 boat and 197 personal licenses for 1992–1993.

The large producers in the state have consolidated. Hillard Bloom and his brother Norman bought their first boat and started Bloom Brothers Seafood in 1948. In 1967 they bought Tallmadge Brothers, and built it into one of the largest producers in the country, with 20,000 acres in the Sound alone. Hillard Bloom, operating from Norwalk, continued to fund and sponsor improvements to bring back oystering in the state. Terry Backer, oysterman, state legislator, and Soundkeeper, said, "He's been a guy who's had a dream and pursued it. He's seeding the future of the industry."

In 1990, when the buyboat *Brier* began to come into the river twice a week, 12 to 20 little oyster scows would cluster around the *Brier* to sell the seed oysters they had dredged from the river bottom in the last few days. Each boat reflected the ideas of its owner-builder. Some had telephone-booth-sized wheelhouses in the stern, others had little outhouse-shaped glass houses in the bow. All had drogues

Workers continue sorting and bagging the catch aboard the Catherine M. Wedmore. *(Courtesy Hillard Bloom, Talmadge Brothers.)*

At the end of a long day and a long career, Jesse Johnson, *one of the last working oyster sloops, heads home in the 1950s.*

and hand winches to bring the haul aboard. Working together to shovel oysters from the "sampans" into bushel-sized wire baskets, they dumped bushel after bushel from boat after boat until the job was done. One of *Brier's* crewmen kept a tally: each bushel brought its seller $7. Then, with a full deckload, the buyboat headed down the river.

In the following years, when the harvest shrank, the *Brier* was replaced by the smaller but much more photogenic *Laurel*, built in Tottenville, New York in 1891, then later by the *Louis R.*, or the little *Greenport* out of Norwalk, or occasionally the *Robert Utz*. All of these were handsome old-time wooden boats—some had started out as steamboats—and their arrival brought hordes of spectators to the dock.

As the years went on, fewer independents showed up at the buyboat—they had indeed become independent, and now sold to out-of-state wholesalers who came in trucks to buy. In the autumn of 1997 the buyboats' pilings were used only five times. About 20 of the seed oystermen licensed by the state, both natural growthers and owners of leased grounds, worked out of Stratford, mostly from Brown's Boat Works adjacent to Bond's Dock.

Buyboat Columbia *noses in to Tallmadge's pilings at Bond's Dock, to wait for independent oystermen to bring their craft alongside. Oysters were loaded by the bushel.*

The Stratford Shellfish Commission was one of the town's most competent commissions: with no political appointees, it was made up of professionals. The commission collected 50¢ a bushel from the seedmen to buy cultch and have it spread. One chairman, Zbigniew Zadrozny, who began oystering in 1982 and sailed from Brown's yard every day, commented, "Anyone who wants to oyster has to like it. Oystermen never stop working in the winter. You stop working, you get cold."

John Volk, director of the state Bureau of Aquaculture in Milford, attributed the return of oysters to Connecticut to modern aquaculture and their reputed high quality. He said that oyster seedbeds in this area—the Housatonic estuary and off Long Beach and Seaside Park—are historically the most productive in the northeast, because of their mix of fresh and salt water, shallow areas, and a firm sea floor, combined with the right nutrients. He called the seed oystermen an integral part of the oyster's growth process; their work in cultivating, hand dredging, and harvesting the seedbeds kept the beds healthy and productive.

The average yearly harvest of Stratford area seed oysters now ran from 30,000 to 130,000 bushels. In three or four years more, these grew into market oysters. Through most of the twentieth century, pollutants in the Sound made it necessary to move the oysters to the south shore of Long Island, to spend those last four years in Great South Bay or Gardiner's Bay, but in the 1990s cleanup programs made it possible for some oysters once again to be marketed directly from beds in the Sound.

The statewide catch in 1998 was 179,000 bushels, down from 525,000 in 1996, 752,000 in 1995, and 894,000 in 1992. The reason seemed to be two protozoan-caused diseases, Dermo and MSX. The state Bureau of Aquaculture observed that the attacks were cyclic, occurring in warmer, more saline water, and spoke of planting the Sound with a strain of oysters more resistant to infection. With ever cleaner waters, the bivalves will be better able to overcome the parasites.

As the twenty-first century begins, a global warming trend has brought an increase in the temperatures of the river and the Sound—45°F in February 1998 instead of the normal 39°F—signifying longer seasons. Shellfish boats still go out from Stratford for oysters, clams, or lobsters on an almost daily basis. *Wicklow*, *Johnny T.*, *Frances Thurston*, *Benny's Shadow*, *Letitia Young*, and *Gypsy* set out at dawn and return at dusk.

State and federal agencies are now working at fever pitch to restore our waters and optimize our shellfish industry. One entrepreneur at Brown's Boat Works is planning to raise oysters in suspended cages. The long term trend is encouraging.

LOG OF THE STEAMER *STRATFORD*

The log of the oyster steamer *Stratford*, from 1904 until April 1911, portrays the daily life of a typical steam-powered oyster dredger working in Connecticut, New York, and Rhode Island waters, preparing grounds, seeding, dredging, hand picking, and supporting a large fleet of sailing craft. Her owner and her master were also not averse to carrying groups of friends and associates on outings up and down the Sound.

Stratford was one of several steam powered oyster dredgers owned by Frederick Starr Beardsley's Stratford Oyster Company, commanded from 1896 to 1927 by Captain George A. Cleveland. Designed by A.J. Hoyt and built in Bridgeport in 1891, *Stratford* was 77 feet overall, and registered at 98 tons. Equipped with powered hoisters, she had a removable house that was installed each October and taken off in March.

George Cleveland was born in Harwinton on January 30, 1852. He moved to Stratford in 1865, and worked as cook aboard Isaac Wheeler's schooner *E.P. Burton*, then on Marcus Hale's schooner *Falcon*. After a trip to the West Indies he became sailmaster of the schooner *Union*. By 1873 Cleveland had enough experience and cash to become master and part owner of the 93-ton schooner *Josephine*. Cleveland soon took over the schooner *W. McCobb*, then from 1878 to 1882 commanded the 66-ton schooner *Anson Brown* in the coastal trade.

On a run up the Sound one cold, blustery day, the *Brown* was carrying 500 kegs, or 12,500 pounds, of gunpowder from New York to the Union Metallic Cartridge Company in Bridgeport. To keep them dry, the powder kegs were stowed in the stateroom, so when the *Brown* lurched to a large wave and the stateroom stove upset, there was great excitement aboard. Quick action by the captain brought order out of panic, and although some kegs were burned nearly through the staves, none exploded, and the fire came under control.

George Cleveland decided he had temporarily had enough of going to sea. He signed on for a year as watchman at the H.J. Lewis Oyster Company, but received a master's license for steam and returned to sea as master of the *Fred Brown*, the *Annie*, and then the *Etta May*. In 1896 Captain Cleveland took command of the steam oyster dredger *Stratford* and stayed for 31 years.

Stratford worked wherever needed. On the day after Thanksgiving in 1906, after taking on 3 tons of coal at Miller's and putting on the deckhouse, *Stratford*:

> Raised steam at 6 25am and went to Wickford, Arived at 4 35pm and laid up.
> Wickford Dec 1 Raised steam at 6am and went on Kingston Ground and
>   buoyed up and caught 500 bushels oysters and went to Providence
>   and unload and put barels and baskets ashore and laid up.
> Providence Dec 5 Raised steam at 5 55am Went on Kingston Ground
>   and planted shels on lot 9 and seed oysters on lot 7 and then caught
>   for Naraganset Oyster Co. oysters and took coal [5 tons] and came to
>   dock and took shels and seed and laid up.

After working for the Narragansett Oyster Company on the 5th, *Stratford* continued planting shells and seed oysters on the grounds and harvesting market oysters for Beardsley's own Stratford Oyster Company. By December 22, when the steamer went to Wickford and then home, the catch for the "shop" totalled 4,450 bushels. On Christmas eve at Bridgeport the crew unloaded oysters for Charlie Wakeley to take to Stratford.

On January 28, 1907, *Stratford* again set out for Wickford and Providence and tended the Rhode Island grounds through winter gales and blizzards until February 21, when, after unloading 8,275 bushels of oysters at Providence and 1,025 onto the schooner *Robert Resnick*, she returned to Bridgeport with 110 bushels of hand-picked aboard. A trip to Greenport on March 6 to 8 found heavy ice in Gardiner's Bay, so after setting a few buoys and dragging for starfish (caught three bushels) it was back to Bridgeport.

A short trip to Kingston yielded some oysters for the Hayes Fish Company in Bridgeport. On March 18, with seed from lots 9 and 18 on deck and the gas boat *Governor* in tow, *Stratford* headed once more for Wickford. After an overnight at Duck Island, a feed pump piston rod broke, forcing *Stratford* to limp into New London for repairs. Then on to plant the seed on Kingston ground, to land ten buoys with their stone anchors at Wickford, to set marks on the grounds, and back to Bridgeport by 4:50 p.m. on March 21.

The vernal equinox gone by, on March 22 Captain Cleveland removed the house, took on six tons of coal, went to lots 9 and 14 for seed for Providence, and on the 26th was back in Rhode Island waters.

The many grounds, or lots, mentioned in the *Stratford's* log, covered parts of three states. In Rhode Island Bay the grounds were Wickford, Kingston, and Jamestown. In Gardiner's Bay, *Stratford* worked at Rose's Grace and South Ferry. Between 1908 and 1910 Rhode Island's production surpassed that of Connecticut,

When built in 1891 the steamer Stratford *was 77 feet long. At overhaul in 1910, they replaced her boiler, then cut her in half and added 25 feet in the middle.* Stratford *spent the rest of her years as a 102-foot boat. (Courtesy Mystic Seaport, Mystic, CT.)*

partly due to the steamer *Stratford* and the seed oyster transferred from Long Island Sound's spawning grounds to the the saltier waters of Rhode Island where they matured for market.

To recover its investment, an oyster steamer's job was to use its greater speed and fancier equipment to work as much as possible with sloops and schooners on the grounds, transferring loads to them to haul to land. *Stratford* worked with hundreds of these sailing vessels.

Year by year, the seasonal tasks repeated. As the "R" months arrived, *Stratford* kept busy planting seed and dredging market oysters for the "shop" and other companies, through the cold winter months. Seed oysters were dredged from their lots and spread in deeper waters to grow to market oysters. In the worst weather, when dredging was impossible, time was spent destroying starfish at the beds. The lots were kept marked by constantly replacing missing stakes at their corners, particularly after storms. An entry in January 1905 says "Took men and went in the woods for stakes." In late spring and early summer, cultch (shells, and sometimes brush) was spread in shallow water waiting for the spat (newly hatched oyster larva) that would come drifting by in late July.

Temperature was very important. Spawning occurred above 68°F. In some years, water temperatures kept reproduction low. At the beds in Long Island Sound, *Stratford* kept a careful watch each spring, to see whether the painstaking

George Cleveland went to sea at age 13 and spent 17 years in sail. With a ticket in steam in 1884, he skippered several steamers, his last 31 years as master of Stratford.

preparation of the ground would pay off. In 1905 readings began on May 26, but it was July 9 before a 70° bottom reading foretold success. In 1906, July 2 gave 70°, but in 1907 it was July 19. In 1908 July 14 showed 68° on the bottom and 69° on the surface. In 1909 water temperature on the bottom never rose above 64°F, but in 1910, the last year of this record, the magic number occurred on July 12, at the noon half flood on lot 48, and all the cleaning, cultching, and starring done that spring paid off.

Stratford's log records many hours of dredging to remove the oyster's greatest threat, starfish—"staring," they called it. Steamboats were ideal for destroying starfish, using tanks of boiling water. Starring was done whenever there was time between other jobs. The process was to drag a curious large mop of baggywrinkle along the bottom. Starfish grabbed and became tangled in the mop, which was then hoisted to the deck and plunged into a vat of scalding water, sprayed with live steam. One entry reads "Went to Pembroke Dock and got stakes and star bars," another describes a blacksmith making the bars, and on another date "men made mops." After a New Year's Day arrival in Bridgeport in 1906, "got ready to go staring." In Narragansett Bay for October the count was 101 barrels of stars. In the sound in November they took four barrels, then after Thanksgiving installed the deckhouse and returned to Rhode Island, where they stayed until December 23 planting seed and hauling market oysters, too busy to drag for stars. Home for Christmas, then back to Providence on January 30, where, after planting seed and shells on lot 9, they resumed "staring" and caught two bushels. The final starfish entry in this log is in August 1910, at Robins Island: 18 bushels on the 4th, a ton on the 5th, and 30 bushels on the 12th.

Stratford spent a lot of time on the developing Rhode Island grounds. On August 20, 1908, on a trip to Greenport out of Bridgeport, Captain Cleveland boasted a party of 21 friends "aboard the good ship *Stratford*." One of the 21 signatures in the logbook is "Chas E Wheeler, Providence, R I." Shang was at the time employed by the Stratford Oyster Company, working at the East Providence oyster plant shared between Captain Fred Beardsley's company and William M. Merwin & Sons, Co. of Milford.

Throughout the winter of 1908–1909 *Stratford* worked out of the plant at East Providence in the Rhode Island beds in the Providence River and Narragansett Bay. Arriving at Providence on December 10, *Stratford* spent the next day planting 150 bushels of seed, then towing the schooner *George F. Carman* in to "the shop," and going out to work Quonset in a driving snowstorm. On the 12th she towed the *Carman* back out to the grounds and planted on two lots. Back and forth, planting on the lots, harvesting, towing in the schooners, unloading at the "shop," coaling up (about 6 tons every five days), the steamer worked with the schooners *Carman, E.M. Robinson, Eva Lewis, Mary Lewis, Lillie Wilson, Mary Patterson, Louisa Polleys*, and the steamboat *Governor*.

Stratford's steam engine was the product of generations of development. Improved materials, higher pressures, and compounding improved the efficiency of steam, but engines of the day remained rugged, simple mechanisms, operable day after day, asking only good coal, clean boiler water, occasional flue cleaning, and plenty of lubrication. Over a six year period, the log has few complaints about the engines. One such occurred on March 19, 1907 when Stratford was towing the *Governor* up the Sound. The feedwater pump piston rod broke and they had to go into New London for repairs. They must have raised steam in *Governor* and towed *Stratford* in.

The hoisting gear, in constant use, required the most attention. On February 26, 1906, the log reports the crew "Laid up and worked on histers," and on the 27th "Laid to dock and overhaled hoisters." On June 12, "Went to dock and repaired hoyster." On June 20, "Broak roler on hang and had to go in and repair." In 1908 the hoisters were overhauled on November 2. On the 23rd both dredges broke, and were sent to the blacksmith shop in Providence for overnight repair. This time they lasted seven months, when the hoisters broke and had to have new stands.

Getting ready for the seed oyster trade in March 1908, the crew spent a few days overhauling, painting, and readying the dredges. That year the annual overhaul began on July 30, with another deck replacement. They took *Stratford* to Port Jefferson on August 3, and hauled her on the ways at John Hawkins's yard, where the work took 11 days. Finally on August 14, they painted the bottom and returned to Bridgeport. Again in 1909, on August 10 they hauled at Hawkins's railway, replaced the stern bearing, and painted the bottom.

Other failures included blown gaskets. On December 1, 1908, "Blowed out hand hole gasket 6:50 off Patience Is. Pulled fires and blew off boiler. Towed to shop at E Providence 2pm." The repair lasted until May 16, when, at Bridgeport, "Hand hold gasket blew out and blew of boyler and laid up at dock all day." Condenser failures were recurring events. On September 30, "Laid at doc. Put in condenser tubes." And on October 2, "Finished condenser. Coaled up."

In August 1910, *Stratford* came into Bridgeport and tied up. The boat was now 19 years old and needed serious work. The crew removed her old boiler, then towed the oyster steamer across the Sound to Port Jefferson and hauled her out to be rebuilt. The plan was to cut the hull in two, haul the two halves 25 feet, 2 inches apart, and insert a whole new section. The work began on September 7 when the saws went to work. By the 23rd the lengthened keel was laid and new ribs were being added. Into a blustery winter the work continued. Deck beams were laid on the afterdeck, and the shear and garboard planks were caulked.

On some December days the log read, "blowing a gail; snowing a blizzard; no work done today." On others the work progressed: "started to spread the after house; finished planking today; caulking all day; finished deck and caulked quarter deck; bunker plates and chane pipe." Later in the month, the log reads, "Snow squalls; joiners would not work; wind nor west a gail and coald; the carpenters would not work." Into January 1911, the yardmen rebuilt the deckhouse and coppered the bottom. On the 7th the coppering was done and bottom paint was applied.

As work continued on the house and rails, the workers slid the steamer onto the ways. On January 18, yard boss Hunt would not launch her, but on the 19th at 2:00 p.m. the lengthened oyster boat slid off the ways and the steamer *Mystery* took her under tow, heading for Rivington Street in the East River. On the 20th *Stratford* was in drydock having a new seacock installed.

On the 21st the steamer *Champion* towed *Stratford* to the foot of Rivington Street where a new condenser heater, boiler, and stack were put aboard. The work was done by 1:30pm and two men came to install the condenser. On the 23rd the ash pans and the circulator pump arrived, and engine overhaul began, together with alignment, boiler installation, and piping work. A new steam steering gear was installed, and on February 6 the engine was fired up to check out the boiler, while gales raged outside.

On Lincoln's Birthday *Mystery* returned and towed the lengthened *Stratford* with her new power plant down the Sound. On February 13 they were back at Port Jefferson, tied up at the town dock.

It took another month to complete the carpentry. The deckhouse, boiler room, pilot house, and rail all needed finishing, and the deck, the house, and the skylight frame all needed canvasing. On March 3 the steamer *Lockwood* took the boat in tow across the Sound to Bridgeport, where she waited for inspection.

Finally on March 13 Captain Cleveland raised steam in the refurbished *Stratford* and headed for Norwalk for yet more finish work. After a 9:40 a.m. arrival, men swarmed over the vessel once more, working on the engine and the steering gear,

At their annual outing on the Stratford *six prominent Stratfordites—David Rhodes, Watson Smith, Ezra Whiting, Henry Stagg, owner Fred Beardsley, and Stiles Judson Jr.—pose with Captain Cleveland.*

painting the pilot house, putting lagging on the boiler, finishing the engine room, setting up the hoisters and the hoisting engine. On April 3, 1911 *Stratford* came home to Bridgeport to install new coal bunkers.

Captain Cleveland commanded the *Stratford* from 1896 through 1927, retiring after 62 years at sea. His spirit is shown by the occasion when he had to put away an aged family cat. He put the cat at the rear of the property, then went back to the house, picked up his gun, and shot the cat. Asked why he shot from so far away, he answered "I wanted to give it a sporting chance." Used to life at sea, he never took to indoor plumbing, and at the family home on Broadbridge Avenue a privy stood in the backyard, solely for his use. When on April 22, 1934 the old man died at the age of 83, the privy came down immediately, and on the spot grew the largest sunflowers ever seen.

DUCKS AND THE DECOY CARVERS

Stratford marshes have always been a food and rest stop for waterfowl on the Atlantic flyway. Ancient records say, "Ye wilde ducks and geese were so plentifulle as to darken ye Sunne when they arose from ye mud flats and marshes. . . . Ye feathers made goode beds and heade rests." The vast salt marsh in the Housatonic estuary and the immense Great Meadows marsh offered, respectively, 600 acres and 1,400 acres of refuge for migratory waterfowl en route. Within memory of living men great flights of birds filled the skies each autumn and each spring. Waterman Howard Hyde remembers setting out decoys for his father and Shang Wheeler early in the twentieth century, when our natural resources seemed endless.

The birds included geese—Canada geese and brant, marsh and pond ducks—black ducks, canvasback, scaup, goldeneyes, mallards, pintails, Labrador, teal, broadbills, whistlers, and old squaws; as well as the diving ducks—mergansers, buffleheads, and scoters (coot); the shorebirds—rail and woodcock; and the now extinct passenger pigeon.

The aborigines lured waterfowl to their nets, stretched across the water's surface, using decoys made by stuffing the skins of captured birds with hay, or weaving body shapes of reeds and mounting real bird heads on them. The local Paugussetts were known to set up stones along the shore for decoys, a small stone atop a larger one.

The very volume of migratory birds encouraged commercial gunners in the nineteenth century. These market gunners used large bore 4 gage and 8 gage guns, worked in teams, and could slaughter more than 100 birds a day. They first used fixed shooting boxes, floating four-man batteries, sinkboxes, and live decoys. Large bore guns and live decoys were finally outlawed.

Recreational hunters practiced line shooting, wherein several hunters would anchor their boats in a line stretching across the river. Shang described such a shoot in the 1890s:

> The gang were polled the night before at the country store, and the party was made up, all agreeing to meet at the Lower Dock at five the next morning to row down to the mouth of the river to line off across its mouth. There were seven boats of us, all rigged about alike as far as the gunning skiffs were concerned. Some of the boys carried a few profile decoys, mounted on lath triangles in groups of three, or on flat boards in pairs, so as to trail off with the tide astern of his boat. Some used one or two exceptionally large stools with the idea that they could be seen a long way off and would start the approaching birds toward his particular point in the line. Some gunners preferred the east end of the line, some the west end, and some the center. Positions were determined by drawing numbers and a small pool—a quarter or half dollar each—was made up for high gun.

In 1863 when Albert Laing came to Stratford, the skies often went dark with flocks of migrating ducks— broadbills, blacks, old squaws. Shooting spots were everywhere: in holes in the marsh, at bars along the shores, and from fleets of boats anchored across the channel. Spots identified on this 1910 chart include the following:

1. *Moneymaking Bar*
2. *Neck Creek*
3. *Sniffen's Point*
4. *Shell Hole*
5. *Mallard Hole*
6. *Fresh Pond*
7. *Broad Creek*
8. *Todd's Pond Hole*
9. *Toleration, or Poverty Bar*
10. *Oldfield Rock*
11. *Mack's Harbor*
12. *Boathouse Creek*
13. *Ferry Creek*
14. *Ford's Hole*
15. *Old Centennial Bar*
16. *Brinsmad'e Island*
17. *Goose island*
18. *Ferry Rocks*

North of the railroad bridge were Culver's Bar, Carting Island, Peacock Island, Long Island, Pope's Flat, and Fowler Island. The names of all the shooting spots were informal and often changed. Many sites disappeared as currents reshaped the land.

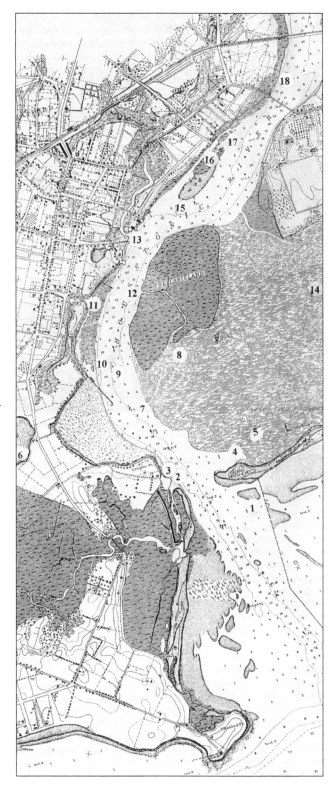

After the usual arguments over distance between boats, we got lined off, and as the sun first stuck his head up over the eastern horizon, the call was passed along the line, "Git down! Lay low!" and here came a bunch of coots, from the east'rd. They got abreast of the middle of our line and then swung in toward the feeding ground back of the beacon. It looked as if #5 (Rad Smith) would get the first shot, and as usual Rad got nervous and couldn't wait until the birds were near enough, but riz up and blazed away with both barrels of his old ten bore.

He didn't touch a feather. They turned off and hauled in again between #7 and #8. Here they got a real reception from Herk Smith, who had a new Scott ten and was a good shot. He tripped up one with each barrel and turned them toward Anse Dart, who had an old-fashioned lever action pump gun—and did he pump it! He just emptied it, killed one dead and straggled down two others.

So it went throughout the forenoon. There were long kills, easy misses, and cheers or jeers. Chasing cripples was the cause of more arguments than all else. "Why don't you kill 'em instead of just slowin' them up?" "Get back in line—you're spoiling our shots."

While rowing home, the alibis, excuses, and ribbing were something to hear. One gem was by Chick Welles, who said, "I don't know what ailed me today—I just couldn't hit a cow in the behind with a snow shovel." Another would lay it to the ammunition—a new load that he was trying. Another would claim that his gun didn't fit because he had too many clothes on. But the payoff came when they reached the dock and counted up the bag. One would have six, another seven. One would say, "That big skunkhead [surf scoter] should be in my bag. He landed twenty feet before you shot!" Then the other would retort, "Whatinell you talking about? You just scared him so as to make my shot tougher." The pool was paid to high gun, and with a "S'long, fellers," each one pulled away for home.

The earliest Stratford decoys were crude and primitive. Few survive. A black dated 1857 and bearing initials WP is typical: It is rough and flat, a "mudder" for use in the marshes where falling tides leave the decoy sitting on the mud. Its style is in contrast to the usual decoy of the time, the heavy full-bodied low-floater known as a "rocking horse."

Over the next century, the Stratford school of decoys evolved into an easily recognizable style. Their two piece hollow bodies made them lighter and they rode higher in the water. They were high breasted to ride well in tidal currents with slushy ice. They had a sleekness in body shape, with narrow breasted entry, flaring into the main body, then fairing into long tails.

It was Albert Davids Laing (1811–1886) who fostered a whole new concept in decoy carving, with beautifully realistic birds, and began what became known as the Stratford school. While many carvers made decoys in one fixed attitude,

The Stratford school of decoy carving evolved from Albert Laing's lifelike birds such as this early sleeping broadbill drake. The line separates the hollow top from the bottom board.

Laing's rig had sleepers, swimmers, feeders, birds at rest with their necks tucked back, others with head high and watchful, and a number of other natural positions. He came to Stratford just as a new generation of rifles and shotguns was turning members of a growing leisure class into recreational hunters.

Laing was born in Rahway, New Jersey, but his family moved to New York in 1820, where he hunted at an early age, in every waterway adjacent to the city. His father was a prosperous merchant, so young Albert had no problem hiring guides and purchasing his own scull, the *Rose*, built in Bridgeport by Henry Robbins and shipped to New York on the Sound steamer *Commodore*. Laing was an early initiate into the growing group of gentleman duck hunters. He moved to Stratford in 1863 and in 1864 he bought the Hale family's house on the river near the lower wharf and began a whole new life.

That first season from October 19, 1863 to May 19, 1864 he scored 625 birds including 467 coot and 96 old wives. In 1865, only 52 birds are specifically listed, but he noted in April, "good broadbill shooting at Fresh Pond," "ducks very plenty on Nell's Island flats," and " 'Alibi' [Edwards] killed 33 broadbills and 56 coot this day." On March 27, 1868 the journal says, "22 broadbill from boat in Coot Bar basin. Picked up for myself." Other hunting spots were Peck's Cove, Goose Island, south of Skate Bar, Quimby's Neck, Half Moon Cove, Old Field Cove, and near the outer buoy. From 1863 to 1871 his total recorded count of kills was 1,085 birds.

Laing decoys were well suited to the Stratford environment. Thomas Marshall believed he made his first decoy in Stratford in 1864. It was hollow, made of a

Albert Davids Laing moved to Stratford in mid-life to enjoy his passions for hunting water birds, fishing, developing fruits and vegetables, and carving decoys.

2-inch-thick top board and a 3/8 inch bottom board. The style did not satisfy him, so he shifted to a decoy made from two 2-inch pieces fastened together with copper nails and white lead. Marshall wrote:

> He made turnbacks with sleeping heads. He made high, medium, and low heads. His development of the Laing decoy was entirely the result of a gentleman's desire to have the best decoy for the area he shot in. Laing had the ability to originate, skill with tools, and an understanding of waterfowl and their habitat peculiar to the area.
>
> Laing used 2 inch pine boards, 6 inches wide and 14 inches long in the bodies of practically all decoys regardless of species. White pine was his principal wood, although some of his decoys were made from white cedar. The two 14" x 6" x 2" boards were planed smooth on one side and laid one on the other . . . held together with two thin nails. Guide lines were drawn on the combined blocks of wood, using a paper pattern. . . . the first rough shape was obtained by cutting with a narrow saw.

> The next shaping was done with a draw knife. . . . A spoke shave, pattern makers, or jackknife was used for the final shaping of the body. It is certain that Laing used additional templates to check the final curve of the breast and where it joined the neck and the stern of the decoy as well as the back and tail.

When the shaping was completed, the two blocks of wood were separated and the core hollowed out with bit and chisel. The resulting Laing decoy weighs less than 3 pounds.

The head was cut out as a side silhouette, then carved with a jackknife and smoothed with sandpaper and fastened to the body with a brass screw. The two body parts were then assembled. Marshall said:

> None of Laing's decoys I have used have leaked, and it was hard to find where the nails were placed. Most of them were made over a century ago, and until I found out how valuable they were I used them in my rig. . . . I believe Laing originated the Stratford style of decoy painting for golden eyes, blacks, and scaup.
>
> There were no straight lines, only curves. The bills of the scoters were painted in detail to show the many colors there with one blending into the next with a finger or dry brush.
>
> Laing decoys are lovely to look at whether they are on the water or on a table. They are practical to use, easy to set out, pick up, and ride well in choppy water and tidal slush ice.

Laing last used his gun on October 18, 1886. His diary for the last day of his life reads, "The swallows returned today." His obituary read:

> Albert D. Laing, a prominent and well-known resident shot himself on Saturday afternoon. The weapon used was a double barreled fowling piece. Mr. Laing had been very much depressed for several months and complained much of headaches. He was a person of decided literary and ample acquirements and spent much of his time reading upon scientific questions of the day. After engaging in various business enterprises, he retired on a competency and came to Stratford. He devoted much of his time to hunting and fishing, in both of which he was very successful.

Laing left his property to Mr. and Mrs. Lorenzo Beers who lived with him and took care of him, and instructed them to sell his 111 decoys for $45. Today their average value is over $25,000. At an auction in 1990 one of his blacks sold for $74,250, and in 1995 a Laing sleeping swan went for $101,750.

After Laing's death, leadership in Stratford decoy carving passed to Benjamin Holmes (1843–1912). Although they knew each other, Holmes and Laing differed in many significant ways. Holmes was born in Stratford in 1843, and was a working man all his life. At age 19 he went to work for carpenter S.R. Bruce to learn the trade, and after 15 years went into the building business for himself. He did some fine carpentry work in town, but became known for his narrow-stern skiffs.

These dorylike boats, about 16 feet in length, made with 18-inch single-plank sides, were low sided but were good heavy weather boats, capable of being rowed, poled, or sculled—great for duck hunting in the marsh.

To supplement his income and occupy the winter months, master carpenter Holmes turned to decoy making, both to order and for speculation. Holmes's early decoys were very similar to Laing's, but later ones had higher, narrow, breasts, greater body thickness, and more rounded tails. To produce birds in quantity for his customers, Holmes used a pattern to shape the plan and profile with bandsaws in his shop. In his basic body patterns, Holmes worked to eliminate sharp angles and to smooth out prominent lines. Individuals from a given run were nearly identical: In fact most of his "mass produced" birds are similar, with forward facing heads.

In 1876 he exhibited a dozen broadbills (scaup) at the Centennial Exposition in Philadelphia, and won top honors. He made large numbers of these "centennial" decoys and shipped them all across the country for $30 a dozen. As more hunters gunned over his decoys, and as other carvers copied his patterns and sold their decoys nationwide, the Holmes style extended across nearly a century of decoy carving, and the influence of the Stratford School spread.

Roswell Edward Bliss (1887–1967), like Ben Holmes, produced decoys for a living and was the most prolific carver of all. A patternmaker by trade, he copied Holmes's patterns to make his birds, turning out decoys in the R.E. Bliss Manufacturing Company shop behind his house on King Street. By 1910 he settled on a pearshaped design, and made production runs of symmetrical forward-facing birds, complete with scrive-line down the center.

Bliss made blacks, broadbills, mallards, and old squaws, then added whistlers, scoters, widgeon, pintails, buffleheads, canvasbacks, redheads, woodducks, teal, brant, and Canada geese—in short, anything any customer wanted. He worked daily in his shop and produced more than 2,000 decoys.

Willard Clinton Baldwin (1890–1979) grew up living next door to his mentor Shang Wheeler. He began to hunt at about 15, and soon began to carve his own decoys, modeled after an old sleeper black he had acquired. Years later he gave them away, saying, "these were made before I learned how to make decoys." Baldwin worked at Singers in the pattern shop (the sewing machine company made all its own iron castings) and ended up managing it and working there for 51 years.

From templates of a Holmes black and a Laing goldeneye, Baldwin made his own handsome decoys, with heads carved in his own less rounded style. His own gunning birds consisted of black, broadbill, and a few goldeneye. He once made a set of 20 balsa blacks for Ralph Welles, and tried a few cork bodies. All of his decoys are of extremely light weight.

Willard Baldwin gave this broadbill drake to a young Todd Lovell with the admonition, "Don't make a lamp out of it."

In Willard Baldwin's later years, young Todd Lovell asked him if he would make a bird for his growing collection. The answer was "No." But three months later Lovell's phone rang, and Baldwin announced, "Come get your decoy." When Lovell asked Baldwin, "What do I owe you?" the answer was, "Nothing. I made it for you. You'll never see it, but inside is an inscription with today's date on it, 'from Willard Baldwin to Todd Lovell.' Don't make a lamp out of it."

Reginald Irving Culver (1897–1975) was the son of oyster steamer captain Robert Culver. At age 15 he became an apprentice to patternmaker and decoy carver Roswell Bliss. His purchase of Benjamin Holmes's remaining blocks from his widow that year, coupled with what he learned from Bliss, started him off in decoy carving. With a pilot's license and a master's license, Culver operated Shang Wheeler's oyster boats, then worked for Moran Towing. His decoys vary widely, with flat heads and low bulging cheeks, most with three-inch body boards, with thick bottom boards.

Some of the decoys carved by hunter Louis Rathmell (1898–1974) were fine enough to be mistaken for Shang's. Charles Ralph Welles (1895–1979) was an engineer, industrialist, old resident of Putney, a hunter, and a fine decoy carver in the Wheeler style. He hunted with and admired Shang. State game warden

Some of Shang's later carvings were classic display showpieces. This colorful wood duck drake done in 1934 was carved of solid pine.

Charles R. Disbrow (1885–1955) was another disciple of Wheeler, good enough to win first place in the amateur division in the North American Decoy Makers' Contest in 1951.

Charles Edward "Shang" Wheeler (1872–1949) was the dean of the decoy carvers. Oysterman Pete Baronoski said that in the days of the vaudeville circuit in Bridgeport, young Wheeler worked as a hand on an oysterboat that on Sundays took the travelling actors sailing on the Sound. Staring at the tall, gangling, scruffy looking deckhand, one vaudevillian said, "You look like you came from Shanghai." He was ever afterward known as Shang.

Born in Westport on July 15, 1872, Shang left home at 16 to knock about the country. He worked at weeding on the Westport onion farms, then roved up and down the coast in search of work. He shipped aboard the salt codder *Dorcas* on the Grand Banks for a season, then came ashore to fashion hollow racing spars for small boats. He found his life's work in the oyster business when he moved to Stratford in the 1890s.

Shang's other love was Captain John Bond's training camp, where he hung around to watch world-famous boxers train and occasionally serve as a sparring partner. (Shang already stood 6 feet, 2 inches and weighed 200 pounds.) Once when a travelling promoter challenged anyone to go three rounds with his fighter, Shang stepped up, decked his opponent in one round, and walked off with a $25 prize.

In about 1907, Shang decided that the oyster business was to be his full-time work. When Sealshipt Oyster Systems made him general manager of its Milford office and docks in 1912, Shang stayed until his retirement in 1946.

It was in this period that Wheeler began to use his spare time to carve. After Laing, then Holmes, evolved their styles, the Stratford school was in its final active stage. The Stratford look tended to be full, the bodies almost round and the beam broad. Surviving Stratford decoys have short, stubby tails, and in most the base of the neck flares out a bit more than the cheeks. Wheeler, however, drew on other sources to expand the ideas and techniques now associated with Stratford.

Shang needed no special equipment. He enjoyed using hand tools, and learned to cut a block with a coping saw or drawknife almost as rapidly and certainly more accurately than most carvers did with a bandsaw. The tools in Shang's shop were simple—rasps, files, augers, drawknife, spokeshave, sandpaper, and his ever present jackknife. Shang did more finishing with this prosaic tool than with any other equipment. He loved to sit and whittle while talking to visitors in his office.

Shang's contributions to the Stratford school were not confined to skillful sculpturing or carving. If anything, his skill as a painter had an even greater impact on the craft. Although he had no formal training, his observations of real birds in real situations, plus his care and patience in painting every feather, recreated the beauty of the natural duck.

Shang's artistry was also evident in his carved fish. Charlie Plumb described one time on a fishing trip when Shang caught a weakfish 3 feet long. They laid it on a plank in Plumb's back yard and Shang traced around it. He then asked Charlie to count the rows of scales, and proceeded to carve a fish from the plank. That carving hung in Plumb's house for years.

Wheeler entered public service in 1921 when he was appointed to a state committee studying stream pollution. He won the first of two terms as a state representative in 1923, then in 1927 went into the state senate. As a dedicated conservationist, he enacted statutes to counter stream pollution and to prevent dumping within 50 feet of waterways. He prompted laws to reduce seasons on a variety of game and fish, and made the use of poisoned bait a criminal offense.

When he retired from political office, Shang became a volunteer political cartoonist in the local papers. Franklin Roosevelt and the New Deal were his favorite targets. But Shang's disdain for the New Deal in no way prevented him from using federal money for a proper cause. When he found out that the marine biology lab in Milford harbor was short of money, he went to work on friends in Washington and came up with the funds. After World War II he campaigned for a state reforestation program to restore a balanced environment.

Shang was never hesitant to enlist someone else in a good political cause. In touch with local politicians, he could often be found in card games at the old town hall or in Seymour Wells's store. Each Christmas, he showed up at Charlie Silliman's with a peach basket full of oysters. In 1926 he persuaded Ray Baldwin to become prosecuting attorney for Stratford, then town attorney. When Baldwin first ran for governor in 1938, Shang ran for state senator from the 26th district in his support, and both won. Shang organized the Stratford Minutemen, a motley group of marchers, whom he led in parade at political functions, dressed in buckskins, coonskin cap, and musket.

By 1947 Shang Wheeler was acknowledged as the finest amateur decoy carver in America. He had won so many prizes that he finally withdrew from competition and showed his work only in exhibition. Today the carvings that he gave away to friends sell for tens of thousands of dollars. In 2001 a carved Atlantic Salmon went at auction for $101,000. His work is an enduring legacy of the man who often said, "You have to stay active to stay alive."

The hordes of migratory waterbirds are gone now, their sanctuaries shrunken by advancing civilization, their marshland retreats polluted by chemicals and biological wastes, whole species wiped out by market gunners early in the century, their nesting sites invaded by mute swans and other non-native birds, their health threatened by manmade poisons, and reduced migration as Canada geese find winter food at golf courses and mallard ducks accept bread crumbs from well meaning humans.

Decoy carvers now carve for pleasure and for shows: few of them set rigs anymore. The few duck hunters out in the marshes today use modern plastic decoys. But there are new efforts to cleanse the water and the air. New reserves are being set aside. There can never be a return to nineteenth century plenitude, but our natural resources are becoming better understood and better protected. And the Stratford school of decoy carvers has carved its niche in history.

Tom Marshall, one of the last duck hunters to use the products of the Stratford school as working decoys, sets out with his dog from his oyster shack. The house behind him is where Albert Laing spent the last years of his life. (Caroline Davenport Mendillo photograph.)

7. An Age of Recreation

In the last century, water dependent industry declined sharply on the river and the Sound. Shipyards, dredging outfits, oyster companies, gravel suppliers, and seaplane builders are gone, and fuel delivery to powerplants is shrinking. Meanwhile, growth of income and leisure time brought a new purpose to Stratford's waters—recreation. It began with prosperous nineteenth-century businessmen who bought large steam and sailing yachts. Commercial watermen began to spend their spare time sailing and racing.

The gasoline engine sparked a whole new type of boat—the powerboat. Yacht clubs, then marinas, evolved to meet the needs of these amateur boatmen. Other citizens flocked to the new public beaches. Marinas, yacht clubs, launching ramps, riverside restaurants and condominiums are still increasing. The age of recreation has arrived. In summertime the channel is crowded with power boats, sailboats, and personal watercraft, and the marshes host kayaks and canoes, and in the winter a few waterbird hunters. Fishermen crowd the public wharves and motor up and down the river casting their lines. Public beaches are cleaner, and water treatment plants are being upgraded. The marshes are recovering, protected by environmental law. Increasing use will tax Stratford's waters, but they will improve.

Gentleman Yachtsmen, Working Sailors

When holidays first arrived in Stratford, residents took to swimming, fishing, and boating. But it was the rich who first had the time—and money—to indulge in pleasure yachts.

In 1864 a sleek new 42-foot sloop could be seen passing up and down the Housatonic. According to Nathaniel Herreshoff, in the summer of 1863 the brothers Herreshoff were cruising in John's *Kelpie* when at Vineyard Haven they met 24-year-old Tom Clapham from Derby and his college chums sailing his yacht *Qui Vive*. Clapham bragged that *Qui Vive* could beat any boat her size, to which the Herreshoffs took exception. The following day, with the yacht *White Wings* as umpire, *Kelpie* trounced *Qui Vive*. When Clapham insisted that they race again, they won again. A letter by Nathaniel says, "This led to Tom Clapham

Looking north from Brown's Boat Works toward the bridges, pleasure boats dominate today's scene.

giving John an order for a larger yacht and starting him in the boat-building business—then at 22 years and without sight!"

Qui Vive II was a light draft centerboarder (the Housatonic was pretty shallow upriver), 42.5 feet overall and 38 feet waterline length. She could ghost upriver on a wisp of wind—which was important on a 10 mile trip against a 7 knot current. Tom owned her for several years.

Not everyone had the luxury of a 42-foot sailing yacht, but many enjoyed their small family sailboats. In 1859 Lewis Russell reported in June, "Bob has been making a tiller for the boat today," "Pa has been puttying up the boat today," and "We are going to launch the boat this week." Then in July, "Went sailing this morn with Jakie Park," and "Went sailing in the afternoon in our boat with Rans Burritt. Moses Beach's yacht the *Flatfish* came in today." In late August, "Went down to the shore after school. Took the N's yawl and went most up to the bridge." In October, "We took the sail out of our boat for the winter today. Took our boat and went up in the creek."

It didn't matter to Nathan Wells how he went out on the water—oysterboat or yacht or barrel. On July 21, 1866 he wrote, "Attended a [sailing] boat race between George Fryer and Isaac Lockwood, from the lower wharf out around the beacon and back, won by Fryer. After which, a blindfold match was rowed from the wharf, across the river to a stake on the Nell's Island shore, [by 14 waterfront men] which was won by Lewis Coe and which made plenty of sport."

In 1871 he recorded, "Independence Day. Went out to the Middleground on the sloop *J.C. Brown*, Capt. Lewis, an invited guest of the Peppermint Club. Had a good time," then on July 13, "My birthday. Went to Charles Island in company with Capt. David Bennett and George Spall on the yacht *Bill Bennet* on a blackfishing trip. Very good luck but a very hot day."

On August 12, Wells reported, "Went down to the lower wharf to see a tub race, and saw three of them paddle across the river and two of them paddle back again—the other came back in a boat. Those who tubbed over and back were Rufus Buddington's son Truman, and William Quinn's son. The third was Truman Hotchkiss's son. The balance of those that entered upset. It made lots of fun."

In 1878 Wells was still crewing in other people's boats. "25 July. Dog day weather begins. Went out to see the new lighthouse on the Middle Ground shoal with Mr. Sedgewick in his boat the *Swan*."

In the waters of the Sound, Connecticut yachtsmen and working sailors came together aboard the sandbaggers. These were shoal draft centerboarders with an enormous spread of sail. The sails were a gaff main with a boom that extended far beyond the stern, and a club-footed jib whose boom could be held out by a whisker pole for downwind sailing wing-and-wing.

They came before any one-design class of boats, but were similar in general lines. Their length varied from 16 feet to more than 32. Many were arranged to be sailed either cat-rigged or sloop-rigged. The name sandbagger derived from the ballast used for trim, portable canvas bags filled with sand and shifted from side to side as required.

Stratford's late harbormaster James Fletcher Lewis, at an age when he said, "I buy the small tube of toothpaste now," put his memories together in a booklet on boat racing in the Sound from 1870 to 1910. Grandson of an oysterman, son of another who existed to race his working boat, and himself an oyster worker, sailor from his birth, expert engine mechanic, and Stratford harbor master, nobody was better qualified than Fletch to describe the races of the sandbaggers. He wrote:

> Long Island Sound was noted for its private and natural beds. The natural beds were worked by sailboats exclusively, and the men who crewed these boats became extremely knowledgeable in the handling of small sailboats. It was from these oystermen that many of the sandbagger crews were recruited.
>
> One of the most noted sandbagger handlers was William A. Lewis of Bridgeport [Fletcher's father]. Captain Bill had so studied the art of small boat racing that it was declared that any boat that he handled was bound to be the winner.

There were several outstanding sandbagger designers. Christopher D. Smith designed boats ranging from 16 to more than 40 feet in length. The team of William Robbins and Son, at the foot of East Main Street in Bridgeport, was one of the cleverest builders. Francis Burritt of Norwalk, a founder of the Indian Harbor Yacht Club and Commodore of the Cedar Point Yacht Club, was an avid racing sailor and a skilled designer of his own racing yachts. Commodore Burritt designed his own *Amateur* in about 1885 and had it built by T.R. Webber in New Rochelle.

Amateur was 32 feet, 6 inches overall, large for a sandbagger. She was planked with oak and framed of hackmatack [tamarack, called beetlebung on Martha's Vineyard]. J. Fletcher Lewis says:

> The commodore sailed her about two years and sold her to my father for $1,000 in about 1887. She had a mammoth rig which was cut down for the purpose of making an oyster sloop of her, and a topsail was added. She was very fast, but it was my opinion that this speed was partly due to the way she was handled. Father always kept her in immaculate condition and he was always looking for a race.
>
> It was the experience of this writer when helping aboard the *Amateur* to be ordered to "get those dredges in and trim the load." That meant that the captain had sighted a yacht which he was desirous of testing the speed of as compared with our sloop. It was fun, but did not enhance our daily pay. However, Captain Bill never had trouble recruiting a crew.

In 1896 it was common practice for the owners of private oyster beds to send schooners or steamers into Bridgeport harbor to buy the set, or young oysters, dredged by the natural growthers. These buyboats would anchor in the harbor, and each would be surrounded by 20 or 30 natural growth sloops "putting out" their catch for the day. Fletcher noted:

> It can be readily seen that if a boat had a good load she still had to be reasonably fast to beat the other boats to the buyer. Remember that many of these boats were converted sandbaggers which had been designed by the most celebrated architects of that period. If these boats were properly maintained, the races which developed between "bed" and "buyer" were exceedingly keen. This rivalry extended far beyond the oyster beds and eventually what was known as the "oyster boat race" developed. It must be noted that all the sandbaggers had long ago been converted to inside ballast [lead pigs or iron slag].
>
> There were several oyster sloops which were reputed to be very fast, and this reputation, enhanced by much loud talk, eventually was the cause of the "oyster boat race." These boats were laid ashore and their bottoms scrubbed and painted, their rigs overhauled, and some even had new sails and rigging. The date of this race is lost, but some of the

246

Captain Bill Lewis converted the sandbagger Amateur *into an oyster sloop in 1887, but he was always ready to yell, "Get those dredges in," and challenge any passing yacht to a race down the Sound. (Courtesy Mystic Seaport, Mystic, CT.)*

contestants were *Amateur, Ariel, Florence B., Emma L., Samuel C. Bond,* and *Marion. Amateur* was the winner, but the rivalry continued, as keen as ever.

I remember, as a small boy, watching a race from Seaside Park in which the inshore mark was close enough to the land for the spectators to watch the crews handling the boats during the turning of the buoy. As the leading boat started to turn, the throat halyards parted at the masthead. Without hesitation, the skipper [probably his father] seized the end of the line, shinnied the mast, reeved the halyards, and then proceeded to win the race by a five minute margin.

Bedell Benjamin's steam yachts were too large to keep at the boat club, so he had his own landing upriver. His last and best boat was the 84-foot Continental, *manned by a four-man paid crew.*

This same skipper had the reputation of always being the first boat over the line at the start of the race. In a race during which the writer was privileged to sail with this skipper [his father] there was a fresh breeze of wind which gave the boats power to maneuver, and in a luffing and jibing match we came clear and were the first boat over the starting line, much to the disgust of the other contestants who had attempted to blanket this boat at the start. Thus, much depended on the skipper and the crew. If a man was a good boat handler he usually kept his boat in top condition, but accidents happened, as in the case of the broken halyard. We also remember a new turnbuckle which parted and dropped the skipper overboard. I would like to record the turnbuckle story, but I am sure it would be deleted.

Yachtsman sandbagger owners often challenged each other to two-boat races, and hired oystering captains to skipper them and oystermen to crew them. Captain Bill Lewis was a popular choice. Two Bridgeport *Post* articles from 1897 tell the story:

Capt. Bill Lewis of Bridgeport successfully piloted the sloop *E.Z. Sloat*, owned in Stamford, in the first of a series of three races with the *B.K. Pigeon*, owned in Port Chester, the race being from Greenwich to

Stamford and return, twice over. The *Sloat*, built in Bridgeport by Capt. Wm. Robbins, is believed the fastest boat of its size in eastern waters. The next race will be Wednesday, and a purse of $400 depends on the outcome of the series.

Capt. Bill Lewis yesterday skippered the sloop *E.Z. Sloat* of Stamford to the second victory over the *B.K. Pigeon* of Greenwich over a 15 mile course, winning by twenty-five minutes and taking the purse of $400.

To give some idea of sandbagger proportions, the *E.Z. Sloat* had a 21-foot hull and a 36-foot mast, from deck to truck. Her boom measured 30 feet and her gaff was 20 feet. The bowsprit projected 26 feet and the foot of the jib was 25 feet, 3 inches. From the point of the bowsprit to the end of the boom, this 21 foot boat measured 52 feet, 3 inches. She carried some 1,500 square feet of sail. Fletcher Lewis's story continued:

> Each summer the large fleet of boats owned by the members of the New York Yacht Club cruised from City Island to Block Island. This fleet included many of the most beautiful sailboats of that period. This cruise was divided into classes and these boats would appear at the west entrance of the Sound and race east toward the opposite end. This display of fast boats was too much for the raceminded skippers of the oyster fleet past which these yachts proceeded. It was a chance to see how the boats in the oyster fleet compared in speed with the elite of the boating world. It was not beneficial to the minds of the owners of these beautiful yachts to have these dirty workboats show that they were, indeed, faster than the yachts.

Fletch went on to point out that it was the skill of the oyster skippers in their sandbaggers as much as the differences in the boats that won races. This was not lost on yachtsmen nor boat designers. Soon new one-design class boats appeared in the Sound to better test the sailors' skills, and amateur boatmen raced their *Atlantics*, *Stars*, and *Lightnings* from Fairfield County harbors. At the same time, the oyster industry declined, and demand for fast one-of-a-kind sloops shrivelled. The day of the sandbagger was gone.

Years ago, winters were sufficiently cold to halt pleasure and commercial boating. In some years the whole Sound froze over. Fletch Lewis recalled that in the winter of 1903–1904 the ice in the river and harbor was nearly 3 feet thick. He wrote:

> We were at a loss as to how to occupy the time after school until some smart boy decided to build an iceboat. If I remember correctly, Harry Ford started the fun with a sloop-rigged frame mounted on Vee shaped runners, two forward and one aft. She went like a streak. That was enough for the rest of us, and Eddie Estabrook, Ort Bedell, and yours

truly followed suit. The workmanship on these rigs was very crude, but in a breeze they were very fast. We finally attracted the attention of the boatmen around the harbor, including my father, Captain Bill. Father was a perfectionist. One day when I was in school, he went to Jesse Wells' blacksmith shop and had three of the most beautiful runners made for my boat, together with a mast step and a tiller. When I came home from school, father was rigging the iceboat. There was a good breeze of wind from the west, and I got aboard and headed out toward the main [Bridgeport] channel. The boat handled beautifully, but those who have been so fortunate as to handle an iceboat of this type know that it is quite different from a boat afloat. This can be learned by experience but, while father was an expert boatman, he had no iceboat experience, and he insisted that he be allowed to sail the iceboat. I made the super mistake of advising him how to handle her. This boat had been clocked by newspaper reporters at speeds higher than sixty miles per hour. To shove the tiller to leeward quickly on an iceboat that has the rudder aft is to invite a first class spill. This is what father did. After he regained his feet and some of his dignity, he started walking toward the shore and forever afterward, "iceboat" was a dirty word.

Arthur Bedell Benjamin, nephew of Canton skipper Pulaski Benjamin, never served at sea but made the sea his avocation, and is described as "a frustrated tow boat master." Born in 1854, son of New York business magnate Frederick Benjamin, Bedell Benjamin spent his life living in the brownstone mansion at South Parade, managing his estate, which grew to make him one of the wealthiest men in the region. This left him with lots of spare time, which he devoted to the young art of photography and to a series of steam yachts, culminating with the 84-foot *Continental*, with a paid crew of four.

The *Continental* was in every respect a bonafide towboat, but was fitted out as a yacht. Benjamin had a pilot's license and was a member of the New York Yacht Club. Although he was a charter member of the Housatonic Boat Club, he kept his steam yacht at his own dock, between Bedell's shipyard and Bond's Dock. Neighbor Alfred Ely Beach reminisced: "He made quite a picture leaning out the wheelhouse window, his hand resting on the steering wheel which . . . was at least six feet in diameter."

Benjamin's photographs show that he cruised all the waters of New England. Charlie Silliman said he always knew when thrifty Benjamin was going cruising: He would come into Jewell's market in the Center and order four steaks (to feed himself and his guests) and four porkchops (to feed the crew).

Beach described him as "steamboat prompt: He would invite his guests to sail at noon, then when he looked at the chronometer in the wheelhouse and saw that it said exactly noon, would blow one prolonged blast on the steam whistle and shout 'Cast off!' As his crew released the lines and *Continental* gathered way, he would look neither right nor left as he steered out into the stream, leaving tardy guests running down the walkway to his private dock."

Bedell Benjamin died in November 1914. *Continental* was sold out of Stratford, and with it ended the era of the gentleman yachtsmen.

THE OLDEST ACTIVE YACHT CLUB IN THE STATE

On May 21, 1887 the Housatonic Club convened its first annual meeting in the brand new clubhouse on the shore of the Housatonic. It was chaired by local merchant Robert H. Russell and lasted 25 minutes.

In early 1887 George Strong came home to live in Stratford. He had sailed on the Sound, and grew to love the peace and beauty of the river. Strong soon induced a few prominent men to organize a formal club of gentleman sailors. That winter, Strong and John Benjamin, John's son Frank, brothers Walter and Arthur Deforest Wheeler, George Leavitt, and Frederick Beach met to plan their club. They chose to build a clubhouse at the edge of the salt marsh owned by Beach's father Alfred Ely Beach, at a spot with a commanding view of the harbor and the Sound, and where their boats could reach the Sound 2 miles downriver on a single tack in the prevailing southwest wind.

That April construction began on a simple two-story clubhouse designed by member Walter Wheeler. It stood on pilings at the end of a 200-foot catwalk

In the spring of 1887 a group of prominent Stratford men built a clubhouse at the riverbank on Alfred Ely Beach's marsh. On May 21 the first membership meeting convened. Today it is the oldest yacht club in the state.

Members kept canoes, rowing boats, skiffs, and shells at the club, but sailboats were the favorites. This cat ketch seems to be shoving off, and its helmswoman is ready to take control as soon as it falls off and catches the wind.

across the marsh. Including dredging, pile driving, and material, it cost $1,204. Both floors had porches on the river end, and a single ramp led down to a float in front. By mid May the house was ready.

The constitution called for ". . . social intercourse and to promote and encourage an interest in yachting." Membership was limited to 100, and—unusual for that time—was open to women. Management of the club was vested in the hands of a seven person governing committee.

At 5:40 p.m. on Saturday, May 21, with 25 of the 41 members (24 men, 17 women) present, that first annual meeting began. The membership unanimously adopted the constitution as written. So, for 115 years the Housatonic Boat Club (HBC) has been governed by a self appointed seven-person board.

Member A. Bedell Benjamin then nominated seven members to the governing committee: his cousin John Benjamin, New York stock broker; John's son Frank; Frederick C. Beach, an executive in his father's Scientific American magazine; grocery merchant Henry Parsons; the Wheeler brothers, New York businessmen; and George Strong, who had started the whole thing.

At 6:20 p.m. the first-ever meeting of the governing committee began. Its first action was to elect John Benjamin President, Henry Parsons Vice President, and

Frederick Beach Secretary-Treasurer. John Benjamin certainly had ties to the sea: He had inherited his home on Elm Street from his uncle Captain Samuel Nicoll, whose actions in the War of 1812 had done so much to influence our country's destiny. His father Captain Pulaski Benjamin documented swift around-the-horn voyages to Canton, helping Navy hydrographer Matthew Maury to reduce sailing time to the Orient. John Benjamin headed the Housatonic Club until his death in 1910.

At the start, the fleet consisted of cats, cutters, cat ketches, and sharpies, with a fleet of canoes and a few Whitehall pulling boats for travelling through the marsh. In the fall, duck hunters at the club kept little sneak boxes on the floating stage. Bedell Benjamin's steam yachts were too large to keep at the club, so he tied up at his own landing upstream. In 1888 James Leavitt introduced the first naptha launch; later Mr. Beach owned one. Naptha launches were popular on the river for a time, but few remain today, because they boiled gasoline to manufacture steam. When they worked they worked quite well, but when they didn't they exploded.

Soon the first gasoline launches appeared, with noisy one-lung engines of 4 horsepower at 400 RPM weighing 240 pounds—Bridgeports, "the motor that motes," or Palmers—leaving trails of smoke. The club's facilities were deliberately spartan. There was no heat, electricity, or running water. A one-holer was tucked under the clubhouse stairs.

The new club had an active first season as its sailors and its paddlers tested the waters. On the Fourth of July, 51 members showed up to dedicate the clubhouse with fireworks, food, and dancing. Steamboater Bedell Benjamin replaced George Strong on the board, and his cousin Pulaski became a member. They arranged to pay A.E. Beach $5 per year as rent, and finished painting and touching up the clubhouse.

The list of members reads like Who's Who of Stratford. Publisher Alfred Beach and family; the wealthy Benjamins; William Samuel Johnson, grandson of the signer of the Constitution, and his son Samuel William and daughter Susan Hudson; John W. Sterling, the man who doubled Yale's endowment, and his sister Cordelia; Dr. Cogswell, Curtises, Fairchilds, Olneys, Russells, Leavitts, Van Voorhises, Gunthers, Egglestons, and all the wealthy merchants and businessmen in town. One local contractor's request to join was tabled.

The 1888 season began with 60 members. Winter weather had been kind to the club. Ice floes in the river did very little damage. On Independence Day the flag, repaired by Mrs. Hudson, flew high. An afternoon regatta, then fireworks and an evening magic lantern show, completed the club's celebration.

The Housatonic Club served as a base for day sailing, cruising on the Sound (in days when it was still possible to gunk-hole, dig clams, and walk or camp along deserted shores), sailboat racing, swimming, fishing, autumn duck hunting, and covered dish suppers, teas, and dances.

The river was clear and clean and members joined for the swimming. In 1893 F.C. Beach donated a shed standing on pilings up at the lower wharf, loaded it onto a small scow, and towed it down to the club to use as a men's bathhouse. Sand from downriver was hauled up to create a beach, and the floating bathhouse could be drawn up against the high bank in the winter.

In 1892 the club incorporated, and in the fall of 1895 the clubhouse was lengthened toward the channel and the pilings were braced to keep the building from swaying when 100 people danced to the orchestra on the second floor.

Small embellishments appeared: Bedell Benjamin donated a framed chart of the river, which is still in place; and a remote-read wind vane and a tidal gauge graced the lower-floor front room.

Sailing regattas and swimming contests were supplemented by fireworks—$30 worth in 1895—club teas, stereopticon shows, musicales, and dances—in 1896, as late as October 10. At the annual meeting in 1897 Secretary Beach noted, "The completion of ten years of existence is an event of which we are all proud, inasmuch as it gives us the assurance that what at first was regarded as an experiment is an established reality."

At the 25th anniversary reception held in August 1912 not much had changed. Two hundred members and former members of the club showed up. George Strong, the man who instigated the club's formation was now an honorary member. John Benjamin was dead, and so was Frank Benjamin, but three members of the original governing committee remained. Club membership still totaled about 60. Gasoline powered boats were beginning to appear in the fleet, and sailboats became more narrow-beamed and deeper-keeled. Catwalks extended north and south from the main float, and individual bathhouses lined the walk. Upstairs the piano was assisted by a Columbia Graphophone, a descendant of the talking machine that Alfred Ely Beach had helped Edison to patent in 1877. Plans were again underway to shore up the pilings to take the strain of the twice-a-month club dances.

In 1917, in response to a request from the Naval Reserve, the governing committee resolved "that the premises and all buildings and other resources of the Housatonic Club be, and hereby are, placed at the disposal of the United States Naval Reserve Force, without reservation." Dues were waived for members in the armed services: club treasurer Lt. Harold DeLacour of the Aviation Division, Lt. N. Hillyer Egleston in the New York National Guard, and Frederick Beach II, grandson of a founding member, were three such members. More club members would soon go off to war. Another era had ended.

The Housatonic Club in the 1920s was a quiet place, "shabby genteel," run by a faded gentry. The membership roster changed, but remained at about 70 persons. Rotting pilings and peeling paint were evident. The officers had trouble collecting the $5 annual dues, and the $600 annual budget ran a deficit. When the house committee asked if they could remove some framed pictures hanging on the walls, the answer was "Yes, but save the glass to cut up for window lights in the bathhouse." In 1924 clubmembers voted a new board, and Louise Shelton became the first woman board member. James A. Wales presided until 1934, when Ernest B. Crocker took the helm.

A handicap race—a group of gaff-rigged sloops and cats—sets off to race down the river. Good racing form and good yacht etiquette are observed—note the ensigns correctly flown at the peak of the gaff.

In the post–World War I period the style of sailing craft completely changed. Shoal draft, wide beam over-rigged "skimming dishes" at the club gave way to narrow-beam deep-keel round-chine sailers. In 1933 member Alfred Gilpin donated a racing trophy to the club in memory of Walter Wheeler. In 1930 the president became the "commodore."

Club members' boats were diverse. In 1925 Roy Lewis purchased the Chinese junk *Amoy* and sailed it to Bermuda. Wooden hulled racers, Victory class, S class, Bergwall's Ghost class, Lightnings, Stars, Comets, Snipes, canoes, and catboats made up the fleet. John Wilson removed the spars from an old catboat, added an engine, and named it *Rexall* for the family drugstore: It was his prescription for relaxation.

By 1937 membership was 145 and growing. After 50 years of operation the club had finally decided that it was really dedicated to sailing, so the name was changed to Housatonic Boat Club. The choice of the word "Boat" instead of "Yacht" reflected a remaining bit of reverse snobbery, and so did the facilities. To

In 1923 John Alden's Malabar IV *won the Bermuda Race dressed in her schooner rig (left). By the time Donald Sammis brought her into the fleet at HBC she was a ketch (right), and her old mainmast was serving as the clubhouse flagstaff. (The Sammis family.)*

reach the main float, one walked the catwalk across the marsh to the rear door of the clubhouse, unlocked the door, walked through the club and down the ramp. Until 1933, oil lamps provided light. Running water was installed in 1946, and even then, until 1955, the pipes were laid across the fields each spring and taken up each fall. The one-holer inhouse outhouse under the stairs still gave a view down to the river. The Fourth of July tea did not officially begin until Mrs. Sterling Bunnell strode down the boardwalk, silver headed cane in hand. Each Memorial Day the blast of a 12-gauge signal cannon at 6:00 p.m. opened the season, until on the 98th opening the commodore stood in front of the cannon and had to have the paper wadding picked out of his leg by a doctor.

A significant event in club history and the start of a new era was the formation of Lightning Fleet no. 6 in 1939. (The first Lightning had been built in Skaneateles, New York in 1938.) The advent of these one-design, simply shaped, mass produced 19-foot day sailers made sailing and sailboat racing affordable to a whole new group of people. Fleet no. 6 ultimately grew to more than 30 boats, and club members raced them all over the world, in Italy, South America, and everywhere.

Member Dorothy Venables captured the flavor of the HBC in an article in *The Rudder* in 1951:

> It is a simple club which started in 1887 as a family group, and in spite of the fact that the membership has increased during the past sixty years to over 200, it still retains the family feeling. Girls grow up, have babies, carry them to the club in baskets, and when they are old enough to stand up and hold belaying pins they graduate to the sailing group. There are

Saturday night covered dish suppers followed by homey entertainment. One formal dance is held each year, a Halloween party, a junior aquatics meet, and duckpin bowling during the winter months.

At the club there are Lightning and handicap races, three or four cruises to Long Island each season, and impromptu sailaways with family picnics down at Milford Point. The Wednesday night river races are a favorite. Starting at the club, the racers round a buoy downriver, another upriver, and terminate in front of the rocking chair brigade. Hot summer evenings find many families at the club for a swim and a simple dinner.

We are not sophisticated. A visiting friend, after looking at the club, said "I thought this was a boat club. Where is the bar?" We have none. From the upstairs porch we can see the moon rise over the marshland and watch its reflection on the river. With the passing seasons we see the marsh grass turn from lime to deep green to brown. We note the changing colors of the river from spring to autumn and watch the sun set over the pines on the hill. It is a simple place and restful.

Among the well known members of HBC have been Ray Baldwin, only man to serve as governor, senator, and state Supreme Court chief justice; Alfred Ely Beach, founder of Scientific American and early subway builder; John Benjamin, a founder of the New York Stock Exchange; Frank Scott Bunnell, after whom a high school was named; aircraft manufacturer Anthony Fokker; Navy Admiral Bancroft Gherardi: Ernest Greenwood, president of Norden; State Senator Stiles Judson IV; landscape architect Charles Downing Lay, who managed Central Park for ten years; bird hunter and decoy expert Thomas Marshall, who asked to keep his shell in the men's bathhouse when he joined; Kenneth Trimmingham, owner of a department store in Bermuda; town managers Sammis and Venables, and local judges Curtis, Kurmay, Stodolink, Trevethan, and Welden.

Storms, ice, hurricanes, and tides have always been a threat to HBC. In the disastrous hurricane of September 21, 1938, water rose 2 feet above the deck. Ten private bathhouses were swept away, and the boardwalk across the marsh was destroyed. But the worst loss to the club was members. Only a week before the storm, a fleet of club boats had sailed to the Thimble Islands to visit Roy and Helen Lewis at their cottage. Then hurricane winds and high water swept their cottage off Frisbie Island and drowned them both.

The worst property damage to the club resulted from the surprise hurricane of 1950. Fortunately the clubhouse had finally been moved onto new pilings in 1948: It was the only structure to survive. All else was demolished— bathhouses, lockers, floats, even the main boardwalk across the marsh. Everything had to be rebuilt. But with the work of many eager hands under the skilled direction of master carpenter Bud Olsen, the club was soon better than ever, with a new sailhouse, a new bathhouse, and in 1960 a new kitchen on the second floor.

In 1955, floods from hurricanes in August and again in September devastated the fleet. That year, the harbormaster and the fleet captain set or hauled all the moorings six times. First a federal dredging project necessitated that every boat be relocated, then replaced. Then followed the hurricanes and the floods. In the rising waters, boats picked up their moorings and floated downstream. Two derelict barges broke loose upriver and swept through the fleet, taking the club's boats with them. The large commercial dredge *General* caught on its spuds and flipped over near Crimbo Point, crushing boats swept against it by the current, and blocking the channel for two years. Joe Venables's S-boat was lost, but was later found and raised. Of John Ross's *Chantey*, only the transom was recovered, washed up on Short Beach. Paul Barry's boat disappeared forever. The outgoing current did not reverse for four days.

More recent hurricanes have been less severe. In 1985 a storm ruined floating equipment and severely damaged decks, again requiring members to rally and repair.

HBC's greatest threat, however, was not weather. In 1952 the club learned that the Beach estate property on which it stood was about to be sold. A special committee, Raymond Baldwin, Al Beach, and Ira Peterson, presented a plan to form a syndicate to purchase the estate for the club. Housatonic Properties, Inc., was created: It bought all the land, then sold the upland portion to the American Shakespeare Theatre. Eleven acres of land to the south and east of Shore Road was deeded to HBC on May 17, 1954. After 67 years, the Boat Club finally owned the land on which it stood.

In 1954 the need for winter boat storage and club parking demanded that the beautiful marsh be filled. From 1956 through 1966 fill was procured from the state highway department, the Town of Stratford, a Fladd & Kahle dredging operation, and industrial sources, for the yard and the club road, and both were raised about 3 feet. In 1975 the town began to oil the road, although the property remains deeded to the club.

In recent years the fleet has changed again. In the 1950s the boats included a Victory class sloop, an S-boat, H-28s, even John Alden's 1923 Bermuda Race winning schooner *Malabar IV*, rerigged as a ketch. Lightnings were made of wood, by Skaneateles or Ventnor, and a few wooden Snipes remained. Now, gone are the wooden boats with cotton sails, replaced by fiberglass and Dacron. Gone is the wonderful smell of sailcloth in what was once the sail loft. Gone are the many Lightnings, although Fleet 6 at the HBC hosted the 1997 Connecticut–Rhode Island regional regatta, and 16 boats participated. Affluence and new materials have given us a fleet of cruising boats with heads and cabins. The boats today are engined, and club stewards take members to their boats in an elegant club launch. The one-design racing class consists of 24-foot fiberglass J 24s, kept on shore and launched only for the races. In 1994 the club bought six JY15s and reinstituted weeknight river races. In 1997 three HBC boats sailed in the Marion-Bermuda race, and one of them won in its class. That year the club began another one-design fleet with Flying Scots.

In 1917 the Pootatuck Yacht Club replaced its building with a beautiful two-deck clubhouse built on pilings and surrounded by a porch. The clubhouse has since been moved onto land and raised into a three-story building. The fleet is berthed at floating docks today.

In the final years of the twentieth century, the club underwent great physical change when the Environmental Protection Agency, as part of its Raymark Superfund cleanup program, removed or covered potentially hazardous materials on the property. In the spring of 2000 the club reopened with the grounds free from contamination. For the first time ever, HBC had its own water and sewer hookups.

After more than 100 years of operation, the Housatonic Boat Club is greatly changed. Government regulations—licenses, mooring site rental, rules by the EPA, DEP, Army Engineers, and the town commissions—restrict the free spirit of sailing. But the club continues to grow. The members come from ever greater distances. They continue to run sailing classes for next generation sailors, and the element of family membership remains—the club still has no bar. In its second century, HBC objectives are unchanged: to share fellowship and love of sailing.

With the dawn of the twentieth century, a new propulsion scheme for boats developed—the internal combustion engine. Boatmen attracted to the new type of boat, the "power" boat, joined forces, and in 1898 Stratford's second yacht club, the Pootatuck Boat Club, was formed.

In 1898 power boaters formed the Pootatuck Boat Club, and in 1902 when the H.J. Lewis Oyster Company moved to Bridgeport, the club rented its old building on Housatonic Avenue.

Nine local citizens—Arthur Beers, Robert Hard, Joseph Houghton, Meigs Russell, Herbert Smith, Hiram Smith, Bruce Weller, Lewis Wells, and David Wohlgemuth—were the founders; they named their club the Pootatuck Boat Club. The first clubhouse was a shed in Peter White's shipyard. In 1902 the club began to rent the Lewis Oyster Company's vacated dock and building. It upgraded its name to Pootatuck Yacht Club (PYC) in 1903. By 1911 Commodore C.E. Rogers could report 83 members and a list of prominent Stratford men on the board, even to fleet surgeon Dr. De Ruyter Howland. Annual dues were $4, and the initiation fee was $5. Their launches and cabin cruisers featured heavy one, two, and four cylinder inboard engines, operable on crude gasoline hardly more than kerosene. The one lungers were make-or-break engines, started by cranking a flywheel, capable of running in either direction by flicking a timing switch. These were manufactured by scores of little companies: the most popular was the Bridgeport. Member Fletcher Lewis was a machinist in the Bridgeport company's factory.

In 1917 the club felt flush enough to have contractor Filmer construct a new two-story building on pilings, with surrounding verandas on both decks. Years later the clubhouse was moved back onto solid ground and raised onto a concrete block foundation. This provided space to construct a series of slips and berths for the growing fleet of ever larger power cruisers. PYC is now in its second century of operation.

Aside from well-to-do yachtsmen, most nineteenth-century Stratfordites kept boats for routine work—fishing, oystering, or gathering salt hay. Gradually these turned into family boats for recreation and excursions in the river and the Sound. Professor Sedgewick kept a sailboat, so did Albert Laing and Lewis Russell. After the formation of the two major yacht clubs in the nineteenth century, some residents joined them, others simply dropped moorings in the river or paid local yards to do it. For many years there were few rules to dictate where or how a boat owner moored, as long as he did not interfere with commercial traffic or access to the wharves and docks. But owners did tend to band together.

In the fall of 1929 ten members of the New Haven Power Squadron met at Burritt's Boat Works to form a new unit of the 15-year-old United States Power Squadrons, a group of boatmen dedicated to improving boating skills through education and training. On November 9 Chief Commander J. Edward Laughton affixed his signature to the charter of the Stratford Power Squadron. Its commander was Benjamin Coe, who would become national chief commander in 1932–1933. Its squadron pennant shows Orion the hunter striding across the sky with Bellatrix, the 13th navigational star, on his shoulder to represent this 13th USPS squadron.

In 1935 an elementary piloting class for the public in Bridgeport's Central High School had 66 students. An advanced piloting class was held in Judge David Cronin's office, and Commander T.F. Davis conducted a lecture course. That year the squadron amended its bylaws to read, "This squadron shall be known as Housatonic River Power Squadron."

At clambake time each summer, members dug a pit in the sand and kept a fire going over heated rocks overnight. The day of the bake, they gathered clams and seaweed, bought lobsters, fish, chicken, corn, and potatoes, and helped the bakemaster sandwich the food in layers of seaweed over the heated rocks. Covered by a moistened tarp, the food steamed for hours, while a chowder, prepared the night before in 30-gallon cans, sustained the hungry horde. At the call, bathers, baskers, and beerdrinkers gathered round to watch the cooks unveil layers of steaming food, first the corn, then clams and fish in cheesecloth bags, then in succession chicken, lobsters, and potatoes. This tradition continued for more than 50 years, on Lordship Beach, Penfield Beach, and then at Russian Beach.

In its first 40 years from 1929 to 1969 the Housatonic River Power Squadron taught more than 2,000 people how to use their boats more skillfully and safely, and became a large and active social group. The large membership meant running the public boating course in three towns. Competent members made good teachers, and squadron textbooks and teaching aids improved.

When in 1989 the United States Power Squadrons celebrated its 75th anniversary and Housatonic River Power squadron celebrated its 60th, USPS circulated a flag, to be passed from squadron to squadron. When it came down the river by canoe to HRPS in July, it was hoisted to the yardarm at the Stratford Marina, 30 feet from the Housatonic River and within 100 feet of where that first meeting had been held 60 years before.

Property of the People

The first brochure of the Lordship Park Association, printed before 1900, describes Stratford's beaches:

> The character of the beach varies. At the point where the bluff reaches its greatest elevation on the shore, there are boulders for some distance out; but west of here, one will find good bathing anywhere at the proper tide. There is also a good bathing beach at the north end of the ridge on the Housatonic River. At one of the longest and best beaches the bathing is excellent at high tide; and as the tide falls, a child may wade out safely nearly an eighth of a mile over a succession of sandbars, exposed at extreme low tide, with shoal water between.

The Lordship Park Association was incorporated in 1896 by William Hopson and others to turn Great Neck peninsula into a summer colony. Hopson and his brother Frank had worked for several years constructing roads and dikes to improve the land—Frank lived in the old Lordship Manor mansion built by Captain Nicoll in 1818. In 1911 the land changed hands again, when more than 500 acres and 3 miles of shoreline went for $500,000 to a development outfit called Wilkenda Land Company.

Key to the vacation community were its shore and beaches. Curving westward from Stratford Point lighthouse along Bennett's cove, the bluffs rose to 40 feet in height. Legend had it that this was where Captain Kidd had buried his treasure in 1699. Beyond the bluffs, stretching to Point No Point, the waves and current had created a wide beach of fine sand. They called it Lordship Beach.

West of Point No Point, a 3-mile long barrier beach stretched to Bridgeport, protecting the fertile shellfish beds in Lewis Gut and the huge Great Meadows saltmarsh. They named this Long Beach.

In the Housatonic River, around the point from the beaches on the Sound, lay another stretch of sandy beach at Half Moon Cove, named, of course, Short Beach.

The first formal attempt to preserve the beaches came in 1923, when an early Planning Board advised the town "to develop Long and Short Beach and to reserve the same for the citizens of Stratford, and that the town handle the rentals direct."

When the Lordship Park Association, Wilkenda, and then the Lordship Company, finally completed development of Lordship Manor, the beach at the end of Washington Parkway had all the amenities. A trolley car left the junction at Stratford Avenue hourly until 11:00 p.m., weaved and bobbed across the marshland on its beeline right-of-way, and rattled down Pauline Street to the beach. On opening day, June 5, 1915, Professor Quilty's orchestra played until late evening upstairs in the new casino, and ice cream and confections were served below. By Independence Day the Lordship Pavilion, with 100 bath houses, a

For centuries the Stratford shore was dominated by 40-foot bluffs at Bennett's Cove. A place where legend said that Captain Kidd buried treasure and where early aircraft flew, the bluffs were cut down in the 1950s to provide gravel for the turnpike, and homes were built on the site.

lunchroom, and an upstairs observatory, was open, and bathers swarmed to the beach. Through the 1920s and the 1930s this wide sandy beach was crowded every summer with bathers arriving on the Lordship Railway Company trolley or bus, or by motor car.

The fierce hurricane of 1938 brought vast change to Lordship Beach. Pounding waves carried the sand out to sea and attacked the shorefront road. Town workers dumped large boulders into the breach, to protect the land and houses from the sea. Several times the sea struck, and each time the town tried again. The end result is a stone seawall along the shorefront road, protected by riprap packed in place, and groins reaching out to sea. The point is stabilized, but the broad beach is gone.

Coastal Survey charts of 1836 and 1855 show Long Beach as a barrier beach extending westward from West Point on Great Neck (Lordship) to end at Bridgeport Harbor. Until West Stratford was ceded to Bridgeport in 1889, all of Long Beach belonged to Stratford. That year the end of Long Beach went to Bridgeport, as Pleasure Beach Amusement Park. By 1904, when a chain ferry

Soon after the trolley line reached Lordship in 1915 beachgoers crowded the broad expanse of sand at Point-No-Point. The pavilion is now gone, replaced by a restaurant, and the house in the distance is now another restaurant.

crossed Johnson's Creek and George C. Tilyou was operating the amusement park as Steeplechase Island (he had earlier created Coney Island), the western end of the spit held one of the finest beaches in the area. In 1919 the City of Bridgeport bought 37 acres of it and leased it out as Pleasure Beach.

In 1902 it was voted "that the selectmen be authorized to lease the beaches of the Town for such terms as they deem proper, not exceeding ten years in duration." Five renters became ten, then fifteen by 1905. By 1936 9,000 feet of waterfront on the Sound and 3,000 on the river at Short Beach were Town owned, and much of this was leased to cottage owners.

On September 21, 1938 the hurricane that laid waste the Connecticut shore struck Long Beach with all its might. "Porches were ripped from buildings, whole walls taken off as though by a can opener. Water, sweeping high above Lewis Gut, struck the cottages along Pleasure Beach and Lordship from the rear, while the hurricane-driven waves battered them from the front." More than 50 cottages were wiped out. The storm cut a gash across the beach, opening a new passage from the Sound to Lewis Gut. For years this new creek through the barrier beach increased the tidal flow in Lewis Gut, replacing Neck Creek inlet, filled in 1928 to build an airport.

To restore Long Beach and stop sand from migrating down the beach., the inlet creek was filled, and in 1966 five new groins—later increased to eight—reached out into the Sound. 600,000 cubic yards of sand were pumped onto the beach. Doc Gunther, then running the Conservation Commission, led an army of environmentalists planting tufts of beach grass to stabilize the soil. Since then, the groins have stopped the westward currents from moving Stratford sand to Bridgeport.

On June 30, 1997, after the Pleasure Beach swing bridge built in 1927 was destroyed by fire, the town cancelled the leases of the last 45 cottages. Barriers across the beach now guard the nesting sites of least terns and piping plovers, protected by the Federal Endangered Species Act.

In 1925 the town claimed title to all the land south of Neck Creek between the riverfront and South Main Street (today's Short Beach). The shore was divided into lots and leased to cottage owners, except for a 400-foot stretch reserved as public beach. Gradually, restrooms, a refreshment stand, and a stone seawall were added. Silt from upriver filled the riverbed until at low tide it was possible to walk out past the beacon. When the river channel was dredged in 1955 sand was used to build up the beach. Finally in 1960 leases were terminated and the whole park, 107.2 acres and 3,335 feet of shoreline, was dedicated to public use. In a $5 million renovation completed in 1988, rest rooms, picnic groves, tennis courts, jogging paths, ballfields, and parking lots were added. The Recreation Department set up headquarters there, and a $3 million sports complex with a nine-hole golf course opened.

Until World War II the town supported only one large boatyard—Bedell's. When leisure time increased and new boats streamed off the line in factories around the country, demand for summer dock space and winter storage surged. The old yard between Bedell's and the Pootatuck Club was modernized as Fladd & Kahle's. Then, north of Bond's Dock, Andy Brown opened his yard, Brown's Boat Works. Andy's granddaughter now owns the yard.

When the Bedells retired, they sold the business to Richard Palmer, who folded in Fladd & Kahle's, (Ralph and Wilson continued to work in the newly expanded yard) and built a large two story building to sell boats, hardware, marine insurance, and anything a boatman might want. They named the yard Stratford Marina.

Edward "Bud" Olsen built a marine store on Ferry Boulevard to cater to the outboard crowd. As recreational boating grew, so did Olsen Marine. About the time Bud retired, Stratford Marina came on the market. Son David Olsen took it over, and the reputation of Olsen Marine moved to the big new yard. Three local marine concerns were now combined at the spot where shipyards had stood since the 1600s, once called Shipyard Point. In 1995 Stratford Marina changed ownership again; Brewer's Stratford Marina has added a new visitor's lounge with a swimming pool and a dockside restaurant.

In 1991 the Osbornes, owners of the Dock Shopping Center between Washington Bridge and the railroad, decided to convert the waterfront at their property into a marina. It was a well protected spot, and the dock built many years before to support the steam locomotives of the old Youghiogheny Coal Company was still structurally sound. Slips were added, and a fenced-in boatyard. At the south end a walkway leads to a public fishing pier.

Fordham's Housatonic Marina has a new store on Ferry Boulevard. Downriver at Crimbo Point, Peter Knapp operates a fuel dock called Knapp's Landing. There is a fine restaurant there as well.

The advent of powerful, reliable outboard motors made possible high-powered boats with light weight propulsion systems and durable fiberglass hulls, capable of being towed long distances and launched close to the scene of use. With so many launching places, Stratford boaters encouraged the town to develop municipal launching ramps.

The launching ramp at Bond's Dock is used extensively by commercial oystermen and clammers, who back their pickup trucks down the ramp to unload bags of clams and oysters from the operators' boats. Kayakers and canoeists paddle from the ramp, across the river to the creeks in the Shang Wheeler preserve. Expert kayakers practice rollovers near the ramp.

The town launching ramp at Birdseye Street was improved in the 1990s. Four boats can now be launched at once, each on a paved ramp. The area has a Coast Guard Auxiliary station, a refreshment stand, and a new fishing pier. Other favorite fishing spots are Bond's Dock itself, in use by fishermen around the clock, lined up elbow to elbow when the word is out that blues are running. Good size stripers are occasionally hauled in at the dock, but bass fishermen are most fond of casting into the Sound from the groins at Long Beach.

Early in the twentieth century, when farmers no longer cut salt hay, when mosquitoes attacked our growing shorefront populace, and when the stench of sewage-clogged marsh waters overwhelmed us, plans came to eliminate our marsh. In 1918 the Bridgeport Chamber of Commerce prepared an intensive plan to convert Bridgeport-Stratford wastelands to "The Port of Bridgeport-Stratford, USA," with an ocean terminal, a deepwater harbor, landing fields for airships, and manufacturing facilities. Great Meadows would disappear, replaced by streets and buildings. A new canal would tie the Housatonic River to Bridgeport harbor. In 1919, opposed by Stratford's representatives in the General Assembly, the bill failed.

But not the filling. The long term project that had begun with Hopson's nineteenth-century "Stratford Dike" continued with development plans of the Stratford Land Improvement Company, and the wetlands were ultimately reduced by half. In 1927 all of the Great Meadows marsh was zoned industrial. In October that year a group of Bridgeport businessmen formed the Bridgeport Airport, Inc., bought 250 acres of the marsh, dredged a seaport basin and filled for landplane operations. By 1988 only 406 acres of marsh remained: 72 percent of the primeval marsh was gone.

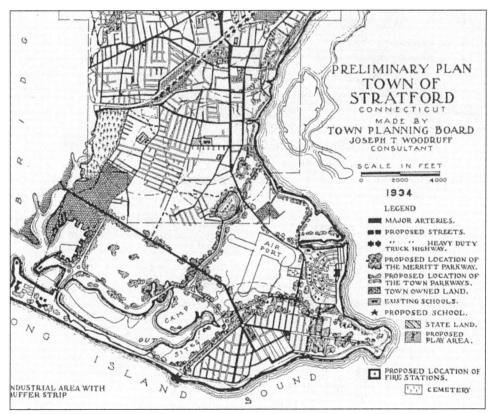

The 1934 Town Plan included the filling of much of Lewis Gut for a golf course and a campground. With a new understanding of the importance of the marshes, all that has been cancelled.

A map in the 1936 Town Plan is remarkably similar to the rejected Bridgeport harbor plan of 1918. Lewis Gut remained, but the marsh would give way to a parkland, filled with campsites, at the east end of the Gut. Near Johnson's Creek the planners sketched a causeway to Long Beach with a bridge across the mouth of Lewis Gut. The 1964 Town Plan proposed to enclose the Great Meadows and the marsh along the Housatonic by hurricane dikes, planned by the Army Engineers at no cost to the town, but when it became decision time, the Town Council vetoed the project.

Construction of our first sewage treatment plant early in the twentieth century offered primary treatment only, but diverted lots of sewage that had flowed directly into our waterways. Sewer Commissioners were appointed in 1917, who hired a consultant appropriately named Clyde Potts. A 1918 report says ". . . it is hoped that by Jan 1, 1919, a portion of the Hollister Heights Section will be relieved [more appropriate wording] as the commission has received permission from the State Board of Health to empty sewage into Bruce's Brook as a temporary expedient." By 1920 the system was in use by a small part of the town.

In 1960 Councilman George "Doc" Gunther's Conservation Committee, first in the state, worked hard to pass state legislation establishing municipal conservation commissions. Legislation in 1961 set the stage for Stratford's Conservation Commission, established by the Council at their December 11 meeting. The new commission went to work immediately to rescue parks, open space, and wetlands. In 1969, with aid of the Commission, the new state Department of Environmental Protection was able to map estuarine wetlands and protect them from exploitation under Public Act 695, sponsored by—now State Senator—Doctor George Gunther.

Because the condition of tidal wetlands is only as good as their feeder creeks and streams, the state legislature followed up in 1972 with Public Act 155, the Inland Wetlands and Watercourses Act that authorized each town to set up its own controlling agency. The Conservation Commission immediately prepared draft regulations for what might have been the first such agency in the state, but the Town Council took no action. Many inland wetland areas succumbed to development until finally, forced by the state, Stratford became the 162nd town to appoint a functioning Inland Wetlands Commission.

After the Great Depression and World War II, conventional wisdom prescribed that the way to conquer the salt marsh mosquito *aedes solicitans* was by ditching and spraying DDT (dichloro-diphenyl-trichlor-ethane). But the straight ditches drained the high marsh, eliminating saline pools and their residents, larva-loving killifish and mummichogs. Broad spraying of DDT also killed the mosquito's nemesis, the dragonfly, and the little fish, and its toxic effect was seen all the way up the food chain. Dead fish floated in the creek at Mack's Harbor whenever the Public Works Department sprayed. Birds could not calcify their eggshells and they stopped having young. Swallows, swifts, and raptor hawks disappeared. Finally in 1962 Rachel Carson's book *Silent Spring* made people aware of this disaster. After Bill McCann became our first Conservation Director, Stratford switched to the biological agent *bacillis thuringiensis* when it could afford it, and a less toxic organic phosphate, malathion, when it couldn't.

In 1985 ditching in the state gave way to an Open Marsh Water Management program, which encourages tidal flushing, wherein the ditches fill with water every tide, refilling high marsh pools and allowing salt marsh minnows to move about in search of mosquito larvae. In 1992 the DEP took over as part of their Wetlands Restoration Program. 1996 was a bad year, but the new style ditching worked, and volunteers led by State Representative Terry Backer placed doughnuts of *bacillus thuringiensis israelensis* in the worst spots.

Congressman Stewart McKinney worked hard to push through legislation to restore the Connecticut shoreline. After his untimely death his successor Chris Shays and Rep. Rosa DeLauro picked up the task: Chimon, Sheffield, and Goose Islands in Norwalk, Faulkner Island, Milford Point, and other coastal open space areas became collectively the Stewart B. McKinney National Wildlife Refuge. In 1994, 330 of the remaining 498 acres of Great Meadows became a part of this, and bit by bit acreage is constantly being added, adding up to 450 acres. The whole

Stewart B. McKinney Refuge totals more than 680 acres. Great Meadows harbors blue heron, black crowned night heron, snowy egret, great egret, ducks and coot, Canada geese, occasional kingfishers, a few piping plovers and least tern, common tern, and marsh hawks. Willet, barn owl, least bittern, king rail, black rail, and pied-bill grebe are visitors. As a federal sanctuary, most of the marsh is closed to human traffic, but eventually pedestrian walkways and parking will be added. The birds, the fish, the vegetation—half the original marsh—are now protected from destruction.

On a sunny Sunday morning in January 2000, nine days into the new millennium, 19 fishing rods projected from Bond's Dock. Nineteen eager fishermen—and boys and women—lined the dock. Elsewhere on the river, at the fishing pier at Birdseye Street, and at the pier at The Dock Shopping Center, as many more were gathered. The herring run was on.

More than 300,000 recreational fishermen now fish Long Island Sound. As the waters of the Sound have warmed, winter flounder have decreased, but in the 1990s the striped bass catch was up from 572,000 to over 1 million. A moratorium on commercial menhadden (bunker) fishing increased stocks, providing food for blues and stripers, as well as great blue herons, egrets, and returning ospreys.

Fewer hunters roam the local marsh today. Encroaching residential zones, fewer flights of migratory birds, and pressure by environmentalists have all reduced waterbird hunting. Still, occasional teams of hunters launch their camouflaged boats at Bond's Dock launching ramp, travel down the icy river with their dogs, and head into creeks in the marsh named for hunter/environmentalist/decoy carver Charles E. "Shang" Wheeler. Sometimes they set up crude blinds, other times they stand or walk the marsh. They come home with a few mallard, seldom with a black or coot or goose.

Great Meadows and Knell's Island marshes are now protected, by law and public ownership. The tidal wetlands act signed by Governor Dempsey in 1969 is paying off as clams, blue crabs, and finfish propagate in water now less choked by fertilizer, chemicals, and sewage.

In 1956 the Town Council–appointed River Improvement Committee, 18 water-oriented citizens of Stratford, recommended a permanent authority to plan, develop, and control the waterfront. It was authorized by the state in 1957. By 1965 Waterfront Authority Chairman Jack Wardman was able to report completion of the Birdseye Street Launching Ramp, continuing development of Short Beach facilities, and commencement of the restoration of Long Beach.

The Stratford Coastal Plan was adopted by the Stratford Planning Commission in August 1990 and incorporated into a new Town Plan in December 1993. Its objective was to emphasize water dependent uses along the shorefront, to use those resources wisely, and to offer access to the general public.

The Connecticut Harbor Management Act became law in October 1984. The Stratford Waterfront Authority became the Stratford Waterfront and Harbor Management Commission, and in April 1991 completed a draft Waterfront and Harbor Management Plan for balanced use of the waterfront and harbor for

Until recently a day tour boat from Bridgeport, Mister Lucky, *came up the river every day.*

recreational and other purposes, and for protection of environmental resources. Approval of the plan took seven years. The 180-page plan was accepted by the Town Council in mid 1994, and approved by DEP in 1997.

As the boating population has grown, regulation has kept pace. Since 1968 all power operated boats are registered by the state. In 1998 state boating licenses were first issued, requiring proof of capability. The harbormaster now assigns mooring spots and collects fees. Stratford, with 9 miles of river and 4 miles of shore, has become a haven for recreational boating.

Federal authorities concerned with the shoreline, waters, and wetlands include the Coast Guard, Army Engineers, and the Environmental Protection Agency. The Connecticut Departments of Environmental Protection and Transportation oversee them too. DEP conservation enforcement officers patrol the shore enforcing size restrictions on stripers. In Stratford, the Town Council, Planning, Zoning, Waterfront and Harbor Management, Conservation, Inland Wetlands, Shellfish, Recreation, and Short Beach Commissions, all legislate. The police and harbormaster patrol. The government is in control.

In 1998 Connecticut beaches were closed 272 times. In Stratford, Long Beach was closed for seven days, and Short Beach for ten. Brown froth from sewage treatment plants was often visible along our shores. Nitrogen from those wastes has been the primary culprit, feeding the growth of algae in the Sound

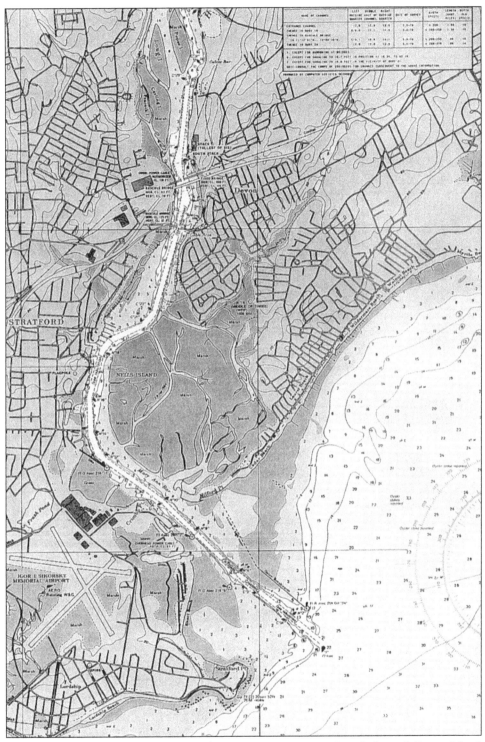

The new millennium has arrived: the Housatonic River, Stratford, and Long Island Sound.

and removing dissolved oxygen from the water. In the summer of 1998 lack of oxygen became critical in the whole western half of the Sound. Fish and shellfish died from hypoxia. But national and state legislation is forcing better waste water treatment.

Sailing up the river from its mouth, the yachtsman views a series of docks, wharves, yacht clubs, boatyards, and marinas to his left. At the first fixed mark in the channel, the river bank is cut by the entrance to the old marine basin, dug for seaplanes in 1928, and once home to keel sailboats, but no longer navigable. Then the Breakwater Key Dockominium, followed by Peter Knapp's fuel dock at Knapp's Landing. Past the old seaplane ramp at the factory and just beyond the jetty is the town's busy Birdseye Street launching ramp and a Coast Guard Auxiliary station. Harbour Woods Condominium's private basin is next, then the Housatonic Boat Club.

Next, the town dock, named for Captain (and saloonkeeper and prizefighter trainer) John Bond, is now reserved for fishermen, townspeople, and special visitors. Visitors to Bond's Dock have included the schooner *Brilliant* from Mystic, Rudy Schaeffer's replica of the schooner yacht *America*, skippered by Stratford captain Jim Thorpe, and a reproduction of the sloop-of-war HMS *Rose*. The American Wind Symphony Orchestra barge *Point Counterpoint II* with hydraulically raised stage has played concerts for audiences on the dock. In 1999 the replica of a Thames barge *Amara Zee* put on the play *Trapped: a Whale of a Tale*, and returned in 2000 with a fantasy called *Shakespeare's Dog*.

Beyond the dock lies Brown's Boat Works, occupied by a fleet of small commercial boats: Stratford's oyster, clam, and lobsterboat armada.

Past Ferry Creek, the oldest shipyard in Stratford—dating from the 1600s—has become Brewer's Stratford Marina, complete with new boat shed, yachtsman's clubhouse, and restaurant. The Pootatuck Yacht Club, with its own berths and floats, was founded before 1900 for the then-new sport of motorboating.

Beyond Washington Bridge (U.S. Highway 1) and under the Moses Wheeler Bridge (Interstate 95) is The Marina at the Dock, with full service for boats to 110 foot length, built on the rugged underpinnings once used by the Youghiogeny Coal Company.

Tidewater Housatonic extends 10 miles to Shelton and Derby, navigable all the way.

Federal and state efforts to clean Long Island Sound and rivers have made major strides. An interstate program begun in 2001 to counter severe oxygen depletion—hypoxia—will reverse the shellfish decline in the western Sound. Since DEP control of chemical discharges into the Naugatuck and Housatonic, fishermen have been able to stand elbow to elbow at Bond's Dock, hauling in herring, blues, and stripers in season. Ospreys have returned to the mile-square Charles E. Wheeler Preserve marsh, 4-foot wingspan fish hawks nest on 12-foot high platforms put up by the Audubon Milford Coastal Center staff. They wheel and soar high above the marsh and waters in search of prey. They thrive on mackerel, stripers, bunkers, bluefish, herring, and alewives—almost any fish.

Since Congress passed the Marine Mammal Protection Act of 1972, harp seals and harbor seals have been spotted in the estuary in the wintertime, and with their related pinnipeds, the gray and hooded seals, there may be several hundred in the Sound. Seven dams in the Naugatuck are being fully or partially removed and fish ladders will be installed, opening the river to ocean-going fish for the first time since 1860. When planned projects are completed, the new century will see a return to the bond between Stratford and the Sea. With clean water, improved boating, swimming, and waterfront facilities, restored marshes, and the return of animal life—salmon, shad, osprey, harriers, eagles, seals, and porpoise—and safe, convenient, public access—long greenways for walkers, hikers, and bikers—Stratford will once again become an outstanding town "at the edge of the sea."

In the nearly four centuries since the Dutchman Adriaen Block sailed his *Onrust* past the Housatonic in 1614 and named it Rodenberg's River, changes to the river and the Sound, natural and manmade, have been immense. With recognition that our waters need protection, with laws and regulations to extend the government's hand, our shoreline lands and waters have indeed become the property of the people. And as we enter a new millennium, Stratford is in harmony with the sea.

In summertime the three-masted schooner Sound Waters *takes groups of 50 out on Long Island Sound to teach sailing and the ecology of the waters.*

BIBLIOGRAPHY

Albion, Robert Greenhalgh. *Square Riggers on Schedule*. Princeton, NJ: Princeton University Press, 1938.

————. *The Rise of the New York Port*. New York: Charles Scribner's Sons, 1939.

————. Baker, William A; Larabee, Benjamin W; and Brewington, Marion V. *New England and the Sea*. Middletown, CT: Wesleyan University Press, 1972.

Alden, Carroll Storrs; and Westcott, Allan. *The United States Navy, a History*. Chicago: J.B. Lippincott Co., 1943.

American Heritage. "Battle at Valcour Island," June 1959, October 1966.

Army Engineers, Corps of. Hearing Minutes. July 24, 1928.

Barnum, Lewis Starr. *Journal of the Voyage of the Ship* Lebanon *from New York to Manila*. Manuscript, 1847–1848.

Barrymore, William A. Letter to his wife Susan from New York, September 25, 1879.

Berg, Henry. *Trondhjems Sjofart*. Johan Christiansens Boktrykker. 1938–1941.

Billo. Excerpts from *Log of Gasoline Oyster Boat* George H Billo, 1925.

Blakeman, Amelia Burr. *Diary 1883–1884*. Stratford Historical Society archives #6083.

Calhoun, John D; Knapp, Lewis G; Lovell, Carol W. *Images of America: Stratford*. Charleston, SC: Arcadia Publishing, 1999.

Chappelle, Howard I. *History of the American Sailing Navy*. New York: Bonanza Books, 1949.

Chatfield, Curtis. *Account Book, c. 1818–1830*. Stratford Historical Society archives #5092-13.

Chitwood, Henry C. *Connecticut Decoys, Carvers and Gunners*. West Chester, PA: Schiffer Publishing Ltd., 1987.

Coast Guard, U.S. Stratford Point Light Rededication Ceremony program. July 14, 1990.

Cochrane, Dorothy Von Hardesty; and Lee, Russell. *The Aviation Careers of Igor Sikorsky*. Seattle: University of Washington Press, 1989.

Coe, David. *Scrap Books c. 1910*. Stratford Historical Society archives #5149.

Coe, John Ebenezer. *1700s Account Book*. Stratford Historical Society archives #4583-18, -19.

As the twentieth century began, Rosedale *was the queen of Bridgeport.*

Coffin, Claude. *The Prehistoric Remains of the Eagle Hill Shell Heap c. 1924.* Milford, CT Historical Society archives.

Coggeshall, George. *History of American Privateers and Letters of Marque.* New York, 1856.

Collier, Christopher, and James Lincoln. *Decision in Philadelphia.* New York: Ballantine Books, 1986.

Connecticut, Colony of. *Public Records of Connecticut.* (Colonial Records).

Curtis, Julia A. *Daybook 1847–1865.* Stratford Historical Society archives #4583-8.

Custom House Registrations. Blunt-White Library, Mystic Seaport #HE 565 U7 C8.

Custom House Registrations. Fairfield County, Bridgeport Public Library Historical Collection.

Cutler, Carl. *Greyhounds of the Sea.* Annapolis, MD: U.S. Naval Institute, 1960.

—————. *Queens of the Western Ocean.* Annapolis, MD: U.S. Naval Institute, 1961.

Danenberg, Elsie N. *Naval History of Fairfield County Men in the Revolution.* Fairfield Historical Society, 1977.

Dayton, Fred Irving. *Steamboat Days.* New York: Tudor Publishing Co., 1939.

DeForest, John W. *History of the Indians of Connecticut.* Hartford, CT. William James Hamersley, 1853.

Delear, Frank J. *Igor Sikorsky, his Three Careers in Aviation.* New York: Dodd Mead, 1969.

Dennison, Archibald Campbell. *America's Maritime History.* New York: G.P. Putnam's Sons, 1944.

Derby Connecticut Commemorative Book, 1975.

Dudley, William S., ed. *The Naval War of 1812, a Documentary History, Vols. I & II.* Washington, D.C.: Naval Historical Center, 1985.

Ellis, Edward S. *History of our Country, Vols. I to VIII*. New York: Francis R. Niglutsch, 1900.

Engers, Joe. *The Great Book of Wildfowl Decoys*. San Diego: Thunder Bay Press, 1990.

Fairchild, John. *Account Book*. 1766 manuscript, Stratford Historical Society archives #4583-5.

Fairchild, Robert. *Day Book* 1824 manuscript, Stratford Historical Society archives #4583-4.

Hamilton, Dr. Harlan. *Lighthouses of Long Island Sound*. New York, 1995.

Hart, Samuel. *Representative Citizens of Connecticut*. New York: American Historical Society, 1916.

HMS *Rose*. Journal manuscripts #ADM/L/R/48 & #ADM/L/R/59. London: National Maritime Museum.

Herreshoff, Nathanael. Letter to William P. Stephens. New York Yacht Club, September 15, 1935.

Hotchkiss, Truman. *Journal of Schooner* Coast Pilot, Oct 1859–June 1860. Stratford Historical Society archives.

————. *Journal of Schooner* Coast Pilot, Feb 3, 1861–July 1, 1863.

Hyde, Howard. *Housatonic History*. 1987 oral history audiotape. Stratford Historical Society archives.

Julia. 1864–1865 Engine room log manuscript. Stratford Historical Society archives #5102-1.

Kelly, Alfred H, and Harbison, Winifred A. *The American Constitution*. New York: W.W. Norton & Co., 1948.

Knapp, Lewis G. *In Pursuit of Paradise: History of the Town of Stratford, Connecticut*. West Kennebunk, Maine: Phoenix Publishing, 1989.

Kochiss, John M. *Oystering from New York to Boston*. Wesleyan University Press, 1974.

Lewis, J. Fletcher. *A History of the Tidewater Housatonic*. Stratford, CT: Lewis Advertising Service, 1962.

————. *Housatonic History*. 1968 oral history audiotape. Stratford Historical Society archives.

————. *Boat Racing—Sail and Power—on Long Island Sound, 1870 to 1910*. *c*. 1970.

Long Island Sound, an Atlas of Natural Resources. 1977 Coastal Area Management Program, Connecticut DEP.

Ludlum, David M. *Early American Hurricanes 1492–1870*. Boston: American Meteorological Society, 1963.

————. *Early American Tornadoes 1586–1870*. Boston: American Meteorological Society, 1970.

Lundeberg, Philip K. *The Gunboat* Philadelphia *and the Defense of Lake Champlain in 1776*. Vergennes VT: Lake Champlain Maritime Museum, 1995.

Mahan, Alfred Thayer. *The Influence of Sea Power upon History 1660-1783*. Boston: Little, Brown & Co., 1890.

————. *Sea Power in its Relations to the War of 1812*. London: Sampson Low, Marshall & Co., 1905.

Marshall, Thomas C. *Albert Davids Laing 1811-1886*. unpublished, 1974–1978.

Mather, Increase. *Remarkable Providences*. 1684.

McClane, A.J. *Field Guide to Saltwater Fishes of North America*. New York: Holt, Rinehart and Winston, 1978.

McEwen, Nathan. 1806–1886 description of his grandfather Nathan Gorham in Orcutt, 1886.

McManemin, John A. *Sea Raiders from Connecticut during the American Revolution*. Spring Lake, NJ. Ho-Ho-Kus Publishing Co., 1995.

Milford Tercentenary Committee. *History of Milford, Connecticut 1639-1939*. Bridgeport, CT: Braunworht & Co., 1939.

Middlebrook, Louis F. *Maritime Connecticut during the American Revolution*, Vols I & II. The Essex Institute, 1925.

Mitchell, Edwin V. *It's an Old New England Custom*. New York: Vanguard Press, 1946.

Morrison, John H. *History of American Steam Navigation*. New York: Stephen Daye Press, 1958.

Musicant, Ivan. *The Naval History of the Civil War*.

Niles Weekly Register. November 20, 1813.

Official Records of the Union and Confederate Navies in the War of the Rebellion. Series 2. U.S. Government Printing Office, 1903.

Orcutt, Rev. Samuel. *History of the Old Town of Derby*. 1880.

————. *A History of the Old Town of Stratford and the City of Bridgeport CT, Vols I & II*. Fairfield County Historical Society, 1886.

Owsley, Frank L; Chitwood, Oliver P; Nixon, H.C. *A Short History of the American People*. 1948.

From the Lewis Gut side of the cottages, Long Beach stretches eastward for 2 miles to Lordship, protecting the gut and Great Meadows marsh from storms.

Patton, Peter C; Kent, James M. *A Moveable Shore . . . Connecticut Coast*. Durham NC: Duke University Press, 1992.

Pearson, David Andrew. *The William Edward Bedell Shipyard, Stratford, CT*. Savannah, GA: Thesis, Savannah College of Art and Design, 1994.

Pendleton, William. *Stratford Weather record book, 1835–1883*. Stratford Historical Society archives #4922-1, -2.

Peters, Rev. Samuel. *General History of Connecticut*. Freeport, NY: Books for Libraries Press, 1781.

Petrie, Donald A. *The Seizure of Siren*. Essay, March 12, 1996.

————. *The Cruise of the Scourge and the Rattlesnake*. Essay, July 17, 1997.

Popick, Rosalie C. *Oliver Wolcott's Ventures in Oriental Trade*. Thesis for Central Connecticut State University, 1985. Stratford Historical Society archives #4943.

————. *Capt. Curtiss Blakeman*. 1988. Stratford Historical Society archives.

Pratt, Fletcher. *The Compact History of the United States Navy*. New York: Hawthorn Books, 1957.

Puleston, W.D. *Mahan, the Life and Work of Captain Alfred Thayer*. New Haven, CT: Yale University Press, 1939.

Record of Connecticut Men in the Military and Naval Service during the War of the Revolution, 1775–1783. 1889

Roscoe, Theodore, and Freeman, Fred. *Picture History of the U.S. Navy*. New York: Charles Scribner's Sons, 1956.

Roth, Matthew. *Connecticut, Inventory of Historic Engineering and Industrial Sites*. Society for Industrial Architecture, 1981.

Russell, Benjamin. *Appointment as Master's Mate for duty on USS* Dandelion, *1863*. Stratford Historical Society archives #5109-3.

Nesting sites like this piping plover's spot on Long Beach are now protected. (Audubon Coastal Center.)

278

Russell, Lewis Howard. *Journal, 1859*. Stfd Hist. Soc. #4624-7e

Selby, John John Selby's Account Book, 1795-1824 Stratford Historical Society archives #1226.

Sherwood, Albert F. Memories of Old Derby. New Haven, CT: Tuttle Morehouse & Taylor, 1924.

Sikorsky Aircraft. *Fifty years of Naval Aviation*. 1977.

Sikorsky, Igor Alexis. *The Technical History of Sikorsky Aircraft and Its Predecessors (since 1909)*. Unpublished, 1966.

Sikorsky Manufacturing Corp. *Sikorsky Amphibion S-38*. College Point, NY: Brearley Service Organization, 1928.

Smith, Chard Powers. *The Housatonic, Puritan River*. New York: Rinehart & Company, 1946.

Snider, C.H.J. *Under the Red Jack*. London: Martin Hopkinson & Co., 1928.

Sobel, Dava. *Longitude*. New York: Penguin Books, 1995.

Stackpole, Eduard A. *The Sea Hunters*. Philadelphia: J.B. Lippincott, 1953.

Staples, Capt. William P. *Journal*, 1920.

Starr, George Ross Jr. *Decoys of the Atlantic Flyway*. Tulsa, OK: Winchester Press, 1974.

Sterling, John W. *The Twenty-Seven Ocean Voyages made by Captain John W. Sterling*. Manuscript of ships' logs 1810–1835. Stratford Historical Society archives #4549-1 thru -9.

————. *Problems in Navigation 1811*. Stratford Historical Society archives #4549-1.

Stratford, Log Book. 1904–1911.

Striddy, William. *Journal*. 1813.

Teal, John and Mildred. *Life and Death of the Salt Marsh*. Toronto: Little Brown, 1969.

U.S. Environmental Protection Agency. *Trip Report—Sediment Coring and Surface Water Sampling at Selby Pond*. 1996.

Waldo, George C. Jr. *History of Bridgeport and Vicinity, Vols I & II*. New York: S.J. Clarke Publishing Co., 1917.

Wells, Bayze. *Journal*, May 1775–Feb 1777. Hartford: Connecticut Historical Society Collections, 1899.

Wells, Nathan. *Diary*, 1866-1890 Stratford Historical Society archives #4961-3.

West, Richard S. Jr. *Admirals of American Empire*. Indianapolis: Bobbs-Merrill Co., 1948.

Wheeler, Charles E. "Long Island Sound." Essay in *Duck Shooting along the Atlantic Flyway*. 1947.

Whitnah, Donald R. *A History of the United States Weather Bureau*. Urbana, IL: University of Illinois Press, 1961.

Wilcoxson, William Howard. *History of Stratford Connecticut 1639-1969*. Stratford Historical Society, 1969.

Winthrop, Governor John Sr. *Journal*.

INDEX

The oyster fleet races home to the buyboat at day's end in this 1905 postcard. The first to arrive received the best prices.

INDEX OF SHIPS

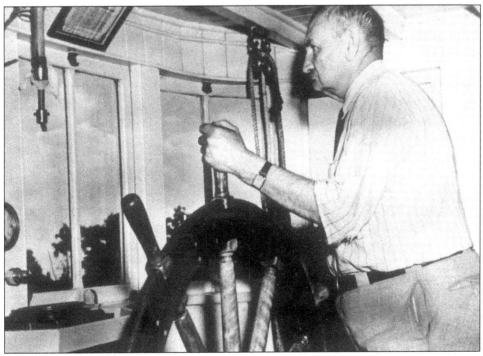

When the burdens of politicking or running the office at the oyster company became too great, Shang Wheeler loved to take the helm of a company boat.

Printed in the USA
CPSIA information can be obtained
at www.ICGtesting.com
LVHW081145221223
766782LV00085B/179